Why Do You Need This New Edition?

If you're wondering why you should buy this new edition of *Steps for Writers: Composing Essays, Volume II, Second Edition*, here are some good reasons.

1. New "Stepping Up" tips at the beginning of every chapter introduce you to the main topic area that the chapter will cover and give you a "heads-up" on what you should master by the end of the course.

2. A whole new chapter on writing examination essays, Chapter 10 (Writing for Examinations), has been added.

3. A new section on outlining is now included in Chapter 1 (Prewriting).

4. A new section on "Key Words" has been added to the end of each chapter. This brief feature will help you to develop your vocabulary and prepare you for future coursework.

5. A new section on tone and voice in Chapter 4, including material on negative/positive connotation, has been added.

6. A sample page of an essay with proofreader's corrections has been added in Chapter 5.

7. A new section, Responding to Ideas in Your Reading, is now included in Chapter 11 (Making a Comparison).

8. A new model research paper in MLA format has been added.

9. The quick reference guide to topics on grammar helps you find appropriate grammar topic areas quickly.

10. Many new exercises have been added that reflect current events and social and cultural developments.

Use *Steps for Writers* alongside Pearson's MyWritingLab (www.mywritinglab.com) and master content like never before while simultaneously accessing the new e-text and other MyWritingLab elements that will improve your overall results!

PEARSON

D0360094

PRAISE FOR
STEPS FOR WRITERS

Composing Essays, 2e

VOLUME 2

"Eggers connects complexity of thought with good writing. I like it better than most developmental texts as it really goes for teaching writing and grammar. It's a good lead-in to higher level writing classes. This one seems more approachable, friendly, and less prescriptive than many (other texts)."

—Jennifer Black,
McLennan Community College

"The Steps for Writers, Volume 2's approach to student writing and emphasis on students using their own experience to confront the challenges of essay writing is excellent."

—Jee Yoon Lee,
Borough of Manhattan Community College/CUNY

"Nearly every text I've used is too much: too much confusion, too much stuff, too many details – and the students get lost. This one, however, gives us exactly what we need: clear instructions, great examples, useful steps."

—Jeff Burdick,
Willow International College Center

"The chapters are all effective; I find Ch. 8 and 9 the most effective. Enumerating and defining terms are skills my students might not have had, and the text is a useful resource in showing the potential of these skills in a variety of rhetorical constructs."

—Bob Lazaroff,
Nassau Community College

"We love the student examples. The topics and writing exercises are relevant and timely. The professional examples offer an opportunity for close and critical analysis. Starting with Enumeration is an excellent idea primarily because competence with this pattern transitions well into all the others."

—Hilda P. Barrow,
Pitt Community College

A native of Indiana, Philip Eggers received his A.B., M.A., and Ph.D. in English from Columbia University. He was professor and chairperson of the English Department at Borough of Manhattan Community College of the City University of New York, where for many years he taught developmental writing and composition, as well as English, American, and world literature. As department chair, he helped create the Writing and Literature Program at BMCC, which is nourishing much undergraduate writing talent. Professor Eggers was elected co-chair of the CUNY English Discipline Council and participated in a CUNY Mellon Seminar and two NEH Summer Seminars. He has presented and moderated at such forums as the CUNY CAWS (City University Association of Writing Supervisors) conferences and NEMLA (Northeast Modern Language Association). He is also a member of Phi Beta Kappa. In addition to a book on Tennyson and articles in scholarly journals on English and American literature, he has written textbooks, including *Writing Skillful Sentences* and *Process and Practice*. Currently, Professor Eggers is teaching as emeritus professor, writing, and presenting talks on literature and composition. He continues to enjoy being a father and grandfather, jogging, exploring global literature, and finding time to travel.

Senior Acquisitions Editor: Matthew Wright
Senior Marketing Manager: Kurt Massey
Senior Supplements Editor: Donna Campion
Production Manager: Jennifer Bossert
Project Coordination, Text Design, and Electronic Page Makeup: S4Carlisle Publishing Services
Cover Design Manager: Wendy Ann Fredericks
Manufacturing Manager: Mary Fischer
Senior Manufacturing Buyer: Roy Pickering
Printer/Binder: Edwards Brothers
Cover Printer: Lehigh-Phoenix Color/ Hagerstown
Cover Photo: © Anderson Ross/Blend Images/Alamy

This title is restricted to sales and distribution in the U.S. and Canada only.

For more information about the Penguin Academics series, please contact us by mail at Pearson Education, attn. Marketing Department, 51 Madison Avenue, 28th Floor, New York, NY 10010, or visit us online at www.pearsonhighered.com/english.

Credits and acknowledgments borrowed from other sources and reproduced, with permission, in this textbook appear on the appropriate page within text [or on page 251-252].

Library of Congress Cataloging-in-Publication Data
Eggers, Philip.
    Steps for writers : composing essays, volume 2 / Philip Eggers.—2nd ed.
        p. cm.
    Includes bibliographical references and index.
    ISBN-13: 978-0-205-07463-1 (alk. paper)
    ISBN-10: 0-205-07463-4 (alk. paper)
    1. English language—Rhetoric. 2. English language—Grammar—Problems, exercises, etc. 3. Report writing—Problems, exercises, etc. I. Title.
    PE1408.E3595 2013
    808'.042—dc23

                                                        2011028489

10 9 8 7 6 5 4 3 2 1—EB—14 13 12 11

www.pearsonhighered.com

ISBN 10:   0-205-07463-4
ISBN 13: 978-0-205-07463-1

PENGUIN ACADEMICS

STEPS FOR WRITERS
COMPOSING ESSAYS

SECOND EDITION
VOLUME 2

Philip Eggers

Borough of Manhattan Community College
The City University of New York

Pearson

Boston   Columbus   Indianapolis   New York   San Francisco   Upper Saddle River
Amsterdam   Cape Town   Dubai   London   Madrid   Milan   Munich   Paris   Montreal   Toronto
Delhi   Mexico City   São Paulo   Sydney   Hong Kong   Seoul   Singapore   Taipei   Tokyo

contents

STEP TWO | Writing Essays Based on Your Own Experience and Perceptions   69

STEP THREE | Writing Essays Based on Your Reading and Research 121

to the instructor

Ours is an exciting and frustrating age in which to teach college writing. More students than ever hope to become novelists, poets, and journalists, but a small and shrinking percentage of them arrive at college with a mastery of basic skills and a rich vocabulary. Furthermore, fewer students come to us with an appetite for reading and the capacity to read college-level texts critically. The disparity between aspirations and aptitude has never been wider. In the past, writing instructors, knowing that many students feared writing and were aware of their deficiencies, often felt the need to reassure students, to help them realize that they could learn to write competently if they could overcome their anxieties. For some students, of course, such anxiety will remain the chief problem. Today's undergraduates, however, have grown up texting one another and witnessing books written by untrained authors becoming best-sellers. A new problem, then, added to the lack of confidence that troubles some students, is the indifference and overconfidence of others. Many do not believe they need writing instruction, either because they think they already know how to write or because they expect someone else to edit and proofread their work.

The graduated approach of *Steps for Writers* is designed to cope with both problems. Students whose confidence needs to be bolstered can begin with basic exercises and assignments that are easy enough to manage. They will be able to experience success before confronting more difficult tasks. Students who are impatient and overconfident will face the reality check of exercises and assignments that will challenge their overconfidence while allowing them to move forward quickly in areas where they are genuinely proficient.

Because every student writer is different, texts and instructors must be flexible. You may choose to follow the sequence of chapters in *Steps for Writers* as the basis for a syllabus, but many instructors prefer not to structure their course on the table of contents of any text. Although you will probably want to follow the general progression of the three major "steps," the sequence of chapters within each step need not be taken as strictly chronological. The experience of learning to write has often been described as recursive, and any book or course should recognize the cycles and repetitions inherent in the process, while at the same time always emphasizing the overarching goal of growth and development. The definition of one mode as more advanced than another has to be somewhat arbitrary, as narrative can be highly complex and argumentation can be simple. Nevertheless, it is usually easier for students to write experiential essays before engaging in analysis, argumentation, or research writing.

Steps for Writers is based on the assumption that we are teaching writing as a means of learning, perhaps as the most important activity in students' intellectual maturation. The importance of writing in recent years has been underscored by state legislatures enacting laws requiring writing in public colleges, by university systems mandating mid-level proficiency tests, and by the SAT and other tests incorporating writing assessments in the measures used for college admissions. Writing across the curriculum has become standard practice in nearly every university. There has been a concomitant emphasis on critical thinking in composition pedagogy, no doubt because we perceive that students are vulnerable to the worst kinds of bias and manipulation, from the blandishments of advertising and the specious claims of political leaders to the urban legends found on Web sites. Along with the emphasis on critical thinking, however, we should incorporate the equally important element of creativity, not just in courses labeled Creative Writing, but in academic and career writing as well. Being able to propose solutions to problems; formulate original thesis statements; and employ vivid, resourceful diction and style requires creative thinking analogous to the inventiveness displayed by poets and novelists. Fiction and poetry, in turn, also involve critical thinking. Resisting the tendency to bifurcate critical and creative writing, *Steps for Writers* encourages students to take an interest in both aspects of their writing and incorporates some fiction and poetry among other kinds of professional writing as prose models. Students are likely to feel empowered and to enjoy their writing more if their logical and imaginative faculties are brought out conjointly.

Acknowledgments

I am deeply grateful to the following professors who, by their comments, have made this a better textbook: Hilda P. Barrow of Pitt Community College, Steven J. Belluscio of Borough of Manhattan Community College/CUNY, Jeff Burdick of Willow International College Center, Patrice Johnson of Eastfield College, Bob Lazaroff of Nassau Community College, Jee Yoon Lee of Borough of Manhattan Community College/CUNY, Selena Stewart-Alexander of Brookhaven College, and Cynthia Wiseman of Borough of Manhattan Community College/CUNY.

I am indebted as well to the Allyn & Bacon/Pearson editors who have contributed indispensably to the project, including Matt Wright and Kristen Pechtol, and to project editor Roxanne Klaas for a superior job of supervising the revisions of the second edition and to Susan Dolter of Clarke University for an expert job of copyediting. I am deeply grateful as well to my colleagues and students at the Borough of Manhattan Community College, from whom I have learned during the course of my career most of what I know about teaching and whose advice and examples have taught me so much about all aspects of writing. Among these colleagues, I especially want to thank Maria do Carmo de Vasconcelos, Joyce Harte, Frank Elmi, Bob Lapides, Nancy McClure, Elliot Podwill, Anthony Drago, Milton Baxter, and Steve Cogan for many years of stimulating exchanges on teaching, writing, and literature.

Developmental Writing Resources

Book-Specific Ancillary Material

Instructor's Exam Copy for *Steps for Writers: Composing Essays, Volume II*, 2/e ISBN 0205074650

The *Instructor's Exam Copy* for *Steps for Writers: Composing Essays, Volume II*, 2/e is the student edition text, but intended for instructors only.

Instructor's Manual for *Steps for Writers: Composing Essays, Volume II*, 2/e ISBN 0205110339

The online *Instructor's Manual* for *Steps for Writers: Composing Essays, Volume II*, 2/e offers additional material to help instructors meet their course objectives. Instructors of all experience levels will find helpful ideas for using the material in *Steps for Writers* so that students can learn the skills they need for successful writing at the college level.

Additional Instructor Resources

The Pearson Writing Package

Pearson is pleased to offer a variety of support materials to help make teaching writing easier for teachers and to help students excel in their coursework. Many of our student supplements are available free or at a greatly reduced price when packaged with *Steps for Writers: Composing Essays, Volume II, 2/e.* Visit www.pearsonhighereducation.com, contact your local Pearson sales representative, or review a detailed listing of the full supplements package in the *Instructor's Manual* for more information.

Media Resources

mywritinglab

Where better practice makes better writers!

www.mywritinglab.com

MyWritingLab, a complete online learning program, provides additional resources and better practice exercises for developing writers.

What makes the practice in MyWritingLab better?

- **Diagnostic Testing:** MyWritingLab's diagnostic test comprehensively assesses students' skills in grammar. Students are given an individualized learning path based on the diagnostic's results, identifying the areas where they most need help.
- **Progressive Learning:** The heart of MyWritingLab is the progressive learning that takes place as students review media and complete the various exercises within each topic. Students move from literal comprehension, to critical understanding, to the ability to demonstrate a skill in their own writing. This progression of critical thinking, not available in any other online resource, enables students to truly master the skills and concepts they need to become successful writers.
- **Online Gradebook:** All student work in MyWritingLab is captured in the Online Gradebook. Students can monitor their own

progress through reports explaining their scores on the exercises in the course. Instructors can see which topics their students have mastered and access other detailed reports, such as class summaries, that track the development of their entire class and display useful details on each student's progress.

- **eText.** The *Steps for Writers: Composing Essays, Volume II* e-text is accessed through MyWritingLab. Students now have the e-text at their fingertips while completing the various exercises and activities within MyWritingLab. Students can highlight important material in the e-text and add notes to any section for reflection and/or study throughout the semester.

Philip Eggers
Borough of Manhattan Community College
The City University of New York

The Steps Approach

Like all writers, you will learn to write in your unique way, and your best writing will bear the stamp of your individuality. There are steps you or any writer should take, however, to learn how to write effective essays and develop good writing habits. This book is designed to help you take those steps and experience the satisfaction of writing correctly and with focus, precision, clarity, and originality. Climbing steps sounds like work and learning to write better does take work. But as you improve, writing will also become more enjoyable. Your enriched vocabulary and increased command of sentence structure and style will give you greater confidence. Freed from the embarrassment of making frequent, basic errors and experienced at developing and organizing your ideas, you will become a more creative and interesting writer.

As you do the individual assignments and exercises in this book, keep an eye on your long-term progress. Learning to write requires a lot of repetition, but the repetition occurs at higher and higher levels. Sometimes it may seem that you are going backward because you find yourself confused about some features of grammar that you have already studied. At other times you may seem to be standing still because you repeat the same mistakes. These feelings stem from the fact that as you take on more challenging writing assignments and acquire more vocabulary, you will be operating on a higher level, where such matters as sentence structure, agreement of subject and verb, and use of pronouns become more challenging. The three-step grammar and writing exercises featured in this book will remind you to keep applying what you have learned as you progress to more advanced work.

Preface to the Second Edition

Students and teachers who have used the first edition of *Steps for Writers* have been enthusiastic about most elements of the book. They like its graduated "steps" arrangement, its compact format, its direct style, and its models of student and professional writing. No text, however, is perfect, and the experience of students and professors is always useful in revealing ways a successful text can be made still better. Furthermore, in a rapidly changing world, textbooks need to keep pace with new directions in teaching, learning, technology, culture, and society.

In this new edition, a number of changes have been made in the organization and format to enhance the effectiveness of *Steps for Writers*. In addition, old material has been replaced and new material has been added to keep students' learning close to the world they are experiencing, with all its rapid transformations in popular culture, world events, politics, sports, and news.

New Features of the Second Edition

- New "Stepping Up" tips at the beginning of each chapter
- A section on outlining in Chapter 1
- A page of proofread text in the Proofreading Aloud section in Chapter 5
- A section on tone and voice, including material on negative/positive connotation
- A new chapter on writing examination essays
- A new section on responding to ideas in your reading in Chapter 11
- Updated content in exercises to reflect current events and social and cultural developments
- Key words at the end of each chapter for review
- A new model research paper in MLA format
- Quick reference guide to grammar topics

Organization

Because this book is arranged in a series of three "steps," with graduated exercises in each chapter, your instructor will probably want you to follow the sequence of units as they are presented. Although there may be exceptions, depending on your particular course and instructor, it makes sense to move in the general direction from Step One through Steps Two and Three. Step One introduces you to the whole writing process, which every writer shapes for his or her own use. Step Two involves writing essays based mostly on your own experience and what you already know of the world around you—your family, friends, school, job, and teams and organizations to which you belong. These compositions do not require extensive use of texts or research, and therefore are the kind of work your instructor may want you to do for your first formal essays. Step Three follows logically from Step Two, with assignments and exercises based on writing that incorporates facts beyond your immediate experience, texts that you read, or research materials that you find.

While *Steps for Writers* is arranged sequentially with an eye to your developing skills, its structure is flexible so that it can be used in a variety of ways. For instance, some courses may lack sufficient time to complete all the chapters. Or, your instructor may wish to arrange the assignments differently, which can be readily accomplished because the order of individual chapters within each step can easily be changed. Remember, too, that if chapters or exercises are omitted from your class assignments, you can still learn a lot by studying them on your own. More than your instructors or your textbooks, you are the one in charge of your own learning. As you take ownership of your own writing, you will learn faster and enjoy it more.

Special Features

A graduated approach. *Steps for Writers* has a number of features designed to help you achieve success as a writer, beginning with its graduated approach to both grammar and composition. Learning to write essays is not like learning chemistry or Russian, where every lesson introduces you to totally new information. You are, after all, writing in a language you already know, even if it is not your first language. Consequently, the knowledge and skills you acquire are not easy to identify and separate from what you already know. In fact, you may have some previously learned misinformation and bad habits that need to be corrected. For that reason you will not always be able to detect your steady advancement as a writer. The arrangement of large and small steps in this book will help you recognize that what sometimes seems like sliding backward is actually an upward climb that will carry you to a higher place.

Before each set of grammar exercises, you will find a Test Yourself exercise that you can do as a follow-up to the grammar lesson. The answers are provided for these exercises so that you can see how well you understand that feature of grammar before you begin the graduated exercises. You will probably find the first step, the basic exercise, fairly easy. At times you may also find that you can do the intermediate and challenge exercises successfully. At other times, however, the intermediate and challenge exercises may be just that: a challenge. Do not be discouraged; very few people have a perfect command of all aspects of grammar. When you have difficulties, be ready to do extra work and seek a tutor if necessary. But do not expect every level to be easy; if it were, you would already be an advanced writer with very little need for instruction or textbooks!

Student models and professional essays. The student models in each chapter will offer you examples of the kinds of writing students actually do that are competent, well organized, and well written, but not beyond what you are capable of doing yourself. Of course, they are not meant for you to copy too closely but to recognize the features of good writing that you as a college student can expect of yourself. Sometimes you may find yourself writing better than the student models, at least in some features. The professional examples will provide texts for you to interpret, analyze, and discuss. You should use them as prose models that demonstrate the range of possibilities in different writing modes. You may be inspired to write better by witnessing how some of the best writers work, just as young athletes learn by watching professionals and Olympians. Sometimes you will find that your best writing is not all that different from the work of published authors, that you have some of the originality and insight they display. Instead of saying to yourself, "I could never do that," you may find yourself thinking, "I can do that myself." That's when writing really becomes enjoyable and you know you are learning.

Embedded proofreading exercises. Grammar is important. However, that doesn't mean you have to study every aspect of grammar from the ground up. As a college student you already know many rules and patterns of English grammar through habit, or, possibly, from instruction in high school. Unfortunately, unless you are a rare exception, that does not mean you can write without making mistakes. Although you may not need a whole course in grammar, you probably still have a few things to learn. On that assumption, this book is designed to incorporate grammar exercises as part of the proofreading process, which should come in the last stage of revision. For quick reference to specific grammatical topics, however, the index at the back will help you find whatever you need to know about fragments, spelling, subject-verb agreement, and so on.

Peer review questions. Your instructor will probably include some small-group work in your writing class or encourage you to share your work with others in a group outside class. Even when your courses do not require you to study with other students in a small group, such study will help you make a habit of sharing your writing with other writers. No writer can predict with any certainty how readers will respond to his or her work; usually some readers will give you helpful advice about how to make your work clearer, more interesting, or more convincing. It takes courage to listen to your classmates' responses, but you'll be glad you did. Each chapter of *Steps for Writers* contains peer review questions that you can use to elicit helpful responses to your writing in the particular mode involved. Use as many of these questions as you can; the answers will probably help you revise and enjoy your writing.

Arrangement by rhetorical modes. The rhetorical modes are the categories of writing that have been identified for many generations as different ways of developing material. Unlike the mythical Procrustes, who chopped off his visitors' feet if they were too tall to fit his bed or stretched them if they were too short, we should not try to make essays "fit" perfectly into one mold. However, composing essays in different modes will ensure that you experiment with a wide variety of writing. Like cross-training in a gym, diverse writing approaches will introduce you to varied kinds of thinking as well as varied ways of using language. Even your grammar skills will be tested differently when you are writing a narrative essay (telling a story) than when you are writing an argumentative essay.

Writing Tips. Each chapter begins with a writing tip that will give you small but important reminders about tactics you should use as you study the writing techniques in that chapter. These preliminary tips are not extended lessons but highlight some of the dos and don'ts at the core of each lesson. You will pick up other tips from your fellow students and instructors as you advance. It might be a good idea to keep a master list of what you learn about your steps to effective writing the hints that you need to remember to avoid your habitual weaknesses and build on your strengths.

Above all, enjoy your writing. There is no gratification quite like writing well and sharing it with your readers.

Philip Eggers
Borough of Manhattan Community College
The City University of New York

VISUALIZING THE ESSAY

Students often ask, "How can I learn to write a good essay?" That is the question this book is designed to answer. But no book can give you one blueprint for the many kinds of essays you may write in college. Just what is an essay? If you already have a notion of what an essay should be, your idea is probably partly right because essays can take so many forms.

When the essay was invented—its inventor is often identified as the seventeenth-century French writer Michel de Montaigne—readers understood that the word *essay* meant "to try": an essay was an *attempt* to do something, an *effort* to explore a topic. An essay was considered worth writing even if the author didn't say everything possible on the subject, so long as he or she put in the effort to explore it. A college essay today is still an adventure in ideas, and it requires the same willingness as in Montaigne's day to explore ideas with effort and an open mind. How, then, can you write a good essay? Don't look for a formula, but be ready to work and be receptive to any facts or ideas that emerge. The right attitude and an effective approach are more important than any blueprint.

There is, however, a classic form for a college essay, which may help you begin writing. Among the many forms of the essay, most follow a familiar three-part structure.

INTRODUCTION: Your introduction is a paragraph, or maybe two, that arouses readers' interest in the topic and gives them a clear idea of what you plan to say in the essay. It should begin with a short statement or question that evokes interest, and then continue with several more sentences that lead up to a clear, forceful **thesis statement**, which announces your essay's main point. The thesis statement is often the last sentence in the introduction.

| **BODY:** | The body of your essay contains several paragraphs, usually three to five, that develop the main point. In this book you will study different ways to develop your points, using description, narration, comparison, persuasion, and so on. Each body paragraph may contain a **topic sentence** that acts as a signpost to guide the reader by introducing the subject of the paragraph. Learning to develop these body paragraphs and connect them with transition words is a major part of learning to write essays. |
| **CONCLUSION:** | Think of the conclusion as your introduction in reverse. You may begin by restating your thesis (though not in exactly the same words). Then find a way to end with interesting statements that leave food for further thought while remaining close to your main idea. Your last sentence, like the first one in your introduction, should be memorable and emphatic—and preferably short. |

The diagram above makes it look as if the parts of the essay are just piled on top of one another. But the adventure of writing an essay is not like stacking cans on a grocery store shelf; it is more like exploring a neighborhood—one that you are acquainted with but that also contains many surprises. As you move from one part of your essay to the next, say to yourself, "This idea leads me to another point, and that point makes me realize that. . . ." An essay is a kind of guided tour from one idea to another. Every paragraph topic should follow from the previous one and every sentence lead to the next. This sequence of ideas and statements is the glue that holds the essay together on the inside and makes the organization of your essay visible "from the outside" to the reader.

Of course, creating an essay that develops out of itself and moves smoothly from beginning to end is not always quick and easy. Writers have many ways of creating essays, progressing from one stage to another from their first ideas through numerous drafts and revisions to a final, completed and corrected composition. We call these methods of creating essays the *writing process*, which also involves a process of thinking and learning. To write well, you will have to discover your own version of the writing process.

The essay below was the final product at the end of one student's writing process. First, to understand what an essay is, let's examine it as a completed whole. Later, we can follow the steps the author, Sarah Chen, took in getting to her completed work.

Student Essay:

The essay below is the kind that supports a main point through illustration—the use of several supporting points, or subtopics. Although this is one of the most common forms used in academic writing, it isn't the only one. This essay is a revised and edited draft. In the section on revising your work, you will see some of the steps the writer took to arrive at her final version.

Why Liberal Arts?

SARAH CHEN

Introduction   Our sociology teacher once asked the class a difficult question. She wanted to know whether we would rather have our college degree without the education or the education without the degree. Most of the students decided that they would rather have the degree, because the jobs they wanted required college degrees. Other students, including me, argued that, in the long run, knowledge is more important than a meaningless piece of paper. We didn't settle the argument, but we had to think a lot about what an education, particularly a liberal arts education, is for. With so much emphasis on career training, we wondered, why should students spend time taking courses that aren't required in their nursing or engineering curriculum? *We came*
Thesis statement   *up with some good reasons why a liberal arts education is more important than ever.*

Topic sentence   *First, there is the question of careers.* Students often make the mistake of thinking they will succeed by getting narrow training for a specific job without

Supporting
example

acquiring a good general education. They want to earn a lot of money in a hurry, and sometimes they do. When computers first came on the scene, people trained as computer scientists and programmers often made a lot of money, sometimes even without any higher education. But then the job market in computers shrank, as jobs were sent overseas, and many of those well-paid workers were laid off. They had no other training or education to fall back on. In the long run, a person with a broad education will be much better able to change jobs and adapt to new technologies than someone with a narrower background.

Topic sentence

Another reason why a good liberal arts education matters is that it promotes participation in society. Jobs and salaries are important, but they are not a person's whole life. Most people gain a great deal from their activities in local organizations, labor unions,

Support by
explaining
an effect

religious institutions, political causes, and other associations. If fewer and fewer people achieve a broad education, our social institutions will suffer. Where will we get the scout leaders, PTA officers, neighborhood spokespersons, and even intelligent voters? Education is not just for the benefit of the individual; it is also necessary for the good of society.

Topic sentence

People need to be broadly educated for the sake of their families as well. Most parents want their children to achieve at least as much as they have accomplished and have at least as good a lifestyle.

Support by
analyzing
a process

Knowing about psychology helps parents raise emotionally healthy children, and knowing about many subjects allows parents to guide their children's education.

As well-educated people, they set better examples for their sons and daughters, causing them to set higher goals for themselves. Since many children do not follow the same careers as their fathers and mothers, parents will be better able to communicate with their children if they know something about the careers they are interested in pursuing.

Topic sentence

Finally, a good education helps individuals to cultivate their own talents. One of the greatest satisfactions in life is the expression of one's own creativity. My aunt, who has just retired from her job as a bank manager, has begun writing poems and composing music for them. She studied music and literature in college but never had time to do much more than listen to concerts and read poetry and novels while she was working. She wrote some poems, but now that she has more time, she is writing a lot of them and composing songs. And she has actually gotten several songs chosen by record companies to be included on CD's by well-known artists. Her success is giving her as much fun and satisfaction as her job ever did. She wouldn't have been able to be creative without a good liberal arts education.

Support with personal experience

Conclusion

All of these reasons won't be enough to stop some students from choosing narrow technical training and ignoring their overall education. But many of those who do will probably regret their choice later and may go back and take courses in subjects they missed out on when they were younger. Luckily, it is possible nowadays to get all sorts of courses online and at local colleges, no matter how old you are. *In whatever way you get it, however, a liberal arts education has a lot of advantages.*

Restatement of thesis

In the essay above, identify the following: (1) the main idea, (2) supporting points, (3) transition words, (4) methods of developing supporting points.

Like most successful essays, this essay has a clear main point, subtopics, and overall structure. In your writing, try to follow the principles Sarah's essay illustrates: state a clear main thesis, develop it in paragraphs that contain supporting material, use transition words and topic sentences to guide the reader, and tie your thoughts together at the end. Sarah's essay is also successful because it takes a stand. Which of her statements do you find most convincing? Which are least convincing? Can you think of a counterargument? What might someone write to express an opposing point of view?

Developing Your Own Thinking, Writing, and Learning Process

Prewriting

STEPPING UP: WRITING TIP 1

Take time to prewrite even when you feel impatient and want to begin composing the essay itself. Thinking and planning now will pay off in a better essay later. Remember: The more thinking and prewriting you do ahead of time, the more material you will have to work with when you compose your essay and the less large-scale revising you may have to do to create a well-developed and well-organized final draft. Remember, too, that the best writers do *more* thinking, planning, drafting, and changing than weaker writers, not less.

Discovering Your Writing Process

Imagine a tower with a spiral staircase inside. Visualize yourself climbing this staircase and looking out a series of windows one above the other. At first, the windows are so near the ground you do not see much of the landscape below, but each time you reach a higher window, the same view, seen from a higher perspective, opens up an ever-expanding prospect. Climbing the steps takes effort, and the view sometimes seems not to change much from one level to the next. But by the time you have reached the top, your efforts reward you with a panorama grander than you could ever have imagined when taking your first steps.

Learning to write is a little like that. It often seems repetitious. It takes effort. You may hear yourself complaining, "Thesis statements again?

Subject-verb agreement—I've done that! Why am I still having trouble with verb tenses?" But each time you repeat a topic, you do so at a higher and higher level as you gain new vocabulary, learn to write with increasing maturity, learn to vary sentence length and structure, and take up the challenge of difficult academic topics. In Langston Hughes's poem "Mother to Son," a wise woman says to her son, "Life for me ain't been no crystal stair." Again, this is true of writing: It will not always be easy, and sometimes you will feel like sitting down on the steps, but as you improve, you will find increasing satisfaction in all stages of the writing process.

Writing is a process of thinking and learning. Accomplished writers often say that many of their best ideas come to them *while* they are writing, not beforehand. Writing a paper on an aspect of psychology or history is often the best way to understand and remember information on the subject. Learning is both passive and active; it is part taking in and remembering, and part organizing, analyzing, and expressing. When you develop your unique writing process, you will also be developing your powers of thinking and learning.

And what is this mysterious writing process? Like all writers, you will find a unique way of making the journey from the first steps of thinking about an idea for a writing project to creating, revising, and polishing your completed work. Experiment and find the methods that work best for you. Everybody is a little different. But, for most writers, there are roughly three main steps in the writing process:

- The many kinds of **preliminary activities** they go through before they get down to systematic composing, many of which are as much about thinking as writing;
- The **composing** process itself, which entails varied modes of organization; and
- The process of looking over their work, **revising**, and **correcting**.

Prewriting Experiments: Freewriting, Focused Writing, Brainstorming, Clustering, Cubing, and Outlining

A number of techniques have been developed to help writers get started, especially those troubled by writer's block. On any specific assignment, certain techniques will work better than others, and you can experiment with the ones described here to see which work best for you. **Freewriting** and **focused writing** are methods of nonstop writing that you do without pausing or self-censoring. Keep writing for five minutes or until you fill up two pages. These methods will not produce a masterpiece, or even an essay, but they may make you less inhibited so that you will begin to write fluently, the way you talk in conversation. The main difference between freewriting and focused writing is that in freewriting you let your mind wander on any subject that occurs to you—just free associate. Focused writing, on the other hand, requires you to stay on one general subject, such as television, sports, your appearance, shopping, politics, or college courses.

Brainstorming is a method best used in a group of people. It involves tossing ideas around for consideration and coming up with anything relevant to the topic. This method is particularly helpful for writers whose words flow easily during speech but who do not put enough content into their writing. Brainstorming will help you if you have trouble making your essays interesting and original, especially if you brainstorm with other lively, talkative people. On the other hand, brainstorming produces an abundance of chaotic facts and ideas. Be sure to follow up your brainstorming with activities that help you organize.

One such activity is **clustering**. Clustering can help you arrange material into groups of subtopics. It is a process of sorting your facts and thoughts into groups, or clusters, by writing them inside balloons like the ones you see in cartoons. A cluster gives you a "picture" of your topic, with its main concept at the center and subordinate ideas branching off from it, like this:

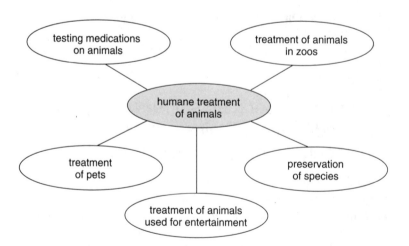

Clustering helps you recognize your essay's main topic, the secondary topics, and the supporting details. If you often mix up important points with unimportant details, clustering is for you.

Cubing, another form of prewriting, sounds like it has something to do with geometry, doesn't it? Some writers like to use the term to remind themselves that not only do topics have many ideas and facts associated with them, but also that they can be seen from many perspectives. If you tend to see a topic from the same angle, cubing may be your most useful prewriting activity. A cube has six surfaces; try to envision a topic from six directions. Imagine you have to write about the World Wide Web and cannot think of enough angles. Try a cubing exercise using these six "sides" of the topic:

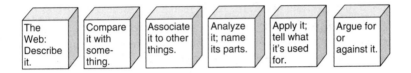

The Web: Describe it. | Compare it with something. | Associate it to other things. | Analyze it; name its parts. | Apply it; tell what it's used for. | Argue for or against it.

This kind of activity usually produces more ideas than you can possibly use in one essay, but if your problem is a one-track mind, cubing may help you develop more tracks and write more intelligent, mature essays.

Outlining is a tried-and-true method of planning that is always useful as a last step before composing an essay. Like many writers, you may prefer freewriting and focused writing as the best ways to begin exploring a topic. But once you have gathered facts and ideas through the methods described above, you should arrange your material into a plan, dividing your essay into main parts and supporting parts. You may not follow every detail of this plan once you begin composing your essay, but it will provide a map for you as you write. If you find yourself continually following every turnoff and losing the main highway, an outline will help you keep the main road in sight. But never use your outline as a rulebook: You may want to make important changes between drafts of your essay. Good ideas will occur to you as you write; be ready to adjust your plan and your outline as you compose. You may even find yourself creating a whole new outline if you decide one is needed.

You have undoubtedly seen elaborate outlines for large projects such as business proposals and academic papers. These usually follow a format using Roman numerals I, II, III, and the like for main headings and Arabic numerals for subheads (A., B., C., etc.). For your own purposes, however, you can use any format that you find helpful. The most important thing is to list your main points in order, as Sarah Chen did in her brief outline on page 8.

Interacting with Your Readers

As you prepare to compose an essay, think about interacting with your readers. First of all, be sure that they understand what you are saying. Their responses will help you clarify confusing statements or sharpen vague ones. You probably have strong ideas about your topic. Readers may agree or disagree with your ideas. Their responses can help you strengthen weak points in your arguments. To find out how others respond to your thoughts on the topic, read aloud some of your best focused writing and get feedback from a number of other people, either in your class writing group or at home. Note unexpected responses, such as points your readers disagree with or passages they find confusing, funny, or moving. Listen to suggestions for added points and examples. Your readers' responses provide a rich opportunity for you to make your writing moving and convincing. Your readers might catch a few mistakes as well.

Identifying Your Purpose

The transitional phase toward actually composing an essay is identifying your purpose in writing the essay. Every essay worth reading has a strong purpose. This purpose—whether it is to portray a person as a hero, compare one film with another, explain how to apply a software program, or persuade your readers to change their college curriculum—can be summed up in a single statement or two. Often this summation takes the form of a thesis statement near the end of your first paragraph. You should always be able to answer the question, What are you trying to say in this essay? Knowing what you are trying to accomplish in your essay is essential to writing effectively, even though that purpose may change as you compose.

Prewriting Activities: A Glimpse of a Student Writer at Work

You've read Sarah Chen's essay in its final form. Like most writers, Sarah went through many steps to get to this final draft. First, her instructor asked the class to think up topics for essays on education. Working in groups, the students brainstormed categories that included the cost of education, education in other countries, problems with high schools in the United States, athletics in college, fraternities and sororities, science education, training for jobs in business, the benefits of a college degree, the difference between community colleges and four-year colleges, and training for nursing and medicine.

The students agreed with the instructor that these topics were too broad and had to be narrowed. Sarah was particularly interested in the topic of community colleges because she currently was attending one and was planning to complete a bachelor's degree later. Instead of trying to write an essay on the broad topic of the differences between two-year and four-year colleges, she decided to try some focused writing to explore her ideas. Here is some of what she wrote:

> *Here I am in a community college. I'm not sure what I'm doing here, but I like my courses, well, most of them. Biology and English are interesting and Western Civilization is ok but we have too much memorizing of dates. I'm more interested in ideas. I'm good at math but my pre-calculus course is a bore, maybe because I had some of the material in high school. So far liberal arts is all right as a major because I can pick classes where I can learn things in different subjects and not have to be too narrow yet. Why do they call it liberal arts? Gina told me in high school she wanted to go to a liberal arts college. I wonder what kind of job she'll get with a liberal arts degree. How did I get on this topic? I'm supposed to be comparing community colleges and four-year colleges. They both have liberal arts, whatever that is. I'm supposed to know. Maybe that would be a good topic to write about. My adviser asked me what I wanted to do in the future, what kind of career I wanted. I told her I wasn't sure but that I wanted to work with people.*
>
> *That was pretty lame, but honestly I don't know yet. I don't think I want to be a nurse or a doctor. I'd rather work with healthy people than sick people. Maybe a teacher or a social worker. I want to make money but I would get bored just analyzing stocks and people's retirement accounts. On the other hand, if I don't make enough money I may not be very happy with the work I'm doing and want to change careers. My uncle told me last week that my generation should expect to have at least six jobs in our lifetimes and be ready to move from one job to another. That sounds scary. I'll have to have*

my resume updated all the time and get recommendation letters. It might be better if I try to do something where I won't have to change jobs every other year. But still I want to get a good education. There are too many interesting subjects for me to just choose one and stick to nothing but courses in that field now. I'm not ready to make up my mind yet. Besides, isn't that what you do in a four-year college?

Sarah continued her focused writing for several pages. Obviously, this kind of loose writing is not an essay, but it did help her realize that what she was most interested in was why she wanted to earn a liberal arts degree. She decided that answering that question would be the main purpose of her essay. Next, she tried arranging her topic into a cluster:

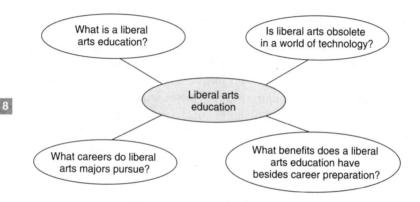

At this point it was possible for Sarah to organize her ideas into an outline that would provide the basis for the complete draft of an essay. Here is her outline.

Thesis: A liberal arts education is more important than ever in today's world.

I. People with a liberal arts education contribute to society.
II. A liberal arts education enriches family life.
III. A liberal arts education makes an individual happier and more creative.
IV. An education in the liberal arts is a good preparation for many careers.

Sarah decided at this point to write a rough draft of her essay without going into detail on each point; she felt confident that ideas would come to her as she wrote. As a result, her first draft was clearly organized but needed a lot of revision. See Chapter 4 to find out how she proceeded with her next steps.

Basic Exercise: Prewriting Experiments

Write for five minutes without stopping. Begin with the sentence, "Some things I like to do alone, but other things I enjoy doing with people." Do not worry about grammar, organization, or anything else—just write without hesitating. Keep writing as if you were dancing or doing aerobic exercises. As with those activities, you gain the benefits of this work (developing fluency) only if you keep moving.

After you have written for five minutes, put your writing aside. Look at it later and see whether you can identify a strong idea that you expressed in the piece. Look also for clusters of ideas that might be organized into groups. Create a cluster diagram, a writing cube, or an outline based on the thoughts you have expressed in your freewriting.

Intermediate Exercise: Prewriting Experiments

Write without stopping until you've filled up two single-spaced pages. Begin with the sentence, "I would like to change a number of things about our society."

Try to stay focused on this general idea; do not worry about grammar or being right about everything you say. The important thing is to develop a flow of words and ideas.

After putting this focused writing aside for a while, look at it again and try to find your most important idea—an opinion that holds your thoughts together. Then identify some subordinate ideas and make a cluster diagram, writing cube, or outline. Omit any topics that seem too far from the main focus of your draft. Save this focused writing and other informal writing, such as journal entries, as possible sources for essay topics and supporting materials later.

Challenge Exercise: Prewriting Experiments

Write without stopping until you have two pages of thoughts about what you've learned in a course you are currently studying or have recently studied. As you did in the previous exercises, concentrate on writing without hesitating: Do not puzzle over grammatical or factual details, just keep writing. As before, put your writing aside for a while, then look at it again. Search for the most important ideas and make a cluster, a writing cube, or an outline to help you identify a main thread of thought as well as supporting ideas. If there are ideas or facts that seem irrelevant to your most important opinions, omit them from the diagram or outline.

Proofreading Practice: Identifying Sentence Divisions in Your Prewriting Activities

Worrying too much about grammar is not appropriate when doing prewriting work. However, once you have substantial focused writing, look it over to see how well you control sentence structure. Experienced writers tend to write in complete sentences that are divided with correct punctuation marks, even when they are concentrating on the flow of ideas. Check your work to see whether you tend to write complete sentences and divide them correctly. If you find that you leave many **fragments**, **run-on sentences**, and **comma splices**, you may need a careful review of sentence grammar. Avoid fragments, run-on sentences, and comma splices by dividing your sentences with the correct punctuation.

Correcting Fragments

Be sure all of your sentences are complete. Remember that every sentence must have a main clause, including a subject and verb that belong together. Remember, too, that a main clause cannot begin with connecting words such as *which, although, because, if,* or *when.* Main verbs cannot be *-ing* forms unless they have helping verbs. (*The person listening* is not a main clause, but *Sandra is listening* is a main clause.) Watch for the extra piece of a sentence that you tag on after completing a statement; it may belong with the sentence and need to be attached to it.

Examine the sentence fragments and their corrections that follow.

Fragment: Hector is an unusually careful person. The kind of student who checks his work three times before turning it in.

Correct: Hector is an unusually careful person, the kind of student who checks his work three times before turning it in.

Fragment: Jennifer signed up for Spanish II. Even though she had never taken Spanish I.

Correct: Jennifer signed up for Spanish II, <u>even though she had</u> never taken Spanish I.

Fragment: Tony took the turnoff for Route 84. <u>Which led to an en-</u>trance to the beltway.

Correct: Tony took the turnoff for Route 84, <u>which led to an en-</u>trance to the beltway.

Fragment: The film ended abruptly after the car chase. <u>And left the</u> audience confused.

Correct: The film ended abruptly after the car chase <u>and left the</u> audience confused.

TEST YOURSELF: **Correct Fragments**

Correct the sentence fragments in the following items.

1. Enid thought Homer was everything she wanted a boyfriend to be. A person who understood her, knew what she wanted, and shared her interests.
2. Teenagers often do not like to follow advice. Especially when it comes from their parents.
3. Marisol decided to visit Mexico in March. Whether her sister could go with her or not.
4. Steven usually reads the news on the Internet. And participates in three online discussion groups.
5. Her cousin is still a senior in high school. She has an associate's degree.
6. Playing golf requires strength, coordination, and concentration. Not to mention endurance.
7. The nutritionist recommended a low-fat, low-carb diet. As well as aerobic exercise three times a week.

Answers: 1. to be, a person who 2. advice, especially when 3. in March, whether her 4. the Internet and participates 5. correct 6. concentration, not to mention 7. diet, as well as

---

Correcting Run-on (Fused) Sentences

Be careful to come to a full stop at the end of every sentence. If you run your sentences together without punctuation between them, they are harder to understand.

Incorrect: The members of the family came to the <u>reunion in May they also</u> went on a cruise of the Caribbean.

Correct: The members of the family came to the <u>reunion in May. They also</u> went on a cruise of the Caribbean.

Another	The members of the family came to the <u>reunion. In</u>
possibility:	<u>May</u> they also went on a cruise of the Caribbean.

The problem with run-on (or fused) sentences is that they force the reader to figure out where one idea ends and the next begins. That's your job as the writer. Do not make the reader do it for you.

To correct a run-on sentence, find where the first sentence ends and insert a period or other end punctuation there. There are more complicated ways to correct a run-on (see "Correcting Comma Splices" below), but let's practice with just dividing run-on sentences into two separate statements.

TEST YOURSELF: Correct Run-on Sentences

Correct the run-on sentences in the following items.

1. Some of the exercises are designed to improve flexibility the last six are intended to build strength.
2. Five courses are available on Monday and Wednesday mornings which one would you prefer?
3. The smartest drivers are usually the ones who win in the end it all comes down to strategy.
4. Byron peered intently at the map for a moment. Then he stood up and gathered the bikers around him.
5. Sharon already knew how to play chess while living in Russia she became an expert.
6. Choosing the right digital camera can be complicated it depends on the kind of photographing you intend to do.
7. The sound track for Gerald's film begins with slow, quiet music suddenly it shifts into thunderous, chaotic noise.

Answers: 1. flexibility. The last 2. mornings. Which 3. who win. In the end 4. correct 5. play chess. While living 6. complicated. It depends 7. music. Suddenly it

---

Correcting Comma Splices

Do not use commas in place of periods. When you get to the end of a sentence and begin a new one, use a full stop. A semicolon (;) can sometimes be used instead of the period.

Incorrect:	The mother in this story tries her best to give her daughter everything a child <u>needs, she</u> works hard to provide food, shelter, and schooling.

Correct: The mother in this story tries her best to give her daughter everything a child <u>needs. She</u> works hard to provide food, shelter, and schooling.

Correct: The mother in this story tries her best to give her daughter everything a child <u>needs; she</u> works hard to provide food, shelter, and schooling.

You may also combine the two statements with the following coordinating conjunctions: *and, or, nor, but, yet, so,* and *for.*

, and	He was fond of Susan, <u>and</u> he wanted to marry her.
, or	You could go to college, <u>or</u> you could play the oboe.
, nor	She isn't happy in her job, <u>nor</u> does she like her apartment.
, but	The first part is easy, <u>but</u> the last section is a killer.
, yet	She liked the film, <u>yet</u> she thought it was too short.
, so	Sam was very hungry, <u>so</u> he ordered a pizza.
, for	No one could find the clue, <u>for</u> it was written in code.

Incorrect: The mother in this story tries her best to give her daughter everything that she <u>needs, her</u> circumstances make it impossible for her to give her daughter the attention she craves.

Correct: The mother in this story tries her best to give her daughter everything that she <u>needs, but her</u> circumstances make it impossible for her to give her daughter the attention she craves.

TEST YOURSELF: **Correct Comma Splices**

Correct the comma splices in the following items.

1. Some students put a lot of their life experiences into their essays, but others prefer not to write about their own lives.
2. The officers of the club made a mistake by calling meetings on Tuesday morning, many students have classes at that time.
3. The new job suits Barbara's schedule, it is only 20 hours a week and she has two days off.
4. The main character in this story reminds me of my girlfriend, she is too dependent on her family and controlled by their opinions.

5. Writing an essay requires planning and revision, you also have to do a lot of critical thinking.

6. The situations of the two mothers are similar, however, they respond to their problems of poverty and lack of support in different ways.

7. Some people do research on the Internet; others, who feel less comfortable with technology, still use only the library.

Answers: 1. correct 2. morning. Many students 3. schedule. It is 4. girlfriend. She is 5. revision. You also 6. similar. However, 7. correct

PROOFREADING EXERCISES: Basic, Intermediate, Challenge

Basic Exercise: Sentence Divisions

Find the seven errors in the following passage. Rewrite the paragraph with corrections.

Latoya decided to look for a new apartment, she wanted to have more space and a better view. Especially a view of the park. She first tried the old-fashioned system of looking in the newspapers for rental ads. There she found three apartments that sounded just right for her, she called all three of them immediately. Unfortunately, they had already been rented. Before she called. Then she thought about looking for an apartment on the Internet. By looking on Craig's List. She found a number of inexpensive rentals. Just like the one she wanted. The second one she called was still available. She hurried over and looked at it. And was delighted to find the apartment of her dreams.

Intermediate Exercise: Sentence Divisions

Find the seven errors in the following passage. Rewrite the paragraph with corrections.

Calvin thinks his economics course was the most interesting course he ever took. Because he learned so much about money, work, government programs, and corporations. Professor Wilson, who taught the course, really knew his subject. And explained a lot about the financial crisis of 2008. At first Calvin thought economics would be boring, he didn't know much about business and didn't like to work with statistics. The textbook was huge and expensive it looked difficult to read. After two weeks, however, he discovered that he could understand concepts like inflation, compound interest, and profit margins. As well as institutions like the Federal Reserve and terms like *credit default swaps*. At the beginning of the course he was a biology major, the course changed his mind about the direction of his studies and his career. Now he is thinking of taking a course in statistics he plans to change his major to business administration.

Challenge Exercise: Sentence Divisions

Find the seven errors in the following passage. Rewrite the paragraph with corrections.

Eileen read a story called "Roman Fever" by Edith Wharton, she liked it because of its surprise ending. The story tells about two upperclass widows from New York, Mrs. Slade and Mrs. Ansley, who have been friends for all of their adult lives. Although they seem to like and admire each other. Mrs. Slade envies Mrs. Ansley partly because her daughter is much livelier and more interesting than Mrs. Slade's daughter. But also because she suspects that Mr. Slade may have been secretly in love with Mrs. Ansley. The two women meet in Rome, they talk about an incident years ago before they married their husbands. Mrs. Slade wrote a letter to Mrs. Ansley, she pretended to be Mr. Slade inviting Mrs. Ansley to meet him for a romantic interlude at the Colosseum. Now, many years later, Mrs. Slade confesses to her friend that the letter was really a fake. Mrs. Ansley, in turn, confesses that she sent Mr. Slade a letter in reply, thinking it came from him. And that they did indeed have that romantic meeting. Mrs. Slade is shocked but still feels superior because, she says, she had her husband during all those years of marriage. But Mrs. Ansley replies that she has had her lively daughter. Who's really Mr. Slade's biological daughter—the result of that one romantic fling. Eileen can't decide which woman is the winner and which is the loser.

Key Terms from Chapter 1 for Review

comma splice, prewriting, run-on sentence, sentence fragments, the writing process

Making a Point

STEPPING UP: WRITING TIP 2

In our age of texting, Twitter, and Facebook, readers are more impatient than ever. Some readers may not pay close attention to all parts of your essay, and if they don't, you can guess which part they are most likely to notice: your introduction and your main point. They expect you to explain your main purpose near the beginning. Be sure not to disappoint them. Better than that, make your opening so interesting and your thesis so clear that they will want to read your whole essay carefully. Be sure that your purpose is evident by the end of your first paragraph.

Thesis Statements

A **thesis statement** is a sentence that explains the main purpose of an essay. It can be just a short, simple sentence stating an opinion or attitude, or it may divide the main idea into two, three, or four parts. A thesis statement has to be broad enough to cover everything contained in the essay but specific enough to explain your purpose.

Simple Thesis Statement

If you are ready for it, an online course can be a good choice.

Developed Thesis Statement

If you are ready for the extra work and have the necessary self-discipline, an online course will provide a different, and in some ways richer, experience than you can have in a classroom.

Although a simple thesis statement is often satisfactory, a developed one provides a map for the rest of the essay and thus guides the reader more. Which of the two thesis statements above gives readers a clearer idea of what to expect in the essay? The developed thesis statement tells us that the writer will discuss the amount of work in an online course, the self-discipline needed to keep up with assignments, and the ways in which learners can get something out of distance learning that they cannot get in a classroom. It makes some specific promises to the reader. The simple thesis statement leaves the reader less certain about what to expect. Remember that if you present a developed thesis statement in your first paragraph, the reader expects your essay to contain just what you promise in your thesis statement!

Thesis Statements Must Take a Position

A thesis statement must state the whole purpose of the essay. Why would the following sentence not make a good thesis statement for the sample essay?

Online courses are now offered at ninety percent of American colleges.

This is a specific factual statement. It might make a good lead-in to arouse interest, but it does not state an argument or explain the purpose of the whole essay.

Thesis Statements Must Be Precise

Although thesis statements must be broad enough to state an essay's main purpose, they should never be fuzzy or confusing. Remember that catchall words such as *bad, good, nice, great, interesting,* and *thing* are not precise. What is good to one person is bad to another; what one person finds interesting another finds tedious. Try to find more precise key words for your thesis statements. Compare these two thesis statements:

A. *Extraterrestrials on Campus* is a bad film.

B. *Extraterrestrials on Campus* is a pointless, tasteless film with a predictable plot and outmoded cinematic techniques.

Sentence A doesn't guide the reader much. It says only that the writer is going to make negative remarks about the film. Sentence B states what kind of faults the writer is going to find in the film.

TEST YOURSELF: Thesis Statements

Determine which sentence in each of the pairs below might make a suitable thesis statement for an essay.

1. A. The Troubled Asset Relief Program in 2008, or TARP, allowed the government to spend up to $700 billion to rescue banks and other institutions.
   B. The Troubled Asset Relief Program in 2008, or TARP, was mostly successful in rescuing banks and other institutions without costing taxpayers as much as expected.

2. A. The Giants won the game 27 to 21.
   B. The game between the Giants and the Chargers was full of suspense and unexpected reversals.

3. A. The current prison system lacks adequate means for rehabilitation and psychiatric counseling.
   B. The state prison at Capital City houses 1,400 inmates.

4. A. Levels of alcohol in the blood can be tested by instruments.
   B. Drunken driving can be controlled better through the use of technology than by new laws.

5. A. My vacation in Morocco was wonderful because I met some remarkable people and visited archaeological sites.
   B. I visited Morocco for two weeks in March.

6. A. Women's fashions this year are reminiscent of those of the 1980s but are very practical.
   B. New fashions for women are interesting.

7. A. Poe's "The Tell-Tale Heart" is a scary story.
   B. Poe's "The Tell-Tale Heart" reveals several features of a psychotic mind.

Answers: 1. B 2. B 3. A 4. B 5. A 6. A 7. B

Introductory Paragraphs

The first paragraph in an essay serves several purposes. Its main purpose is to arouse interest and to let the reader know what the essay is about, usually in a thesis statement. Starting with the thesis statement in your first sentence, however, is usually too blunt. Capture the reader's attention first, and then lead up to the thesis statement in some way. Think of the three-step design as a useful pattern for your first paragraph: lead-in, tie-in, and thesis statement.

Starting with the Three-Step Design

Begin your paragraph with an effective **lead-in**. This attention-getter can be one of several types:

- A question
- A quotation or other amusing remark
- A short, thought-provoking statement
- A surprising fact or statistic
- A problem or riddle

After capturing the reader's interest with a creative lead-in, find a way to focus that interest on the subject. The two or three sentences in which you do this are your **tie-in**. Finally, move smoothly from your tie-in to your thesis statement. The three-step design—lead-in, tie-in, thesis statement—is not a universal formula, but it may help you to begin essays effectively.

Model Introductory Paragraph

Taking a course online can be a rich experience if you are ready for it. Because I was not quite prepared to change my study habits, my first distance learning course almost became a disaster. However, I was able to make some adjustments in my attitude and routine quickly enough to learn a lot in the course. From my experience, I would advise anyone planning to take a course online to keep one important consideration in mind: Distance learning does not require you to be a computer scientist, but neither is it an easy way out of difficult courses. If you are ready for the extra work and have the self-discipline to complete assignments regularly, an online course will be a different, and in some ways richer, experience than you can have in a classroom.

To create organized paragraphs like this, you may have to do some prewriting experiments to identify your main idea and supporting details. You will probably write a rough draft of your introductory paragraph and revise it after you have composed the rest of your essay.

Avoid Bad Starts

Watch out for these common problems with introductions. It may be tempting to use these methods, but they usually produce weak essays.

- Do not begin by apologizing.

> *In this essay I am supposed to write about the effect of instructional technology. I never took a distance learning course and I don't have very good keyboard skills. All I can say is that online courses are very important for some people and are here to stay. Every time I look at the schedule of classes, I see whole lists of courses given online. Sometime maybe I will try to take one of them. I wish I knew more about technology.*

This kind of introduction reads like a piece of focused writing in which the writer is searching for something to say about the topic. The paragraph has no organization, no lead-in, and no thesis statement. Do not tell the reader what you do not know; explore what you *do* know through prewriting techniques until you find a good way to begin.

- Do not bore your reader by mechanically previewing too much of your essay.

> *I am going to discuss instructional technology in this essay. First, I plan to talk about how important distance learning is to some students who can't attend regular classroom courses. My next paragraph will be about how computers can be used in classrooms. Then I will discuss different kinds of courses that use technology. Finally, I will stress how important technology will be in higher education over the next decade.*

This writer calls too much attention to her plan. No viewer at the beginning of a film wants to know the entire plot and all the cinematic and audio techniques used in making it. Be clear about your intentions, but do not bore the reader.

▪ Do not begin with grandiose statements that fail to lead into your thesis.

> *Since the beginning of time human beings have invented new technological advances that have helped and hindered the progress of education toward perfection. In our postmodern times, nothing has had a bigger impact on the way people learn than one single invention: a machine called the computer. This machine will be remembered as the greatest learning tool of all time.*

This writer shows enthusiasm but needs to focus his ideas. *Show* rather than *tell* the reader what is important and exciting about your subject, and concentrate on a topic that is limited enough for you to discuss in depth.

TEST YOURSELF: **Introductory Paragraphs**

Read the three sample paragraphs that follow. Identify the paragraph that is carefully organized; find the lead-in, tie-in, and thesis statement. Explain why the other two fail as introductory paragraphs.

Paragraph A

Poetry is one of the most wonderful things in the world. Since the beginning of history, people have written poems. There are many kinds of poems, long poems, and short poems. Everybody likes to read poems and most people like to write them. Without poetry, where would we be? Poetry is the best way to spend your time. If you read and write poems, you will be a better person. Poetry will be around until the end of time.

Paragraph B

Can a poem written in conversational language express deep meaning? Robert Frost's poem "The Road Not Taken" reads like an ordinary person talking to us, but gives us wisdom to guide our lives. Its plain language allows the reader to concentrate on the details of the poem and to imagine being in the situation it presents: facing a choice between two roads, which really stand for the choices we face in life. The conversational style of this poem allows the reader to find personal meaning in imagined experience.

Paragraph C

In this essay I am going to talk about the topic of poetry. As a child I liked to read poetry. My sister used to read poetry to me before I could read. I don't know much about how to write about poetry, but it's always hard to get started writing about anything. I don't like poems that have big words I can't understand. The poems I like are simple, but they say a lot in ordinary language. I'm not going to write about technical stuff like rhyme schemes and what kind of accents there are in every line. Poetry is hard to write about.

Answer: Paragraph A makes grandiose, overgeneralized statements and would not lead in well to an essay. Paragraph C apologizes for the writer's confusion and wanders in several directions. Paragraph B focuses on a specific poem and makes a clear point that could be developed in an essay.

WRITING EXERCISES: Basic, Intermediate, Challenge

Basic Exercise: Thesis Statements

Identify the sentence in each pair that would make an effective thesis statement for an essay. Explain why the other sentence is not effective as a thesis statement.

1. A. On my trip to Las Vegas I lost $300.
   B. My trip to Las Vegas taught me two lessons: Plan ahead and don't gamble.

2. A. News magazines cover stories in more detail than television news.
   B. I like to read news magazines and watch television news.

3. A. Soccer is played in almost every country.
   B. There are three reasons why soccer is becoming more popular in U.S. schools.

4. A. My sister's experience with three diets shows which one really works.
   B. My sister is really overweight and needs to go on a diet.

5. A. A lot of people shop online nowadays.
   B. Several tips will help you become a smarter online shopper.

6. A. To improve credibility, the Olympics needs improved judging and drug testing.
   B. London was chosen as the site of the summer 2012 Olympics.

7. A. This essay will be about physical therapy.
   B. Education and training requirements for a career in physical therapy are rigorous.

Intermediate Exercise: Thesis Statements

Rewrite these sentences to make them more effective thesis statements. An example follows.

Original sentence: Aiden's first year in college was a good experience.

Revised sentence: Aiden's first year in college changed him from an adolescent to an adult.

1. Ted has two brothers and three sisters.
2. The mall where I worked had thirty-six stores in it.
3. Reading novels takes a lot of time.
4. Biology 101 is a good course.
5. Lebron James is a famous basketball player.
6. I like to watch *Dancing with the Stars* on television.
7. You see people reading e-books everywhere.

Challenge Exercise: Thesis Statements

Write precise, developed thesis statements for essays on these topics.

1. Teenagers and their parents
   Thesis statement: _____

2. Marriage and divorce
   Thesis statement: _____

3. College courses
   Thesis statement: _____

4. Choosing careers
   Thesis statement: _____

5. Television sports
   Thesis statement: _____

6. A film you enjoyed
   Thesis statement: _____

7. A band or singer you like
   Thesis statement: _____

   _____

Proofreading Practice: Agreement of Subjects and Verbs

Watch Those S-Endings

Writing a thesis statement always involves matching a subject, either singular or plural, with an action. As in all sentences, the verb in a thesis sentence must agree in number with the subject. Most errors in subject-verb agreement involve missing s-endings on nouns or verbs. Sometimes writers put s-endings where they should not be.

Examine the following typical errors in thesis statements.

Incorrect singular statement: Technology help students become active learners.

Corrected form: Technology helps students become active learners.

Incorrect plural statement: Technological innovations helps students become active learners.

Corrected form: Technological innovations help students become active learners.

Remember the **one-s pattern**: In most sentences, either the verb has the s-ending (singular) or the noun subject has the s-ending (plural). For example:

Singular: An outstanding student submits work on time.

Plural: Outstanding students submit work on time.

TEST YOURSELF: **Subject-Verb Agreement**

Find the errors in s-endings in these sentences. Add s-endings where they are missing and eliminate s-endings where they do not belong. One sentence is correct.

1. Sarah's cousin like Sarah's new hairstyle.
2. Three players wants to join another team.
3. Some candidates refuses to accept public funds.
4. Spring vacation this year begins on Tuesday.

5. Most essays needs strong introductory paragraphs.

6. The professor always assign a long reading over the weekend.

7. Cars with ample interior space sells well.

Answers: 1. likes 2. want 3. refuse 4. correct 5. need 6. assigns 7. sell

---

PROOFREADING EXERCISES: Basic, Intermediate, Challenge

Basic Exercise: Subject-Verb Agreement

Find the seven errors in the following passage. Rewrite the paragraph with corrections.

Shirley plans her weekdays in three stages. She usually spend her whole morning in college classes. She always take notes and participates in discussions. At one o'clock she always feel tired and hungry, so she heads for the cafeteria. That is where she meets her friends Jennifer and Jonathan. They both live in town and commutes to campus. In the afternoon, from 2:00 until 6:00, her job in the law school library take up all of her time. After work, she relax and has a light dinner. Then in the evening she and her friends often goes to parties, discos, or movies. Her schedule keeps her active and socially busy, and she needs the weekend to rest and do homework.

Intermediate Exercise: Subject-Verb Agreement

Find the seven errors in the following passage. Rewrite the paragraph with corrections.

Wise investing depend upon several factors. It involves your income, needs, and willingness to take risks. Some people invests their money only in stocks. Other opportunities also exists. Municipal bonds, mutual funds, and term savings accounts all offers investment advantages. The right kind of investment for you mean considering several elements. Tax benefits from municipal bonds appeals to some investors. Stocks present possibilities for high income but with high risk. The investor who wants to avoid risks often choose mutual funds. Corporate bonds also offer high income possibilities but also with greater risk than municipal bonds.

Challenge Exercise: Subject-Verb Agreement

Find the seven errors in the following passage. Rewrite the paragraph with corrections.

Some expert believe that one of the chief problems in American education is the inability of student to understand and evaluate knowledge. Howard Gardner, a professor of education at Harvard University, in a book called *The Unschooled Mind*, write that too many students think according to stereotypes. In the social sciences, for example, they bring to the study of a problem their assumptions about human nature based on their own experience. In the arts, they often retains tastes acquired in childhood and nourished by popular culture and do not acquire more complex and subtle ways of appreciating music, art, and literature. When they analyze a historical event or evaluate a poem or piece of music, too many students rely on their habitual responses, which derives from a narrow range of biases and preconceptions. Therefore a major challenge of education is to help students develop the power to analyze, evaluate, and appreciate new problems, situations, and experiences by drawing on a deep understanding of academic disciplines. Although acquiring factual knowledge is part of learning, memorization of information do not guarantee that students understands the meaning and value of the factual knowledge they have acquired.

Key Words from Chapter 2 for Review

introductory paragraph, subject-verb agreement, thesis statement

Developing Your Body Paragraphs and Making Conclusions

STEPPING UP: WRITING TIP 3

Students often ask their instructors how long an assignment should be, as if the only goal were writing a lot of words. If you think of your essay as a 750-word hike, you'll probably head for your goal with blinders on, counting your words but ignoring many of the ways you could enliven your topic. Instead, try to create a different mental picture of your project—not as a journey but as an empty canvas to be filled with colors and shapes, a meal to be prepared with varied ingredients, or a garden to be planted with many flowers and vegetables. Imagining such nonlinear tasks will help you think in terms of variety, richness, and the interrelation of parts. Be resourceful about adding material to your composition anywhere—in the beginning, the middle, or the end.

Explaining and Illustrating Ideas in Body Paragraphs

The most common problem with many writers' first drafts is lack of development. Think of development as explaining and illustrating ideas, not just adding words. Even writers with a fluent command of English and smart ideas may fail to say enough about the topic they discuss. There is no way of getting around it: explaining and illustrating your ideas takes work. There are techniques to help you develop your ideas, but no quick and easy ones. Development requires thinking, composing, and revising.

Applying Techniques of Development

You will find it easier to develop ideas if you acquire a variety of development methods. One approach is to **analyze** and **explain** your topic. If your subject has complicated and controversial aspects, do not rush over this part of the essay. Explain the complexities and controversies; go into detail in explaining your point. Another technique is to give **examples**, either from **personal experience** or **general knowledge** acquired from the news media and your reading. A third is to **draw analogies** by comparing your subject to some parallel thing or concept. You may want to **acknowledge your reader's viewpoint** if it is likely that many people will disagree with you or have a different perspective on the topic. In most of the best writing, there is some **appeal to emotions** as well, which can be done through your style, the examples you choose, or the way in which your writing strikes a responsive chord in the reader's feelings.

In research essays, you will use **published sources of information**, such as books, articles, and postings on Web sites. Beware the "data dump," however. It is tempting to take passages from print materials or Web sources and paste them into your essay without thinking carefully. If you want to borrow material from printed or Web sources, as you're often expected to do in college essays, read these sources carefully and evaluate their content. Passing along whole blocks of writing from another source may give you a sense of power, but it will not impress a reader unless you select the information carefully and present it effectively to fulfill the purpose of your essay. In addition, if you neglect to give credit to the author of your borrowed material—whether intentionally or not—you will be guilty of plagiarism.

Following are methods of development used by writers.

Analyzing a Topic

Here is one student's analysis of an issue in education.

> There are many reasons why students with good abilities do poorly in school and college. Sometimes they have personal problems that hold them back, causing them to undermine their own progress. Their peers, especially ones who have a negative attitude toward school, may influence them. Some students believe that it is more important to earn money than to earn a diploma or college degree. They may put off completing their education so they can buy the clothes, jewelry, and electronic equipment they want. Other students have learning disabilities and, even though they are very intelligent, may not get the special help they need to succeed in school. Finally, many students attend schools in which the instruction is not in their native language. They may take a number of years to catch up to native speakers and not reach their full potential right away.

Remember to use your powers of critical thinking to explore and analyze the range of your topic. Brainstorming, focused writing, or cubing may help you recognize the many aspects of your topic.

Using Personal Experience

Here is a passage in which the writer draws on personal experience to make a point about the power that books exercise in the minds of children. Mike Rose explains how reading and writing were connected in his youth as he told stories to his friends in the street.

> Reading opened up the world. There I was, a skinny bookworm drawing the attention of street kids who, in any other circumstances, would have had me for breakfast. Like an epic tale-teller, I developed the stories as I went along, relying on a flexible plot line and repository of heroic events. I had a great time. I sketched out trajectories with my finger on Frank's dusty truck bed. And I stretched out each story's climax, creating cliff-hangers like the ones

*I saw in the Saturday serials. These stories created for me a
temporary community.*

—Mike Rose. *Lives on the Boundary* (New York: Penguin, 1989): 21

Mike Rose's book is mostly about his own life, so naturally he writes
about personal experience. For some college-level writing assignments,
however, using personal experience to support a main idea may not be
appropriate. If you are not sure what to do on a specific assignment,
discuss it with your instructor.

Using Analogies

Here is a passage from *The Black Swan* by Nassim Taleb, in which
the author identifies unexpected events in history as "black swans"
because they are so rare. He first talks about real black swans and then
makes the analogy to "black swan" events.

> *Before the discovery of Australia, people in the Old World were
> convinced that all swans were white, an unassailable belief as it
> seemed completely confirmed by empirical evidence. The sighting of
> the first black swan might have been an interesting surprise for a
> few ornithologists (and others extremely concerned with the coloring
> of birds), but that is not where the significance of the story lies. It
> illustrates the severe limitation to our learning from observations or
> experience and the fragility of our knowledge. One single observation
> can invalidate a general statement derived from millennia of
> confirmatory sightings of millions of white swans. All you need is
> one single (and, I am told, quite ugly) black bird.*
>
> *I push one step beyond this philosophical-logical question into
> an empirical reality, and one that has obsessed me since childhood.
> What we call here a Black Swan (and capitalize it) is an event with
> the following three attributes.*
>
> *First, it is an outlier, as it lies outside the realm of regular
> expectations, because nothing in the past can convincingly point to
> its possibility. Second, it carries an extreme impact (unlike the bird).
> Third, in spite of its outlier status, human nature makes us concoct
> explanations for its occurrence after the fact, making it explainable
> and predictable.*

—Nassim Nicholas Taleb. *The Black Swan:
The Impact of the Highly Improbable* (N.Y.: Random House, 2010)

Explain or look up in the dictionary the meaning of these words: unassailable, empirical, invalidate, millennia, confirmatory.

Comparisons of this kind help us understand a topic better, but an analogy is *only* a comparison and therefore doesn't prove much about the original subject. Notice how Taleb not only explains the parallels between black swans (the birds) and black swan events, but also points out one way in which the two differ. What is the one way in which black swan events are *not* analogous to black swans in nature?

Acknowledging the Reader

Below is a passage from the famous "Letter from Birmingham Jail" by Dr. Martin Luther King, Jr. Notice how he begins his letter by recognizing the objections of the clergymen to whom the letter is addressed and appealing to their religious convictions.

April 16, 1963

My Dear Fellow Clergymen:

While confined here in the Birmingham city jail, I came across your recent statement calling my present activities "unwise and untimely." Seldom do I pause to answer criticism of my work and ideas. If I sought to answer all the criticisms that cross my desk, my secretaries would have little time for anything other than such correspondence in the course of the day, and I would have no time for constructive work. But since I feel that you are men of genuine good will and that your criticisms are sincerely set forth, I want to try to answer your statements in what I hope will be patient and reasonable terms.

I think I should indicate why I am here in Birmingham, since you have been influenced by the view which argues against "outsiders coming in." I have the honor of serving as president of the Southern Christian Leadership Conference, an organization operating in every southern state, with headquarters in Atlanta, Georgia. We have some eighty-five affiliated organizations across the South, and one of them is the Alabama Christian Movement for Human Rights. Frequently we share staff, educational and financial resources with our affiliates. Several months ago the affiliate here in Birmingham asked us to be on call to engage in a nonviolent direct-action program if such were deemed necessary. We readily consented, and when the hour came we lived up to our promise. So I, along with several members of my staff, am here because I was invited here. I am here because I have organizational ties here.

But more basically, I am in Birmingham because injustice is here. Just as the prophets of the eighth century B.C. left their villages and carried their "thus saith the Lord" far beyond the boundaries of their home towns, and just as the Apostle Paul left his village of Tarsus and carried the gospel of Jesus Christ to the far corners of the Greco-Roman world, so am I compelled to carry the gospel of freedom beyond my own home town. Like Paul, I must constantly respond to the Macedonian call for aid.

Moreover, I am cognizant of the interrelatedness of all communities and states. I cannot sit idly by in Atlanta and not be concerned about what happens in Birmingham. Injustice anywhere is a threat to justice everywhere. We are caught in an inescapable network of mutuality, tied in a single garment of destiny. Whatever affects one directly, affects all indirectly. Never again can we afford to live with the narrow, provincial "outside agitator" idea. Anyone who lives inside the United States can never be considered an outsider anywhere within its bounds. . . .

—Martin Luther King, Jr. Excerpt from "Letter from Birmingham Jail."

Dr. King then goes on to explain why his nonviolent campaign against racial segregation is necessary and right. Before making his argument, however, he captures the attention and sympathies of his readers by talking directly to them and understanding their point of view, even though he disagrees with it. By basing his argument on their shared principles, he can more effectively persuade them that his cause is just.

Appealing to Emotion

In the following passage, Dr. Sherwin B. Nuland, in the midst of giving a scientific explanation of Alzheimer's disease, appeals to the reader's emotions to convey how devastating the disease can be for the families of those who are stricken. See how many emotions you can identify in his discussion.

In the case of Alzheimer's disease, it is rarely the patient who recognizes the need for company in the journey through travail. But there is probably no disability of our time in which the presence of support groups can help so decisively to ensure the emotional survival of the closest witnesses to the disintegration. . . . There is strength in numbers, even when the numbers are only one or two understanding people who can soften the anguish by the simple act of listening.

That anguish consists of many parts, and some of them cannot be dealt with unless with a sympathetic and knowing listener. Is it possible that the burden of this disease does not become a source of resentment and sometimes repugnance to everyone it drags along in its loathsome wake? Can anyone maim a great piece of his or her life without seething? Is there a single person who can forbearingly watch as the object of his or her brightest love involutes into incomprehension and decay?

–Sherwin B. Nuland. From *How We Die: Reflections on Life's Final Chapter* (New York: Knopf, 1994): 106

Using Public Sources of Information

One task you are certain to be assigned in college courses is to use researched materials from the Web or the library to back up the arguments in your papers. This research can be done for any subject. Below is a brief example of how to use a source to make a point about a short story.

In Alice Walker's short story, "Everyday Use," patchwork quilts serve as a central symbol as well as the subject of a family quarrel. Over the centuries quilts acquired symbolic importance in African American culture. According to Houston Baker and Charlotte Pierce-Baker, quilts "crafted from bits of worn overalls, shredded uniforms, tattered petticoats, and outgrown dresses" came to represent the "patterned wholeness in the African diaspora" (309). Walker incorporates this traditional symbolism for the purpose of revealing the strength as well as the inner tensions of African American families. She also causes the reader to think about the meaning of the word heritage.

Notice that when you use sources this way, you must fit the quoted matter into your sentences grammatically, enclose it in quotation marks, and refer to its source in parentheses. (Usually the author's last name and the number of the page on which the quoted material is found are given in the parentheses, but in the above example the authors are already mentioned in the text of the paragraph so they do not need to be repeated.) At the end of your paper, you must create a **bibliography**, or list of sources. The source referred to above would look like this on your list:

Baker, Houston A., Jr., and Charlotte Pierce-Baker. "Patches: Quilts and Community in Alice Walker's 'Everyday Use.'" *Alice Walker: Critical Perspectives Past and Present*. Ed. Henry Louis Gates, Jr. and K. A. Appiah. New York: Amistad Press, 1993. 309–316. Print.

For a complete lesson on using research materials, see Chapter 15.

Choosing Modes of Development

Writing is often classified into categories called **rhetorical modes**. The **narrative** mode is storytelling, whether fiction or nonfiction. The **descriptive** mode refers to writing that paints a word portrait of a person, place, or institution. There are several kinds of **expository** modes, such as **process analysis, enumeration, definition**, and **classification. Comparison and contrast** is a writing mode often used in academic work, and **persuasion**, also called **argumentation**, is a familiar form of writing in editorials and political writing.

These categories identify the purpose of the essay and generally establish the method by which it is structured. Most essays fit loosely into one of these types, but these categories are not completely separate, like biological species. A single essay usually draws on several of these modes and combines them for a total effect. For practice, however, it is useful to group essays into these modes to explore varied kinds of writing.

Some college writing assignments require a particular mode. In other cases, you may have some choice, such as an assignment that requires an expository presentation but does not specify exactly how you should arrange and develop it. Being familiar with the different modes and choosing the one that will be most effective is a key to successful writing. It is also important to familiarize yourself with the best techniques to use in different modes, as well as some of the problems they may present, both as writing strategies and as grammatical challenges.

Concluding Paragraphs

Concluding paragraphs should look in two directions—backward to sum up what you've said, and forward to suggest further thought. Like introductory paragraphs, they are usually short. Your concluding statements should leave the reader with a sense of completeness and a desire to think more about the subject. Like the opening, the ending of your essay should be dramatic, witty, imaginative, amusing, or thought-provoking. It might pose a question, a prediction, or a paradox. It should remind the reader of something you said at the beginning of the essay, but it should not merely repeat words or restate ideas from the first paragraph. Think of the concluding paragraph as an upside-down version of the introductory paragraph. It may begin by reemphasizing the main idea (but not by restating the thesis sentence word for word) and end with statements that wrap up the discussion with humor, emotional appeal, or insight.

Conclusions to Avoid

- **Do not introduce important ideas that are not supported in your essay.** If you try to complete your essay in one hasty draft, your "concluding" paragraph may be the one in which you discover important new ideas. If this happens, either rethink the whole essay, using material from this "concluding" section as the main point expressed near the beginning of your essay, or rethink the concluding paragraph to make it fit the essay you have written. Consider this attempt at a conclusion to our imaginary essay on distance learning.

    So we can see that technology has become very important in higher education. In fact, businesses and government agencies use technology just as much as colleges do. Try to imagine banks without ATMs, transit systems without computer programs, and police departments without cellular phones and data files. Technology has changed every part of our lives today.

    This paragraph jumps off the track. The essay is about online courses, but at the end the writer suddenly becomes interested in other uses of computer technology. The concluding paragraph is a bad place to change your topic, just when you should be stressing the points already made.

- **Do not end with a detailed, monotonous summary.** Another kind of conclusion that does not succeed in a short essay is the mechanical summary. Sometimes a very long piece of writing, such as a book or dissertation, especially if it is complicated, needs a summary to help the reader digest and remember the points it made. In a short college essay, however, such a summary is a great way to bore the reader. Consider this paragraph as an ending to our essay on computers in higher education.

> *In summary, I have discussed in this essay some of the ways that computers make higher education more efficient. The first advantage I discussed was taking courses at home. In the next paragraph I talked about asynchronous discussions in online courses. Then I explained the advantages of having access to professors through e-mail. When you have read what I explained about these advantages, you will understand why it is important to take more courses online.*

This paragraph emphasizes the writer's plan when the focus should be on the topic itself. Give the reader a sense of order and make some indirect reference to your opening, but do not overdo the repetition.

- **Do not fade at the end.** Often when you have put a lot of effort into writing an essay, you may be tired and not want to put much effort into your final paragraph. Remember that some readers will look to your conclusion for a concise, forceful statement of your purpose and expect it to be some of your best writing in the essay. Do not disappoint them.

Model Concluding Paragraph

Here is a more successful concluding paragraph for our essay.

> *Online courses, as I discovered, can be exciting because of the features you cannot experience in a classroom. In threaded discussions you can see what everyone else is thinking, and the remarks are saved, unlike a class discussion, where many students remain silent and no record is kept. You also receive more feedback from both the instructor and your classmates than you are likely to get in a traditional class. Materials from Web sites make the course richer as well. If you are ready for the extra work and have the self-discipline to keep up with the assignments, these advantages of distance education are for you.*

Note that the writer makes an indirect reference to the advice given in the model introductory paragraph above—that students should be realistic about the demands of online courses. This link to the introduction creates a sense of completeness.

WRITING EXERCISES: Basic, Intermediate, Challenge

Basic Exercise: Using Personal Experience

Begin a paragraph with the sentence provided below. Develop the idea with at least six additional sentences, using personal experience as a method of development.

> An important change in my life taught me a lesson about myself.

Intermediate Exercise: Using an Analogy

Begin a paragraph with the sentence provided below. Develop the idea with at least six additional sentences, expanding your analogy as a method of development.

> My family is just like a _____ (fill in the blank with a word such as *team, circus, sitcom, soap opera, corporation*, etc.).

Challenge Exercise: Acknowledging Your Reader

Begin a paragraph with the sentence provided below. Develop the idea with at least six additional sentences, acknowledging your reader's viewpoint as a method of development. Explain why others believe what they do and why you think they are mistaken.

> Many people believe that making a lot of money is the most important goal in life.

Proofreading Practice: Special Problems with Agreement

While developing your thesis, you should write sentences that are varied and interesting. Varying sentence styles, however, requires careful matching of subjects and verbs. This is a good time to review this aspect of grammar because not all of your sentences will follow a simple pattern of subject-verb-object and there are some special problems with agreement.

Forms of Be, Have, and Do

The common helping verbs *be, have,* and *do* present special difficulties with agreement because they have more forms than other verbs. Instead of just adding an *s*-ending, *be* has these forms.

	Singular	**Plural**
First person:	I am	We are
Second person:	You are	You are
Third person:	He, she, it is	They are

Note: In the past tense, *be* is the only verb that can cause agreement problems because it has two forms:

She was   They were

Have has two forms in the present: *has* for third person singular and *have* for all other subjects.

He has   They have

Do also has two forms: *does* for third person singular and *do* for all the others. Be careful about *don't* and *doesn't* as well.

She does   They do
She doesn't   They don't

TEST YOURSELF: *Be, Have,* and *Do*

Tell whether the forms of *be, have,* and *do* are correct. If not, supply the correct forms.

1. Students who doesn't join the program will lose out.
2. Raul thinks he have the best chance to win.
3. One of the old highways are going to be resurfaced.
4. Not all of the stores does business on Saturday.
5. Margaret always has a positive attitude.
6. Every workshop in the lab are going to last one hour.
7. Most of my friends does their banking online.

Answers: 1. don't 2. has 3. is 4. do 5. correct 6. is 7. do

Subjects that Come after Verbs

You may have difficulty with sentences that do not follow the ordinary subject-verb-object order. When a verb comes before the subject, you have to match the verb with the subject that appears later in the sentence.

Verbs come before subjects in several kinds of sentences.

1. Questions containing reversed word order

   Are there any new workers here today?
   v   s

   Where **have** the clinics been established?
       v   s

2. Sentences beginning with *there* or *here*

   There **have** been several problems with that model.
     v   s

   Here **is** a beautiful photograph of Hilary as a teenager.
   v   s

3. Sentences beginning with descriptive phrases

   Behind the gate **were** three armed guards.
         v   s

   Projected on both screens **was** a clever icon.
          v   s

Notice that in such sentences you should not try to match the verb with the word right before it so that the combination sounds right. You must find the subject *after* the verb. In the last sentence, not the *screens were* but the *icon was* projected on the screens.

TEST YOURSELF: **Subjects that Come after Verbs**

Tell whether the verb forms are correct. If not, supply the correct forms.

1. There isn't many ways to get to the airport.
2. Why have Shirley registered for both courses?
3. On the back of the computer was two USB ports.
4. What was the vice president and his advisors thinking?
5. Here is a good example of special treatment for visitors.
6. Among the first deliveries was some suits and dresses from Italy.
7. Where does the atmosphere end and outer space begin?

Answers: 1. aren't 2. has 3. were 4. were 5. correct 6. were 7. correct

Special Subjects

Some subjects are hard to match with verbs because they seem to be plural but are singular grammatically or because they are singular when used one way and plural when used another.

Singular Pronouns	**Singular/Plural Words**
everyone	all
anyone	half
someone	some
everybody	most
anybody	more
somebody	

Write *everyone has* some kind of special talent, not *everyone have*. *Each*, *either*, and *one* are also singular, even though they are often followed by plural phrases, as in the following examples.

<u>Each</u> of the students **<u>knows</u>** (not *know*) about the change in the syllabus.

<u>Either</u> of the women **<u>has</u>** (not *have*) the right to participate.

Some words are singular when they refer to amounts and plural when they refer to numbers.

<u>All</u> of the money **<u>has</u>** been deposited. (singular—an amount)

<u>All</u> of the employees **<u>are</u>** required to wear passes. (plural—a number)

Group Nouns

Nouns that refer to groups of people present a special problem. Words such as *army, family, team, jury, chorus, union, committee, company,* and *organization* seem to be plural because they refer to many people; however, they have plural forms (*armies, families,* etc.), so the singular forms should be used with singular verbs. An *army invades* another country, or the *team has* a winning season. When you refer to such words as single units, using the singular form, use singular verbs as well. However, when you use the word to refer to the individual members of the group, it is permissible to use a plural verb. Some writers find it awkward and consider it incorrect to write a sentence like "The *team are* taking their places on the field." It is less objection-able to write "The *players are* taking their places," or "The *members* of the team *are* taking their places." Just be sure to tell the differ-ence between the group as a unit (singular) and separate individuals (plural).

Verbs Separated from Subjects by Prepositional Phrases

A verb will often be separated from its subject by a prepositional phrase. Do not be confused by such phrases. *A subject cannot be part of a prepositional phrase.* If you try to match the verb with a word next to it, you may miss the subject and choose the wrong verb form. Notice the difference in the following sentences.

1. The musicians **are** busy rehearsing.
      s   v

2. One of the musicians **is** not here yet.
   s   v

In sentence 2, the subject *one* is separated from the verb *is* by the prepositional phrase *of the musicians.* You must mentally cross out the phrase and match the subject with the verb: One . . . **is** not here yet. What are prepositional phrases? They are phrases made out of the little relational words like *in, of, with, for, to,* and the like. Problems with agreement occur most often with sentences beginning with the construction *One of the . . . .* Remember that the word *one* requires you to use a singular verb form: One of my favorite films **is** *Avatar.*

TEST YOURSELF: Special Subjects and Group Nouns

Determine whether the verb forms are correct. If not, supply the correct forms.

1. One of the best ways to buy jewelry are to shop online.
2. Everybody has to participate in one form of community service.
3. The program are scheduled to appear on Pay Per View television.
4. One of the smartest students never ask any questions.
5. All of the income from the single track downloads go to charities.
6. Someone has to speak out against the new policy.
7. The side effects of this medication usually appears within two weeks.

Answers: 1. is 2. correct 3. is 4. asks 5. goes 6. correct 7. appear

Basic Exercise:
Special Problems with Agreement

Find the seven errors in the following passage. Rewrite the paragraph with corrections.

Everybody in Steven's family have a nickname. Most of them has names associated with their personal features. His brother Wade, for instance, is heavyset so they call him Wide. His cousin Larry, who is tall, is called Lofty, and his female cousin Kathy, who is always busy at her computer, is called Keys. Some of the others has been given names that are the opposite of their traits. For example, one of his sisters have been nicknamed Skinhead because she has beautiful long hair. The family have named Uncle Manuel, who is unusually aggressive, Mouse, and his sister Serene, who is very quiet, Siren. Among all these nicknames are one that Steven is not sure about—his own. His cousins all call him Star, but he doesn't know whether it is a term of admiration or a joke. He hopes that all of his family members thinks he really is outstanding, but he suspects they may be making fun of him.

Intermediate Exercise:
Special Problems with Agreement

Find the seven errors in the following passage. Rewrite the paragraph with corrections.

Many people likes to communicate with their friends through social messaging on Facebook or through e-mail rather than writing letters or talking on the telephone. One of the reasons are that electronic messages are much faster than sending a letter. Another reason is that when you send an e-mail or leave a message on Facebook, the other person don't have to be there at the other end. Almost everyone leave telephone messages too, but on the telephone you don't have time to compose a message, and voice messages has to be short. Among the other advantages of digital communication are the fact that you can send pictures, Web links, and attachments of all sizes. Last of all, there are the advantage of being able to save your own messages and the ones you receive without having to copy them.

Challenge Exercise:
Special Problems with Agreement

Find the seven errors in the following passage. Rewrite the paragraph with corrections.

American democracy is sometimes called the worst system of government, except for all the others. Among its most problematic features are the electoral system. Instead of voting directly for President and Vice President, American voters actually choose statewide electors, who casts all their votes for the candidate whose party wins the most votes in that state. And that candidate then gets all the electoral votes of that state, even when the total votes in that state is almost equal. Many voters then feel that their votes doesn't really count. In addition, during the campaign, the candidates tends to ignore the states that they are sure to win or lose and concentrate on the so-called "swing states," where their speeches and television appearances makes a big difference. And when a candidate wins the popular vote but lose the election because of the electoral count, as in the year 2000, there is sure to be much anger and resentment.

Key Words from Chapter 3 for Review

bibliography, body paragraphs, concluding paragraphs, rhetorical modes, subject-verb agreement

Global Revising: Doing an Extreme Makeover

STEPPING UP: WRITING TIP 4

Learn to revise effectively. Beginning writers, fearing that making a lot of changes in their work will make them look incompetent, often avoid large-scale revisions. To encourage yourself to make effective changes, remember that the best writers are those who make the most revisions in their work, not because their early drafts are sloppy or full of mistakes, but because they set high standards and are not content until their final product is the best it can be. Follow their example.

The Importance of Revision

Like most college writers, you may find that your biggest chore is developing your thesis effectively and adequately. When you have done that, you will probably feel that your work is nearly finished. However, there is more to revision than just adding material, correcting a few errors, and transferring your essay from handwriting to the keyboard. The real revision begins after you have a complete and well-developed draft. The difference between an acceptable but unexciting essay and a superior one (which often means the difference between a grade of B and a grade of A) lies in the process of making changes in your thinking and wording.

Moving from a Draft to an Essay:
A Glimpse of a Student Writer at Work

You have read Sarah Chen's essay "Why Liberal Arts?" in its final form. Before reaching that final draft, however, Sarah did a lot of work thinking about the subject, as you saw in the section on prewriting activities. After doing some focused writing and clustering, she created a rough draft based on her outline. Read the draft below and notice the comments afterward, which were made by Sarah's instructor and helped her produce the final essay you read in the introduction.

Liberal Arts in the Modern World

A good education is one of the most important things for anybody in this day and age. Most people say that you need a good education to survive but they don't think about what it means to get a good education. Is it really necessary nowadays to get a broad education?

Is making money the only thing? Our sociology teacher asked us which we would choose—a good education without a degree or a degree without an education. But some students don't think into the future. They forget that the job they are training for could become outdated, and then where are they? They don't have a good education to fall back on. People who have a broad education are better in other ways, too. They participate in society more intelligently than uneducated people, and they make better parents and family members in general.

It is also important for an individual to lead a happy life by being creative. Some people who have a good education do this on their jobs, and sometimes they take up hobbies that allow them to express their creativity in other ways. There is no doubt that making money by getting job training in business or computers is what many students want, but it may be more important to become a better educated human being while you can as a college student.

Most students major in business, accounting, engineering or some other major which will get them ready for a high-paying job. They think that the only thing that matters is making money. Maybe a liberal arts education is a better preparation for jobs than they realize.

If you recall from the section on prewriting, Sarah developed an outline for her draft. It looked like this:

Thesis: A liberal arts education is more important than ever in today's world.

    I. People with a liberal arts education contribute to society.
   II. A liberal arts education enriches family life.
 III. A liberal arts education makes an individual happier and more creative.
 IV. An education in the liberal arts is a good preparation for many careers.

Sarah's instructor praised her for following her outline, but offered some additional suggestions.

- The draft is very short and needs more development of each section.
- Each of the four points in the outline should be developed into a full, separate paragraph, not squeezed together and left without enough explanation.
- Maybe the last topic about career preparation should come first, and that would leave the point about individual happiness as an effective closing. What do you think?
- The introduction should be more focused and interesting: maybe the story about the sociology class would make a good introduction.
- The conclusion should be separate from point number four about creativity; it should wrap up the entire essay.

Sarah decided that she needed to make her essay much longer and rethink her outline. She decided to change her introduction and to put the first topic of her outline last. As writers usually do when they make global revisions, she made major rearrangements in her plan and added a lot of material. Reread Sarah's essay on page xxix and see how much planning and revision went into producing her well-organized final draft.

    Sarah also made some wording and grammar corrections in the draft, but these have been left out to emphasize what revision really is—re-visioning your work, looking at it again, and doing a makeover. You've seen people on television whose appearance is transformed in astonishing ways by experts at extreme makeovers. Always try to do the same with your early drafts and make the final version better written, better organized, and better developed.

Testing Your Thesis:
Looking for Digressions and Weak Spots

When you examine your draft, first look at your main point—your thesis. Do not be afraid that the essay will collapse if you question your thesis. Read your essay as if you were a stranger who hasn't seen it before and disagrees with what you say. You can almost always make your point sharper and stronger by paying attention to how others respond to it.

What does it mean to test your thesis? Challenge it; give it the "Oh, yeah?" treatment. Let's say you are arguing in favor of lowering tuition at your college. Your position is one with which most other students will agree. But what would the college administration say? Think about why tuition is so high at most colleges. What costs are involved? Do you propose a way to bring down the costs? Should students do without something to reduce tuition? Should the college find other ways to bring in money? These are thoughts that you should explore in your essay. It is not enough just to take a position; you must consider the ways in which your ideas are necessarily connected to facts in the real world. Anticipating possible "Oh, yeah?" responses from your reader and addressing them will make your essay stronger and more credible.

Achieving Continuity Through Transitions

Read your draft through to see whether it moves logically and smoothly from beginning to end. Does every sentence flow naturally from the one before? In the process of rethinking your work, you may leave out some necessary explanations between statements or between paragraphs. You may have written sentences that seem to contradict each other, and you may have made statements that are downright confusing. One general rule is that the reader cannot read your mind, only what you write on the page. Did you ever remark, "What the writer is trying to say is . . . "? As a writer, you must *actually* say what you mean and not make the reader guess what you are *trying* to say.

For practice, begin reading a page from a book, preferably nonfiction, written by a professional writer whose work you especially like. Read a few sentences slowly, then stop, covering up what comes next. Try to figure out what the writer will say next. Do this several times, noticing how carefully he or she moves from one thought to the next. Make a conscious effort to do this in your writing as well.

Improving Your Style: Breaking Up, Varying, and Combining Sentences

Read your work carefully aloud, noticing the rhythm of your sentences. Are they varied: some short, some long, and many in between? Do they have a natural flow, like good conversation? Be watchful for a tendency to write repetitively in short sentences that always begin with the subject followed by the verb. That habit will create an impression of immaturity. The opposite habit—launching into meandering, shapeless sentences connected by *and* or which—will create the impression that you aren't sure what you want to say and haven't organized your thoughts.

Interacting with Your Reader (Reading Aloud to Others)

One of the best ways to benefit from the revision process is to have classmates read the draft of your essay and give their opinions. If they argue with you about the points you make, so much the better. Probably you will find that some readers agree and others disagree. That will complicate your process of revision but not weaken it. You have to decide how to deal with the objections raised by those who disagree and how to incorporate supporting points made by those who agree.

Some writers do not want others to read their drafts, at least not until they're finished with their final revisions. One reason may be that these writers believe that getting help from other students is a form of cheating. On the contrary, this kind of help, which is often called *feedback*, is not only not cheating, it is one of the best ways to improve your work. No matter how many classmates' opinions you listen to, you have the final responsibility for the ideas you put forward in your essay and the facts and arguments you use to support those ideas. Cheating would be having someone else write the essay for you.

You may feel shy about reading your work to others. This is understandable, especially with an early draft that probably contains some writing errors and questionable statements. If you are working with other students whose early drafts are also incomplete, try to avoid grading or being judgmental. If you work in a group, think of it as an editorial staff, as if your essays were articles to be published in a magazine and you want to make all of them as readable and convincing as possible.

Finding the Right Tone and Voice: Positive and Negative Connotation

One feature of writing that your readers can help you improve is finding the right tone and voice and maintaining it throughout your essay. A successful essay not only conveys an idea and supports it but also expresses your attitude toward the topic through your choice of words and phrases. If you achieve a consistent tone, one that you intend to convey throughout the essay, the reader will hear your voice expressing the attitude you intend—serious, ironic, angry, or funny—from the beginning of your essay to the end. When you choose words, remember that a word has both a *denotation*, its actual meaning or dictionary definition, and its *connotation*, the emotional and social overtones associated with it. The words *woman* and *lady* both refer to female adults, but *lady* is also associated with a traditional society in which *ladies* were generally of the upper class and behaved according to strict rules of behavior. Similarly, *man, guy, dude,* and *gentleman* all refer to male adults, but all have different social and emotional associations. When you read your work aloud to a writing group of friends or classmates, pay attention to any comments about your attitude toward the subject: Are there passages where you become unintentionally negative, superior, formal, funny, or hostile? If so, which words convey attitudes that you may not have expressed directly?

Compare the connotations of these statements. Which one has a positive connotation and which a negative one? Which words convey positive or negative connotations?

A. Esmeralda is a conceited character who always knocks the way her friends dress.

B. Esmeralda is a person with high standards of style whose friends appreciate her advice on fashion.

PEER REVIEW QUESTIONS

In order to give responses that help you and your classmates improve the drafts of your essays, be sure to include comments on the items in the following checklist.

1. Here is my impression of what you say in your essay. (In four or five sentences, summarize your overall response to the essay.)

2. Your introduction is interesting. ☐ Yes ☐ No
   Your introduction makes your main purpose clear.
   ☐ Yes ☐ No
   The sentence that most nearly states your main purpose is the following:

3. You develop your main point well. ☐ Yes ☐ No

4. Your method of developing ideas is the following:

5. Your conclusion (is/is not) effective for the following reason:

6. What I like best about your essay is the following:

7. I recommend you make the following changes:

WRITING EXERCISES: Basic, Intermediate, Challenge

Basic Exercise: Achieving Continuity

Complete the paragraph below, beginning with the sentence provided. Write at least five more sentences and end with the one given. Try to make every sentence in the passage follow from the one before.

When I get up in the morning, I go through a number of steps to get ready for work or classes. . . . When I finish doing all these steps, I am ready to begin my day.

Intermediate Exercise: Achieving Continuity

Complete the paragraph below, beginning with the sentence provided. Write at least five more sentences and end with the one given. Try to make every sentence in the passage follow from the one before.

There are several ways to make friends in a new place. . . . If you try all of these techniques, you are sure to meet all the new friends you want.

Challenge Exercise: Achieving Continuity

Complete the paragraph below, beginning with the sentence provided. Write at least five more sentences and end with the one given. Try to make every sentence in the passage follow from the one before.

My favorite television show has several features that make it interesting. . . . All of these features together make it one of the best shows on television.

Proofreading Practice: Subordination

To achieve more variety in your sentence patterns, you should practice **subordination**. Subordination means using **subordinate clauses** to place some statements at a lower level of importance by beginning them with **subordinate conjunctions**. These are words that make the statement tell *how, when, where,* or *why* something happened, rather than *that* it happened. For example:

Main Clause (whole sentence: tells *that* something happened):

We arrived late. An accident occurred on Route 87.

Subordinate Clause (part of a sentence: tells *why* something happened):

We arrived late because an accident occurred on Route 87.

Because an accident occurred on Route 87, we arrived late.

When you begin a statement with *after, although, as, because, even though, since, when, whenever, whereas, wherever,* or *while,* you are making it a subordinate clause. Such clauses can begin sentences or end them, as in the example above. If your sentences seem too mechanical and repetitive, you may be able to improve your style by using more subordination.

TEST YOURSELF: Subordination

Underline the subordinate clauses in these sentences. One sentence has no subordinate clause.

1. Whenever Jennifer drives past the mall, she wants to stop and look at the sales.
2. James knew he would pass the course because he had reviewed for the final exam.
3. As winter approached, the fuel prices began to rise.
4. The film began while Jason was buying popcorn.
5. Although most people like Amy, few of her friends understand her.
6. The management decided against using a wireless network, whereas their competitors were already doing so.
7. Jeremy began exercising a month ago and has now lost twelve pounds.

Answers: 1. Whenever Jennifer drives past the mall 2. because he had reviewed for the exam 3. As winter approached 4. while Jason was buying popcorn 5. Although most people like Amy 6. whereas their competitors were already doing so 7. no subordinate clause

PROOFREADING EXERCISES: Basic, Intermediate, Challenge

Basic Exercise: Subordination

Read this passage. In the blanks write subordinate conjunctions such as *after, although, as, because, even though, since, when, whenever, whereas, wherever,* and *while.* Be sure that the ones you insert make sense and allow the paragraph to read smoothly.

Waverly is a rescuer of animals. She likes to collect injured and lost animals and makes some of them her pets. _____ she finds a bird with a damaged wing, she takes it in. _____ she is able to make it better, she lets it go. _____ she is constantly bringing in stray cats and dogs that are limping or injured, she often has as many as a dozen animals in her house.

Most of them she has been able to place in other people's homes once they are well again. _____ some of her neighbors disapprove of her having so many pets, she doesn't care what other people think. _____ she began this project, she has, according to her count, saved more than a hundred small animals. She has had to look up a lot of information about small animals _____ she is in the process of feeding and caring for them. It is no surprise that her mother once suggested that she should become a veterinarian _____ she already knows so much about healing small creatures.

Intermediate Exercise: Subordination

Rewrite this passage, converting the underlined statements to subordinate clauses and combining them with sentences before or after them. Use subordinating conjunctions such as *although, because, when,* and *while* to change these statements to subordinate clauses.

Karen is the president of her class. She has to organize many activities and get other students to work on projects and committees. Some of the student leaders she works with are helpful and hard working. Others are not. She has discovered that the best way to get others to be positive and contributing is to praise them for whatever they do well. Samantha manages a Web site for the school. Karen tells her how impressive it is. Mike designs a poster for homecoming week. She tells him how great it looks. Such remarks do not prevent her from offering constructive criticism. It's needed. Karen has created a positive feeling in student government. She has been able to accomplish a lot. Karen graduates from college in June. Her leadership in student government will help her succeed in her new job.

Challenge Exercise: Subordination

Rewrite each of these passages, combining the short sentences by using subordination.

1. Some of the terms used by philosophers are simple and clear. Others are hard to define and used differently by different writers.
2. *Empiricism*, for instance, is not a controversial term. Its meaning is reasonably clear and simple. Applying it to particular philosophers may not be simple.

3. We call an analytical approach *empirical*. We generally refer to analysis based on evidence gained through experience.

4. On the other hand, a term like *existentialism* is harder to define. It has been used by thinkers in many different ways.

5. Terms used in theology are especially controversial. Their meanings are often connected to strong beliefs and feelings.

6. Recently coined words, such as *semiotics* and *deconstruction*, are even harder to define and understand. They continue to be useful and necessary in discussions of literature and the media.

7. Philosophers want the public to appreciate and understand their work. They should explain the meaning of their terminology simply and clearly.

Key Words from Chapter 4 for Review

combining   sentences,   subordinate   clauses,   subordinate conjunctions, subordination, transitions

Putting on the Final Touches

Improving Word Choice and Eliminating Wordiness

Be precise. Be concise. From the writer's point of view, the term *precision* means saying exactly what you mean. *Conciseness* means saying it as briefly as possible.

Before submitting your final draft, examine it sentence by sentence to see whether you can improve your choice of words. In the process of composing, it is wise not to stop to consider all the synonyms available to you because doing so can distract you from your larger purpose. As a result, however, some of the words you chose probably weren't the best. As you carefully read your last draft, hunt for words that do not fit, either because their meaning (denotation) is a little off or because they create the wrong tone or suggestion (connotation). Some words have negative connotations, some positive, and some neutral. Be ready to substitute more accurate or suitable words for the ones you have written. Use a thesaurus, either in book form, such as an edition of *Roget's Thesaurus*, or as a word-processing function on your toolbar (click on Tools, then Language, then Thesaurus).

Another way to improve your word choice is by reducing wordiness, which simply means removing unnecessary words. Wordiness doesn't result from writing too much; rather, it results from using too many empty words, roundabout phrases, and pointless repetitions. Wordiness usually comes from an attempt to sound impressive rather than to communicate something important. When you have an urgent message, you are less likely to waste words conveying it. Wordiness can also come from not having enough to say but being required to write a specific number of words—say 500 or 1,000—for an assignment. When that happens, of course it is tempting to "pad" your essay with unnecessary words.

We've all read pieces that skirt around a topic and use pompous words and phrases but say very little that's new or thought-provoking. If you find yourself lapsing into that pattern, do not settle for merely tightening up your style. Rethink your main purpose; find some fresh ideas and examples. No display of fancy language can hide a lack of content.

Lack of conciseness often occurs in long sentences, particularly ones that express complicated ideas. Here is an example.

> *In the story "The Lottery" by Shirley Jackson the author tells us about a woman who is the one chosen by lottery to be stoned and she protests that it is unfair to stone her but it is not because she objects to the outrageousness of the lottery which she does not but just because it was unfair that she was chosen instead of somebody else.*

The problem with that sentence is not just that it is too long but that it is loose and baggy. A shorter, more concise sentence would be better.

> *In "The Lottery," Shirley Jackson portrays a woman who is chosen by lottery to be stoned and who objects, not because the lottery is cruel, but because she is the victim.*

TEST YOURSELF: Eliminating Wordiness

Rewrite these sentences, making them more concise.

1. There are three ways by means of which you can travel to Chicago: you can ride there on the train, you can fly in an airplane, or you can drive in your own car on the highway.
2. In his poem titled "The Raven," the author, Edgar Allan Poe, writes about a bird called a raven that keeps saying continually again and again the word *nevermore*.
3. According to how much the test counts when the instructor figures out the final grades in the class, more psychological pressure the test puts on students when they take it.
4. Two people may think they love each other but do not really understand each other's true personalities and therefore are not really in love.
5. One point of similarity between the main characters in these two stories is that they are both women who have vivid imaginations and they are both unhappy women as well.
6. We will never find a solution to this problem unless and until the parties on both sides find it in their hearts to go half way and begin to see it from the other person's point of view and reach a compromise.
7. The length of the readings in this assignment adds up to a lot more than most people would be able to finish reading over a single weekend.

Possible answers: 1. You can travel to Chicago by train, airplane, or car. 2. In Edgar Allan Poe's poem "The Raven," a bird repeats the word *nevermore*. 3. The more the test counts as a percentage of the final grade, the greater the stress it places on students. 4. True love is possible only between people who understand each other. 5. In both stories the main characters are imaginative but unhappy women. 6. This problem can be solved only if both parties are willing to compromise. 7. This reading assignment is too long to complete in one weekend.

Using Your Spelling and Grammar Check

Technology is helpful when it comes to correcting writing errors, but you must not rely on it alone to catch and correct mistakes, because it can create as well as correct problems. Using your spelling and grammar checks is a must. The spelling check will catch most typographical errors and misspellings, but it cannot identify errors in word choice. For instance, it cannot catch *their* instead of *there*. There is another danger in relying totally on your word processor's spelling check: that you will not become a good speller.

Proofreading Aloud: Locating Your Patterns of Error

Proofreading requires patience and close attention. It is a kind of courtesy you pay to your readers. Many people do not proofread their e-mail messages, which may be considered acceptable when you are informally e-mailing friends. Formal academic essays require more care, however. To proofread effectively, read your work aloud, s-l-o-w-l-y. This isn't the time to rush; if you do, you may miss errors that you could easily correct. In addition, reading aloud will help you identify sentence divisions. When your voice drops, that is probably the end of a sentence: Be sure to place a period there. Reading aloud also helps you feel the rhythm, or lack of rhythm, in your writing. If something in your writing bothers you when you read aloud, try reading it to someone else; perhaps that person can help you identify the problem.

One purpose of reading aloud is to help you notice recurring patterns in your writing. Do you frequently run sentences together or write fragments? Do you make errors in verb form that you can hear, such as "you was" or "she has went"? Many of our writing errors are not random, but fit into a few patterns that occur frequently.

Sample Page of an Essay with Proofreader's Corrections

People make a mistake when they refer to celebrities as role models.
Athletes
Athaletes like Michael Vick and Tiger Woods are held up by the media

as examples of behavior for young people to follow, and if they act
badly   *, at least*
bad, it is considered a tragedy for the whole country. At least for the

teenagers who might be influenced by their actions. Female perform-

ers like Lady Gaga, Janet Jackson, Christina Aguilera, and Rhianna are
scrutinized
also scrutinize on television and in the press for any slips of decorum,
           substances   *assumed*
indecent remarks, or arrests for use of illegal substance. It is assume
       rests
that the morality of the country rest on the shoulders of these stars
     models
as a model for the younger generation to imitate. There is no doubt

that most young people admire such celebrities and are influenced by
them. *, especially* Especially when it comes to style. *, but they* But they probably are not the

most important influences on the lives of teenagers and young adults.
Their There own parents and older siblings and relatives, classmates, teach-

ers, counselors, and community leaders do much more to shape the
lives of young people *than* then the famous individuals they see on tele

vision, and the movies, *in the movies* and on the computer screen. Teenagers do

not expect to become the next LeBron James or Rhianna, but they do
expect to follow patterns of life *similar* similiar to the people they know in

their personal world. If these people—their family members and mem-

bers of their communities—set examples that *inspire* inspired them, they will

not be *led* lead into self-destructive paths just because Lindsay Lohan is

back in rehab. The opposite is also *true: it is* true, it is unlikely that teenagers

who see only bad examples of behavior such as *violence* voilence and crime in

their immediate world will be *inspired* inspire to follow the path of maturity

and success just because their favorite athlete or hip-hop star sets an

example of intelligent behavior. The people who should be called role

models are the adults nearest them in their daily lives. *lives because* Because the

roles they play are closest to the ones that teenagers will assume as

adults and parents *themselves* themself.

Computerized grammar checks are still not totally reliable. They
identify some errors but not others, and they often see errors that do
not exist. Do not substitute the grammar check for your own sound
grasp of grammar. Instead, use the grammar check only as backup
after you have done your own careful proofreading.

Basic Exercise: Putting on the Final Touches

Read the passage below and revise the underlined words or phrases, eliminating wordiness or making corrections in spelling or grammar.

In my opinion, I feel that most of my classmates would like there campus to be more user-friendly. Most of the students realizes that often it is usually difficult to go from one class to another and get there on time without being late. The student government has propose a new schedule that would leave 15 minutes between classes. That way students would not feel to pressured and would not have to hurry all the time.

Intermediate Exercise: Putting on the Final Touches

Read the passage below and revise the underlined words or phrases, eliminating wordiness or making corrections in spelling or grammar.

Many people have strong emotional feelings about using stem cells for medical research. It is a fact that some people argue that progress toward finding cures for Parkinson's disease and other serious illness can go forward only if embryonic stem cells are use. Other people raise religious objections and insists that using embryos violates the holy sanctity of human life. Candidates for public office sometimes try to use this controversy to gain votes, and talk show debates often flare up on the subject. People on both sides of the issue, pro and con, should know more about the scientific facts involved.

Challenge Exercise: Putting on the Final Touches

Rewrite the passage below, eliminating wordiness and making corrections in spelling or grammar.

In "The Guest," a short story written by the author Albert Camus, a schoolteacher named Daru is ordered to guard an Arab prisoner. This man has killed someone, and Daru is suppose to take him to prison. Daru does not want to become involved, and he treats the Arab man as a guest rather than a prisoner. Instead of taking him to jail, Daru take the prisoner outside and points in two directions, one leading to prison and the other to freedom. The Arab walks off toward the prison alone by himself. When Daru returns back to his schoolroom, he reads an angry message written on the board. Even though he did not turn the prisoner in, the prisoner friends threaten to take revenge. This story expresses the author's disgust at violence and also in addition his belief in the freedom of the individual to make choices in an absurd world.

Proofreading Practice: Spelling

To become a better speller, take charge of the problem yourself. Many writing courses do not devote much time to spelling, so you cannot expect class work alone to improve your spelling ability. Do not expect to improve without making repeated efforts. Only a few people can spell correctly without effort; the rest of us need to do old-fashioned work on the words we often misspell.

How can you improve your spelling? Follow these recommendations.

- Learn the patterns and rules. Although English spelling is irregular and most of its rules have exceptions, you will do well to recognize some basic patterns.
- Drill yourself on frequently misspelled words. Study tricky words, or spelling "demons," especially those in your area of work or study. A corporate employee should never misspell *business* or a nurse misspell *medicine.*
- Use your spell check effectively but do not trust it totally. The better a speller you are, the more your spell check will help you catch typos. However, it will miss many *homonyms*, words that sound alike and look alike but have different meanings.
- Master the homonyms—the look-alikes/sound-alikes. Be especially mindful of the homonyms that occur regularly in writing (*to, too, two; there, their, they're; weather, whether*).
- Take personal responsibility for your spelling. Do not expect a book, a course, a teacher, or spell check to work magic for you. Make lists of your own most often misspelled words and master their correct spellings.

Spelling Patterns

The first step toward spelling competence is to learn the main patterns of English, even though these patterns may have exceptions.

Pattern 1: ie and ei Words

You probably have heard, and may know, the old rule:

> *i* before *e*
> except after *c*
> or when sounded like *a*
> as in *neighbor* or *weigh*

Knowing the jingle helps, but be prepared for the many exceptions. Study the patterns.

1. *i* before *e: Believe.* Most words with an /e/ sound do follow the rule when there is no *c* before the combination.

achieve (*ch*, but not *c*)	pierce
friend (even though pronounced *eh*)	priest
fiend	relieve
grieve	reprieve
lien	retrieve
niece (the *c* comes after *ie*)	shriek
piece	thief

2. Except after *c: Receive.* Despite exceptions, this pattern usually holds true, too.

   ceiling, conceited, conceive, deceive, perceive, receipt

3. Or when sounded like /a/: *Weigh.* Combinations that are sounded like /a/ or /i/ are usually spelled *ei*.

   eight, freight, height, neighbor, vein, weight

Some exceptions to the rule: A few words take *ie* even though it comes after *c*.

   financier, society, species

4. A few *ei* words with the /e/ sound and no *c* before them can fool you, too.

   either, leisure, neither, seize, weird

Pattern 2: Keeping or Dropping the Final e

When adding an ending to a word with a final *e*, keep the *e* if the ending starts with a consonant.

arrange + ment = arrangement
hope + ful = hopeful
nine + ty = ninety
sincere + ly = sincerely
face + less = faceless
manage + ment = management

Drop the *e* if the ending starts with a vowel.

give + ing = giving
have + ing = having
erase + ure = erasure
locate + ion = location
guide + ance = guidance

Exceptions: To keep a *g* or *c* soft before a vowel, we sometimes keep the *e*.

age + ing = ageing or aging
manage + able = manageable
service + able = serviceable

The word *judgment* does not keep the *e* except in British spelling. *Dyeing* keeps the *e* to prevent confusion with *dying*.

Pattern 3: Doubling Final Consonants

This rule is somewhat complicated, but it does not have many exceptions and applies to many common words. Learn the pattern.

The rule applies to words like *begin, control*, and *occur*. When you add an *-ed*, *-ing*, or *-er* ending to these words, do you double the final consonant? Yes: *beginning, controlled*, and *occurred*.

What do these words have in common? The rule says that they end with a single consonant (not *ck* as in *shock*, or *st* as in *post*) preceded by a single vowel (not a double vowel, as in *break* or *meet*). And the accent must be on the last syllable (not earlier, as in *travel*, where the *l* does not have to be doubled, or *pivot*, where the *t* is not doubled).

To sum up, these words contain

- A single final consonant: begi<u>n</u>
- A single vowel preceding the final consonant: beg<u>i</u>n
- An accent on the last syllable: be<u>gin</u>

Many common words follow this pattern. When you become familiar with it, the rule is extremely useful. Here are only a few examples.

beginning	forgetting	referred
committed	occurring	stopped*
controlling	omitted	throbbing*
excelling	preferring	

TEST YOURSELF: Spelling Patterns

Some of the following words are spelled correctly and some are not.
Write *C* next to the correctly spelled words. If a word is misspelled, spell it correctly in the blank. Review the rules first; don't simply guess.

1. belief _____   5. commited _____
2. occurance _____   6. movement _____
3. arrangment _____ 7. achieve _____
4. definitly _____

Answers: 1. correct 2. occurrence 3. arrangement 4. definitely 5. committed 6. correct 7. correct

---

Twenty Common Mix-ups

The following words are often misspelled because they contain combinations that are easily confused with those in similar words. Study the groups carefully, looking for the trouble spots.

1. ability   (The last two do not contain *ability*.)
   responsibility
   possibility

2. accumulate   (Study the *c*'s and *m*'s in these common
   accommodate   words.)
   recommend

3. across   (Both are often misspelled; notice the
   address   single *c* and double *d*.)

4. alone   (These simple words are often carelessly
   along   mixed up.)

---

* The rule applies to one-syllable words as well.

5. amount
   among
   (Be careful not to write *amoung*, even though *among* rhymes with *young*.)

6. arithmetic
   athletics
   mathematics
   (Do not add an extra *e*, as in *atheletics* or *athelete*, but don't forget the *e* in *mathematics*.)

7. believe
   receive
   (These two most common *ie/ei* words do follow the rule.)

8. committee
   committing
   commitment
   (Note the single *t* in *commitment*.)

9. definitely
   immediately
   (Do not confuse *-itely* with *-ately* words.)

10. develop
    developed
    envelope
    (There is no such word as *develope*.)

11. divide
    decide
    (There is no such word as *devide*.)

12. familiar
    similar
    (The extra *i* in *familiar* gives it an extra syllable.)

13. fulfill
    foretell
    (Do not spell it *forfill* or *forefill*.)

14. necessary
    occasionally
    professional
    (There is only one *c* in *necessary*, one *s* in *occasionally*, and one *f* in *professional*.)

15. pastime
    part-time
    (Do not double the *t* in *pastime*.)

16. accidentally
    publicly
    (Do not add an extra syllable—*publically*)

17. relevant
    prevalent
    (Two difficult words; notice the *e*'s and *a*'s and the *l*'s and *v*'s. Both words contain the name *Eva*.)

18. separate
    desperate
    (Do not replace the first *a* with an *e—seperate*)

19. surprise
    suppose
    (Do not write *suprise* or *surpose*.)

20. till
    until
    (Do not add an extra *l—untill*)

TEST YOURSELF: Spelling Mix-ups

Each of the following groups contains one misspelled word. Circle it and write the word correctly in the blank.

1. adress
   necessary   _____
   till

2. accomodate
   publicly   _____
   fulfill

3. prevalent
   receive   _____
   surpose

4. desperate
   pastime   _____
   devide

5. occassionally
   familiar   _____
   across

6. responsability
   professional   _____
   recommend

7. definitely
   possibility   _____
   amoung

Answers: 1. address 2. accommodate 3. suppose 4. divide 5. occasionally
6. responsibility 7. among

PROOFREADING EXERCISES: Basic, Intermediate, Challenge

Basic Exercise: Spelling

The paragraph below contains seven misspelled common words. Find and correct them.

Paula and Beverly wanted to arrange a baby shower for there friend Annette. They had similiar ideas about how to plan the event, but they couldn't decide on were it should take place. Each of them beleived it should be held at her home as a supprise party. Finally, since they couldn't dicide, they tossed a coin, and Beverly won. Then they got together and made the necessary arrangments.

Intermediate Exercise: Spelling

The following paragraph contains seven misspelled words. Find and correct them.

Writing well is a skill that you should develope to help you in your career. In business, law, and medicine, effective writing is neccessary. Students who do not beleive this is true are often surprised to discover too late that they lack this important proffesional competency. They may have to learn the hard way—by recieving criticism of their work—that writing well is expected on many jobs. In the business world it is understood that the committment to writing goes along with the strickly technical aspects of a job.

Challenge Exercise: Spelling

The paragraph below contains seven misspelled common words. Find and correct them.

Many scholars have puzzled over the extraordinary developement of Shakespeare as a poet and playwright. There was little in his imediate surroundings as a boy and an adolescent that could explain his astonishing achievments as possibly the world's greatest writer. He was probably educated strickly and traditionally at the school in his hometown of Stratford, but his experience in theater was probably limited to performing plays at school and watching traveling companies of actors that occassionally visited his hometown. We will probably never know what brought him to London and lead him to join the theater companies there. We do know that he became highly sucessful as a writer and part owner of the theater. When he retired to Stratford, he bought the largest house in town.

Key Words from Chapter 5 for Review

conciseness, consonants, homonyms, precision, proofreading, thesaurus, vowels, wordiness

Writing Essays Based on Your Own Experience and Perceptions

Describing a Situation, Person, or Group

STEPPING UP: WRITING TIP 6

Descriptive writing is a little like painting a picture in words. Pictures usually contain many details, and you may have been told to "put a lot of details" into your descriptive writing. That is good advice if you remember that some details are important and some are not. Too many meaningless details will get in the way. Descriptive writing is like a cartoon or sketch that captures and highlights the most recognizable and characteristic features of the subject. To create an indelible impression of the person, place, or organization you describe, include vivid, memorable details.

Visualizing Your Subject and Giving It Meaning

Writing a descriptive essay requires the same care that a painter takes in creating a landscape or portrait. But words are not pictures; your readers have to imagine everything you describe. Unlike pictures, words require readers to use all five senses in their imaginations. To describe a person, place, or group well, use specific images invoking the five senses to create in readers' minds the most vivid experience you can. Like drawing and painting, descriptive writing has meaning. A picture or an essay conveys a message through what it portrays. A portrait or photograph may make you feel sad, excited, puzzled, or angry; a descriptive essay may cause you to admire, like, or detest a person. Whether or not you announce your meaning, the way you describe something and the way you organize your material will create meaning and will affect your readers. In order to convey the meaning and impression you want, read an early draft aloud to several friends or writing group members to discover whether your intention comes across.

Student Essay: Describing a Person

My Abuelita

LOURDES FERNÁNDEZ

The person who has influenced me the most has been my grandma, my Abuelita. She has done a lot of good things for me in my life, and she taught me a lot, but some of her ways were hard for me to accept. She was always there for me, sometimes when nobody else was, and I will always be thankful for her help in my life. She was my angel, although sometimes I used to think she was my bad angel. I now realize that she was always strong, loyal, and wise.

First let me tell you the good things about my Abuelita. She is a very big person, but not in height, only in the person she is. She can be described as strong emotionally and spiritually. She came to the United States from the Dominican Republic without speaking any English. She worked in Washington, D.C., cleaning people's houses until she met my grandfather. He got a job in New York City, so they moved there and had six children. She had the strength to raise all of them to be educated and hard workers, and all the time she worked long hours. Sometimes she did sewing at home, and later she cooked in a restaurant, and on weekends she was on the cleaning staff in an office building. No matter how hard things got, she never gave up, and she always found ways to solve problems.

I call her loyal because when her children got in trouble or didn't do well in school, she always supported them. When they were wrong, she didn't let them get away with it, but she always let them know she loved them and would do anything to help them get their problem solved. And with me she became my number one parent when my dad was out of the country and my mom was in and out of the hospital. She gave me many words of wisdom, telling me that all I had to do was imagine where I wanted to be in life and hold onto that dream until I finally made it come true. She told me stories about people in Santo Domingo and corrected my Spanish. She made me feel smart and successful even when I had trouble with my chemistry class and when I ran for student vice president and lost. Nobody was ever more helpful to me.

Maybe this sounds like she was perfect and we always got along. That isn't true. She still has some ways that I don't agree with. She was very old-fashioned in her thinking and usually disapproved of my choices and opinions. She wouldn't let me date until I was sixteen, and she frowned at most of the clothes I wanted to wear. She said they made me look like a loose woman and she sometimes would forbid me to leave the house until I changed into something "proper for a lady." And she hated almost all the music I liked and tried to teach me all the religious songs she sang every day. My first boyfriend she wouldn't let into the house because she called him a good-for-nothing and a bum. After I stopped seeing him I partly agreed with her, but still I didn't like the way she criticized me about him.

I now know that she was only trying to do what was best for me and teach me right from wrong. Even when we disagreed, she always loved me and wanted me to reach my goals. She will always be in my heart as the person who helped me become the person I am. When I have children, I want to be a parent just like her, except maybe I'll have better taste in clothes and music.

Lourdes found a way to organize the body of her essay into two main parts, which she divided into separate paragraphs. First she described the good things about her grandmother in two paragraphs; then she described the traits that were not so good in another paragraph. There are a number of ways you can organize a descriptive essay. Which of the patterns mentioned below did Lourdes use?

Organizing a Description

Descriptive essays can be organized in different ways. They can be arranged **spatially**, meaning that you move from front to back, side to side, far to near, and so on. Or, you can use a **chronological arrangement**, or arrangement in time, showing how a person has changed from childhood to maturity, or how you experienced the situation or place you want to describe, beginning with your first impressions and moving to a time when you understood it more clearly. Still another possibility is to arrange your material **topically**, according to different features of the subject, such as a person's appearance, personality, and accomplishments. Early drafts of a descriptive essay are often jumbled, as you try to include all the important details about your subject. This initial chaos is fine, but be sure that your later drafts have a clear plan of organization. In descriptive writing, revision usually entails a lot of rearranging.

Here is a description of a place. What plan or organization does it follow, and what details make the description memorable?

Example by a Published Author: Using Details

How beautiful, she thought. What a beautiful house. There was a big red-and-gold Bible on the dining-room table. Little lace doilies were everywhere—on arms and backs of chairs, in the center of a large dining table, on little tables. Potted plants were on all the windowsills. A color picture of Jesus Christ hung on a wall with the prettiest paper flowers fastened on the frame. She wanted to see everything slowly, slowly. But Junior kept saying, "Hey you. Come on. Come on." He pulled her into another room, even more beautiful than the first. More doilies, a big lamp with green-and-gold base and white shade. There was even a rug on the floor, with enormous dark-red flowers. She was deep in admiration of the flowers when Junior said, "Here!" Pecola turned. "Here is your kitten!" he screeched. And he threw a big black cat right in her face. She sucked in her breath in fear and surprise and felt fur in her mouth. The cat clawed her face and chest in an effort to right itself, then leaped nimbly to the floor. (89–90)

—Toni Morrison. From *The Bluest Eye.*

What do the details of the interior of the house tell you about the people who live there? How does that description make you feel? Pecola, a young girl in the novel, experiences two opposing feelings in this paragraph. Explain what these feelings are and identify details that communicate each emotion.

WRITING EXERCISES: Basic, Intermediate, Challenge

Basic Exercise: Descriptive Writing

Write an essay describing a place that you visit frequently. This may be an office where you work, a gymnasium where you work out, a store or mall where you shop, or a diner where you eat. Think first of the feeling this place arouses in you. Then, using a prewriting activity that works for you, select the details that most strongly evoke this feeling. After writing a first draft, find a way to organize your material, either by moving from one location to another (near to far, right to left, etc.), by clustering your details according to the senses (sounds, visual impressions, smells, etc.), or by grouping details according to other categories (obvious details, less noticeable details, and details that create false impressions). Use your creative powers in selecting categories and in choosing descriptive vocabulary.

Intermediate Exercise: Descriptive Writing

Write an essay portraying a person who has had a powerful influence on your life. Begin with a focused writing exercise in which you write freely for several pages about this person, jotting down everything that comes to mind about him or her. Look over your work and identify what it is about that person that has influenced you for good or bad, or both. Organize your material by clustering, cubing, or outlining, so that you can bring out different aspects of this person's character and behavior. Quote or paraphrase (put in your own words) this person's most memorable sayings, and describe how this person behaves in different situations. If the person's physical qualities affected his or her influence on you, be sure to describe them as well. Remember to make your introduction and conclusion especially vivid as you create a complete impression of this person in the reader's mind.

Challenge Exercise: Descriptive Writing

Describe a course you have taken and completed, either in high school or in college. First collect all the facts about this course you can think of, either by brainstorming or by doing several pages of focused writing.

Then identify your main point about this course—what you gained from it and why it is worth describing. Group your material using a cluster or cubing exercise, sorting out different aspects of the course such as the teacher's style, your relation to your classmates, the books and other materials used, the course content, the skills required, and the facts and insights you acquired. In your revised draft, be sure that your introduction and conclusion state clearly and emphatically what made your experience of taking this course worth writing about.

Essay Topics: Descriptive Writing

1. Describe a natural scene that inspires you.
2. Describe a person who deserves to be better known.
3. Describe an organization or team of which you have been a member.
4. Describe a character on your favorite television program.
5. Describe a painting, statue, or special exhibit in a museum near you.
6. Describe a storm that you witnessed.
7. Describe a recent invention that has made life better.

PEER REVIEW QUESTIONS: DESCRIPTIVE WRITING

1. Here is the impression I think you are trying to convey in your description:

2. Your introduction is interesting.   ☐ Yes   ☐ No
   Your introduction makes your attitude toward your topic clear.   ☐ Yes   ☐ No
   The sentence that most nearly expresses this attitude is the following:

3. You create an overall impression well.   ☐ Yes   ☐ No

4. The following details create a vivid impression of your subject:

5. Your conclusion (is/is not) effective for the following reason:

6. What I like best about your description is the following:

7. I recommend you make the following changes:

Proofreading Practice:
Adjectives and Adverbs

People often confuse adjectives with adverbs, and vice versa.

Telling the Difference between Adjectives and Adverbs

The most common mistake people make with adjectives and adverbs is to write *good* when they mean *well*.

Not: This engine runs good.
But: This engine runs well.

Good is an adjective; *well* is an adverb. What is the difference?

Adjectives tell *which*, *what kind of*, or *how many*; they modify nouns or pronouns.

a perfect evening
a foolish idea
the final chapter
a rapid message

Adverbs tell *how*, *when*, and *where*; they modify verbs, adjectives, and other adverbs.

The evening went perfectly.
He acted foolishly.
They finally arrived.
She talked rapidly.

Another common mistake is to omit the –*ly* ending on adverbs. Many adjectives can be converted into adverbs by adding –*ly*.

Adjective	Adverb
a quick meal	We ate the meal quickly.
a real diamond	a really fine diamond
a bad feeling	They arranged it badly.
The answer was correct.	They answered correctly.

Remember to use adjectives after forms of *be* (*is*, *are*, *was*, *were*). Adjectives in this case modify the subject. Also use adjectives after verbs of the senses such as *feel*, *smell*, *sound*, and *taste*.

1. The film sounds <u>exciting</u>. (*Exciting* modifies *film*.)
2. The pastry smells <u>delicious</u>. (*Delicious* modifies *pastry*.)
3. I feel <u>good</u> this morning. (*Good* modifies *I*.)
4. The bread tastes <u>stale</u>. (*Stale* modifies *bread*.)

Do not confuse these adjectives (called **predicate adjectives** because they come after the verb, not before the noun) with adverbs that come after verbs.

1. The script reads <u>smoothly</u>. (*Smoothly* modifies *reads*.)
2. The chef makes pastry <u>expertly</u>. (*Expertly* modifies *makes*.)
3. I dress <u>quickly</u> in the morning. (*Quickly* modifies *dress*.)
4. She writes stories <u>frequently</u>. (*Frequently* modifies *writes*.)

Some Tricky Adverbs

Certain adverbs are often confused with adjectives. Be on the lookout for these.

Adjective	**Adverb**
<u>most</u> people	<u>almost</u> always
She feels <u>bad</u>.	She sings <u>badly</u>.
an <u>easy</u> job	He does it <u>easily</u>.
an <u>everyday</u> task	He swims <u>every day</u>.
a <u>slow</u> pace	Drive <u>slowly</u>. (*Slow* is also accepted as an adverb.)

TEST YOURSELF: Adjectives and Adverbs

Choose the correct form in each sentence.

1. Day care workers have to be (real, really) mature.
2. These computer games help children learn (easy, easily).
3. Some people feel (bad, badly) after their favorite teams lose.
4. Pilates exercises have become an (everyday, every day) activity for many people.
5. Toner cartridges are (most, almost, mostly) as expensive as printers themselves.
6. Some children behave (violent, violently) after their parents argue.
7. To choose a major (careful, carefully), you should talk to students in the program.

Answers: 1. really 2. easily 3. bad 4. everyday 5. almost 6. violently 7. carefully

---

Basic Exercise: Adjectives and Adverbs

Practice using *good* and *well* correctly. Supply the adjective *good* or the adverb *well* for each item. Remember that *well* may be an adjective meaning "healthy" or "not sick."

1. Jessica did the assignment _____.
2. She had a _____ memory and could write _____.
3. After being absent during an illness, she had gotten _____ again; now she was expecting to earn a _____ grade on the final exam.
4. It felt _____ to have a challenging task.
5. She remembered _____ how hard high school had been.
6. A career in some medical field now looked _____ to her.
7. It was a _____ way to help people and it paid _____.

Intermediate Exercise: Adjectives and Adverbs

Supply the missing forms.

Adjective	**Adverb**
Example: She is <u>stylish</u>.	She dresses <u>stylishly</u>.
1. His reply was slow.	He replied _____.
2. The problem was <u>easy</u>.	She solved the problem _____.
3. The ending was _____.	The play ended <u>happily</u>.
4. We gave it <u>careful</u> thought.	We considered it _____.
5. He felt _____ about the job.	He did the job <u>badly</u>.
6. They created a <u>good</u> plan.	They planned _____.
7. The supervisor was <u>efficient</u>.	She supervised the office _____.

Challenge Exercise: Adjectives and Adverbs

Compose sentences using the following words and phrases.

1. good
   well
2. especially
   special
3. bad
   badly
4. probable
   probably
5. careful
   carefully
6. real
   really
7. everyday
   every day

Key Words from Chapter 6 for Review

adjectives, adverbs, chronological arrangement, descriptive writing, spatial arrangement, topical arrangement

CHAPTER

Telling a Story to Make a Point

STEPPING UP: WRITING TIP 7

Narrative writing follows a chronological pattern; that is, it follows a time sequence. However, when you tell a story, don't assume that your narrative has to march along with clocklike regularity. You will want to use your Fast Forward button at times, your Pause button at others, and occasionally even your Rewind. Although narrative writing is sometimes seen as the easiest mode, don't underestimate how creative you can be with it and how complex it sometimes is. Try reading a story like William Faulkner's "A Rose for Emily" to see how a great writer moves skillfully back and forth in time.

Organizing Chronologically

Telling a story, or **narration**, is one of the most important ways of developing an idea. It can be the easiest way to organize material, because narration is simply telling about a series of events in the order in which they occurred. Often, however, your story will not be that simple. Parts of it might need to be told in detail, minute by minute, while other parts can be skipped. One paragraph might concentrate on an important moment, while another might sum up events that happen over several months or years. Sometimes you want to include quoted conversations or to pause and describe a person or situation.

Narrative rarely moves like clockwork, at a steady, measured pace; in fact, it may even begin near the end of the events, flash back, tell a story, then work its way to where the story concludes. Although narrative writing can be one of the simpler modes, it also can be quite complex. Be ready to rethink and revise your story to emphasize its effect on your reader and the meaning you want the reader to derive from it.

Telling a Meaningful and Moving Story

Many people write memoirs, and it is sometimes said that every human being's life contains a novel. That is, everyone's life has meaning, and if the story were told well, readers would grasp that meaning and respond emotionally to it. The way you tell a story is what gives it meaning. The best novels and short stories are read and reread because they are especially rich in meaning. Make the story you tell so full of meaning and emotional impact that the reader will want to read it again. Your first draft may flow easily as you simply tell your story. But then you should read it a day or two later as if someone else wrote it. Which parts need to be dramatized more? Which section moves too slowly? How can you experiment with the time sequence to create suspense, distance, uncertainty, or emphasis?

Student Essay:
Telling a Story to Make a Point

This essay was written by a student who uses a story of his experience in the military to examine his own attitudes. Rodney Vega uses narrative development to support an important point about himself and about tolerance in relating to others. In doing that, he makes his essay meaningful to anyone reading it, since we have all had to reflect on things in ourselves that may need improvement. This essay does not show all the stages of the writing process that Rodney went through. As a successful final draft, it provides the kind of goal to aim for. The essay tells a story but also, like all effective essays, makes an important point. Notice that the essay has a clear introduction, thesis, and conclusion, and several paragraphs begin with topic sentences that guide the reader.

A Weighty Experience

RODNEY VEGA

Introduction

Throughout my military career, I traveled to many places and had encounters with all sorts of people. Some were religious, others atheist; some were tough, others timid; some were bright, others not quite. However, I was never prejudiced toward anyone regardless of these varied characteristics. When it came to physical appearance, however—in terms of one's weight—it was a completely different issue. I despised overweight people and considered them both lazy and careless, particularly if they were in the military. In addition, to me, being overweight was a liability. I would have hated to lose someone in combat simply because they couldn't keep their grubby little fingers out of the cookie jar. *So I thought, until I had an experience that totally changed my attitude toward overweight people.*

Thesis Statement

Shortly after my promotion to sergeant, I was assigned to train a unit of fifteen recruits who were deemed "unfit" by Marine Corps regulations. I wasn't enthusiastic about the assignment, but it did present a golden opportunity: not only could I show off my outstanding physical conditioning, but I was also allowed to mock the overweight soldiers. I searched on the Internet for "fat" jokes and insults I could use the next day. Not surprisingly, a group of trainees soon complained to the department officer about my training techniques, claiming that they could not stand my verbal abuse anymore.

Body Paragraphs Using Narrative to Support a Thesis

The officer immediately called me in to discuss my methods. I argued that my training techniques were within regulations and involved the same psychological methods that drill instructors use to motivate overweight recruits. He did not dispute my argument and allowed me to continue with my training methods. After several months, new soldiers were assigned to my squad while others passed the program and were processed out. However, I had become intensely disliked by many and even overheard rumors of people making obscene puns on my name. But I didn't care; in fact, I pushed even harder.

Topic Sentence

My sense of superiority, however, was soon to be challenged. One morning a new soldier appeared unexpectedly in my unit. Anxious as always to show off in front of new people, I was more intense in training than ever. I enjoyed scaring the "Twinkies," as I called the newly assigned overweight soldiers. We began that morning as usual jogging at a slow pace for two miles while I shouted cadences about cakes, Krispy Kreme doughnuts, and ice cream. Then I made everyone do the standard Marine Corps three-mile run to test their individual fitness. My true intention, of course, was to humiliate the new individual. As always, I was far ahead of everyone on the track, but after the first mile, something happened. To my amazement, someone was closing in on me, and fast. I couldn't believe it: it was the newbie! There was no way I was going to be beaten, so I gave it my all. But after two miles the new recruit was sitting at the finish line waiting for me.

Topic Sentence

In the attempt to redeem my pride, I tried to deny what was happening. I claimed that I had severe stomach pains. How could I admit that a "fat body" had defeated me in a race? And to make matters worse, the fat body was a young woman who had given birth just a few weeks before! I cancelled training for the next two days, claiming that I needed to recover from the stomach pains. At our next meeting, I tried even harder, running like a train down the track; but to my extreme disappointment, she arrived at the finish line before me again. After one more humiliating loss, knowing that everyone in my division was silently mocking me, I began to admire her persistence and determination—and I began to like her too.

Topic Sentence

I tried a new way of making an impression. I ceased the verbal hazing and began treating the recruits with respect as real Marines. Everyone was surprised and wondered what caused my change of heart. They soon began to think highly of me. That, however, was just a bonus, as my real intention was to win the friendship of the young woman. As the days and weeks passed, I formed friendships with some of the people in my program by treating them as people just like me. As I got to know them, I realized that some were struggling with depression or medical conditions. They were not all sitting in bed with cheesecake and Doritos watching television. After listening to their stories, I became sympathetic toward their situations.

Conclusion

After seven months, I was replaced by a new sergeant and went on to other assignments. *In the process of training others, I was the one who changed the most.* The people whom I once ridiculed and made stereotypes of had not only proven themselves capable of enduring my rigorous training but had convinced me that I was no more special than they were. Because they helped me see my true self and what I had become, they in a sense saved me from myself. I've learned to accept others because of that invaluable experience. However, even though I gained much from that experience, I never succeeded in obtaining what I set out to get by changing my attitudes and behavior: I never got to date the young woman.

1. In your own words, explain the main lesson of Rodney's essay.
2. What change takes place in his attitudes, and what causes the change?
3. Approximately how much time elapses in the period covered by the essay?
4. Identify details that Rodney includes to give the essay interest and humor.
5. How does he use the element of surprise to hold your interest?
6. How does his introduction pull you into the story?
7. What does his final paragraph add to the story?

Example by a Published Author

Here is a narrative that covers a significant period of time and tells about a meaningful experience.

Up In the Tree

Yasunari Kawabata

Keisuke's house was on the shore where the great river began to enter the sea. Although the river ran alongside the garden, because of the somewhat elevated embankment it could not be seen from the house. The old shore, lined with pines and slightly lower than the embankment, seemed part of the garden, its pines the garden pines. This side of the pines, there was a hedge of Chinese black pine.

Michiko, forcing her way through the hedge, came to play with Keisuke. No, she came just to be with him. Both Michiko and Keisuke were fourth graders. This ducking through the hedge, instead of coming in by the front gate or by the garden gate in back, was a secret between them. For a girl, it wasn't easy. Shielding her head and face with both arms, bent over from the waist, she would plunge into the hedge. Tumbling out into the garden, she would often be caught up in Keisuke's arms.

Shy about letting the people in the house know that Michiko came every day, Keisuke had taught her this way through the hedge.

"I like it. My heart pounds and pounds like anything," Michiko said.

One day, Keisuke climbed up into a pine tree. While he was up there, along came Michiko. Looking neither right nor left, she hurried along by the shore. Stopping at the hedge where she always went through, she looked all around her. Bringing her long, triple-braided pigtails in front of her face, she put them into her mouth halfway along their length. Bracing herself, she threw herself at the hedge. Up in the tree, Keisuke held his breath. When she'd popped out of the hedge into the garden, Michiko did not see Keisuke, whom she had thought would be there. Frightened, she shrank back into the shadow of the hedge, where Keisuke could not see her.

"Mitchan, Mitchan," Keisuke called. Michiko, coming away from the hedge, looked around the garden.

"Mitchan, I'm in the pine tree. I'm up in the pine tree." Looking up toward Keisuke's voice, Michiko did not say a word. Keisuke said, "Come out. Come out of the garden."

When Michiko had come back out through the hedge, she looked up at Keisuke.

"You come down."

"Mitchan, climb up here. It's nice up here in the tree."

"I can't climb it. You're making fun of me, just like a boy. Come down."

"Come up here. The branches are big like this, so even a girl can do it."

Michiko studied the branches. Then she said, "If I fall, it's your fault. If I die, I won't know anything about it."

First dangling from a lower branch, she began to climb.

By the time she'd gotten up to Keisuke's branch, Michiko was gasping for breath. "I climbed it, I climbed it." Her eyes sparkled. "It's scary. Hold me."

"Hmm." Keisuke firmly drew Michiko to him.

Michiko, her arms around Keisuke's neck, said, "You can see the ocean."

"You can see everything. Across the river, and even up the river . . . It's good you climbed up here."

"It is good. Keichan, let's climb up here tomorrow."

"Hmm." Keisuke was silent a while. "Mitchan, it's a secret. Climbing up the tree and being up here in the tree—it's a secret. I read books and do homework up here. It's no good if you tell anyone."

"I won't tell." Michiko bowed her head in assent. "Why have you become like a bird?"

"Since it's you, Mitchan, I'll tell you. My father and mother had an awful quarrel. My mother said she was going to take me and go back to her parents' house. I didn't want to look at them, so I climbed a tree in the garden and hid at the top. Saying, 'Where's Keisuke gone to?' they looked all over for me. But they couldn't find me. From the tree, I saw my father go all the way to the ocean to look. This was last spring."

"What were they quarreling about?"

"Don't you know? My father has a woman."

Michiko said nothing.

"Since then, I've been up in this tree a lot. My father and mother still don't know. It's a secret," Keisuke said again, just to make sure. "Mitchan, starting tomorrow, bring your schoolbooks. We'll do our homework up here. We'll get good grades. The trees in the garden are all those big camellia trees with lots of leaves, so nobody can see us from the ground or anywhere."

The "secret" of their being up in the tree had continued for almost two years now. Where the thick trunk branched out near the top, the two could sit comfortably. Michiko, straddling one branch, leaned back against another. There were days when little birds came and days when the wind sang through the pine needles. Although they weren't that high off the ground, these two little lovers felt as if they were in a completely different world, far away from the earth.

of North Point Press, a division of Farrar, Straus & Giroux, Inc.

–From *Palm-in-the-Hand Stories*. English translation c. 1988
by Lane Dunlop and J. Martin Holman. Rpt. By permission
of North Point Press, a division of Farrar, Straus & Giroux, Inc.

1. How much time does this story encompass?
2. Explain why Keisuke first began to hide in the tree.
3. Explain why Keisuke and Michiko like to spend time together in the tree.
4. Is this a children's story or a story for adult readers?
5. How does the story change when Keisuke mentions his parents?
6. Describe the landscape and how the two children interact with it.
7. Why do Keisuke and Michiko want to be in a world far away from the earth?

WRITING EXERCISES: Basic, Intermediate, Challenge

Basic Exercise: Narrative Writing

Write an essay telling the story of a trip you have taken. Arrange the story in chronological sequence: before, during, and after; tell about getting there, being there, and returning. Although this is one of the simplest ways of organizing an essay, it requires some balancing of the parts: Do not spend all of your time telling the reader how you got to your destination, leaving no time for the rest of the story. Tell the reader in detail what you did when you were at the place you visited and what your return trip was like. Include factual details in all three parts, but be sure your essay has an overall point. First write a draft telling about the trip, then look it over and decide what you gained from the experience, and make this point in your introduction and conclusion.

Intermediate Exercise: Narrative Writing

Write an essay in which you relate an important change in your life. This may be a change in residence, such as immigrating to the United States or moving from one city to another; in a relationship (such as marriage or divorce); in employment, physical appearance, health, or membership in a group (either joining or leaving). Develop each part of the story fully: Explain the circumstances that led to the change, tell about how you felt during the change, and analyze what that change has meant in your life. You will probably need to write several drafts to ensure that each part is detailed enough and complete, so that the whole story interests the reader. Your introduction and conclusion should help the reader understand the meaning of the experience.

Challenge Exercise: Narrative Writing

Write your intellectual and philosophical autobiography. Tell how your opinions developed during an important part of your early life, such as childhood or adolescence, and explain who or what influenced them. Then explain what events, persons, educational institutions, or reading changed your attitudes. Identify clearly what opinions you now hold on politics, religion, family, and careers. Your introduction and conclusion should make your memoir interesting and meaningful to any reader.

Essay Topics: Narration

1. Tell the story of a search for something important to you and how you found it or failed to find it.
2. Tell about an experience in which you met a challenge successfully.
3. Tell about a job experience from which you learned something.
4. Tell about buying a product or service that you were dissatisfied with and how you responded.
5. Tell about an experience of being in the hospital and what you learned from it.
6. Tell about the experience of finding a place to live and what advice you would give others looking for housing.
7. Tell about witnessing a crime, act of violence, or accident; tell what happened, how you responded, and what you learned from the experience.

PEER REVIEW QUESTIONS:
NARRATIVE WRITING

1. Here is the point I think you are making in your story:

2. Your introduction is interesting. □ Yes   □ No

   Your introduction and conclusion make your point clear.
   □ Yes   □ No

   The sentence that most nearly expresses your point is the following:

3. Your story is interesting and easy to follow.   □ Yes   □ No

4. Each paragraph in your essay moves the story one step further toward a climax.   □ Yes   □ No

5. You use the following transition words and phrases:

6. What I like best about your narrative is the following:

7. I recommend you make the following changes:

Proofreading Practice: Past Tense

Verb Tenses in Writing: Some Guidelines

1. Stay in the same tense as long as the time you are writing about does not change.
   Example: Karen peered at the controls, started the engine, and prepared for an exciting race.

2. If the time changes, the verb tense *should* change, even in the same paragraph or sentence.
   Example: I once believed that money makes people happy, but now I realize that I was wrong.

3. Tell about the plot of a play, novel, or story in the *present tense.*
   Example: The main character in this story makes mistakes before she finds the right man for her.

4. Statements about eternal truths may be in the present even when you are telling about past events.
   Example: The child learned quickly that not all people in this world can be trusted.

5. If you are writing about experiences that you remember, statements such as "I recall" or "I remember" are in the present.

The events happened in the past, but you are recalling them now.

Example: I remember (not remembered) how hot the summers were in Arizona when I was a child.

In narrative writing, most of your sentences will be in the past tense. In the **past tense**, verbs fall into two categories: **regular verbs**, which take *-ed* endings, and **irregular verbs**, which change their spelling and do not take *-ed* endings.

Past Tense of Regular Verbs	**Past Tense of Irregular Verbs**
succeeded	became
walked	bought
kissed	saw
stampeded	drank
murdered	sang
worshipped	took
doubted	drove
discussed	broke
wandered	spent

-ed Endings in the Past Tense

One of the most common writing errors is dropping or forgetting to add *-ed* **endings** on regular verbs. Be careful to edit for *-ed* endings when writing in the past tense.

When *Not* to Use *-ed* Endings

If you tend to omit *-ed* endings in the past tense and are trying to check for missing *-ed* endings in your final draft, remember that there are a few places where *-ed* endings should *not* be used.

Do not use *-ed* endings after *did* or *to*:

Did you discuss (not *discussed*) the salary?
They tried to reach (not *to reached*) the exit.

Do not use *-ed* endings after other helping verbs such as *may, might, can, could, would, must,* and *should*:

She might like (not *liked*) to participate on the panel.
He could learn (not *learned*) a lot from you.

The Past Tense of Irregular Verbs

Irregular verbs never take -ed endings. Instead, they change in different ways—go changes to *went*, think to *thought*, and so on. Most of these past tense verbs you know by habit, but some cause frequent mistakes. Look over this list to see whether you recognize the past tenses.

Present	Past	Present	Past
be (am, is, are)	was, were	make	made
become	became	meet	met
begin	began	pay	paid
bring	brought	put	put
buy	bought	quit	quit
choose	chose	rise	rose
cost	cost	seek	sought
do	did	sell	sold
cut	cut	send	sent
feel	felt	shine	shone
fly	flew	sing	sang
get	got	spend	spent
give	gave	stand	stood
go	went	steal	stole
have	had	swim	swam
hear	heard	take	took
keep	kept	teach	taught
know	knew	tear	tore
lay	laid	think	thought
lead	led	throw	threw
lie	lay	write	wrote
lose	lost		

PROOFREADING EXERCISES: Basic, Intermediate, Challenge

Basic Exercise: Past Tense

Find and correct the seven errors in the use of the past tense in the passage that follows.

Last year when Ella was 15 she notice that her 11-year-old brother James was acting in a peculiar way. He was always going out for short walks all the time, and he would get angry if anybody ask him why he went out. At first she believe he was starting to hang with a gang and would get into trouble, but he spend too much time at home for that to happen. Once when she was coming home she saw him smoking a cigarette across the street from their house. He didn't see her watching him while he snuff out the cigarette butt before he went back inside. Ella was not happy to realized that he was developing a nicotine habit, but she feel a little relieved that he wasn't doing something worse.

Intermediate Exercise: Past Tense

Find and correct the seven errors in the use of the past tense in the passage that follows.

A tropical storm began forming out in the central Atlantic Ocean. Soon it gather strength and headed toward the Caribbean Islands. People in Haiti and the Dominican Republic start to board up their windows and to move their belongings into the safest shelters they could find. Soon, however, the storm changed direction and turn toward the coast of Florida, where people seek to evacuate the coastal areas as meteorologists predict 120-mile-an-hour winds by the next morning. Fortunately, the winds subside somewhat and many of the residents along the coast escape serious damage to their homes, and few people were injured.

Challenge Exercise: Past Tense

Find and correct the seven errors in the use of the past tense in the passage that follows.

The psychologist Abraham Maslow did much to change our views of human nature. He began as an experimenter who spend most of his time studying emotional illness. He wrote a book on abnormal psychology but then become dissatisfied with approaches that analyzed only disturbed persons. Instead, he choose to examine the characteristics of the unusually healthy person. He contribute significantly to modern psychology and brought a new emphasis on health and potential rather than sickness. He realize that many mysteries are still unsolved in the psychology of the healthy personality. He teach for many years and was a popular professor at several universities. Certain of his concepts, such as self-actualization and the hierarchy of needs, take their place among the leading ideas of modern psychology.

Key Words from Chapter 7 for Review

chronological, narration, past tense, regular and irregular verbs

8

CHAPTER

Enumerating Examples

STEPPING UP: WRITING TIP 8

Developing and organizing your essay by listing a series of examples is called *enumeration*. Keeping your points in order by numbering them can guide your reader, but it can also call too much attention to your essay's structure, making it seem mechanical and pedantic. It is sometimes better to number your paragraphs by using words like *first*, *second*, and *third* in your early drafts but burying them by using more attractive words like *another*, *next*, *further*, and *finally* in your later drafts. Be clear about your purpose: If you want to overwhelm your readers with the extent of a problem, give many examples. If your main purpose is to put across a simple point, use a few vivid examples instead.

Enumerating Examples as a Mode of Development

One of the simplest and best ways to develop ideas in an essay is to provide a series of examples to illustrate the point you are making. Generally, this means writing a paragraph, perhaps two, on each example, with an introductory and concluding paragraph tying them together. It is easy to organize an essay of this type, but it is not as easy to make it interesting: You must use creativity to produce a lively essay instead of a mechanical list. Try to write a thought-provoking introduction, make transitions between your paragraphs, and choose examples that are sufficiently different from one another to avoid repetition.

Student Essay: Enumerating Examples

Read Reginald Stevens's essay and then answer the questions that follow it.

International Students Upgrade American Colleges

REGINALD STEVENS

One of the main reasons people come to the United States is to receive a college education which they can't get in their own countries. Some Americans may think that these foreign students are occupying places that should be taken by students born in the United States, and sometimes they make remarks about foreign students who have trouble with English. What they should realize is how much better American colleges are because of international students. *A few examples of students I know would convince anybody that international students improve the quality of colleges in the United States.*

Thesis Statement

First Example

One of my friends is Carlton, a sophomore student from my country of Guyana. Carlton is studying to be a lawyer and wants to start his own practice in my country, where he hopes to enter politics someday. He is an honors student and has been on the dean's list every one of his four semesters. In most classes he does more work than anybody else, and he helps other students after class when they don't understand the lesson. Some people say he is a politician already, and he is thinking about running for student government because he has been a leader of the debate team, and after every debate someone comes up and tells him he should be in politics.

Second Example Another international student who contributes a lot to my college is May, a student I met in chemistry class. She will be graduating next semester and is applying to veterinary schools. Her family comes from South Korea, and she has been in this country for just five years, but she speaks English really well, and she won a creative writing prize for a short story she wrote. May wants to stay in the United States. Her dream is to move to California and have her own veterinary practice, where she can care for rare animals that are becoming extinct. She organized a group of students to travel to the Galapagos Islands to study unusual species, and she was the president of a club for students interested in protecting the environment. As a senior project she helped the science department create a new course in ecology.

Final Example An even better example I know of an international student who has contributed to the betterment of our college is my friend and classmate Natasha. She spent one year in a technical college in Moscow, and then her family moved to the United States. Like many other foreign students, she had to learn English in a hurry to continue her college education. In fact, her first semester she took only an ESL class and an advanced course in Russian literature. But after a year, she began to speak and write English well enough to earn high grades in all her courses. She is an outstanding pianist and has been the accompanist for the glee club since her second semester. She joins as many activities as she can and still does all her academic work. She helps the theater club with music and set design and has played three outstanding roles in school performances. Recently she was accepted into one of the best graduate theater programs to study directing. What makes her unique is that she not only added a lot to the school as a student, but she wants to come back some day and teach in the theater department after she makes a name for herself as a director.

Conclusion   It is true that international students like these compete with American students for admission to colleges, but there is a place somewhere for any qualified student. They also compete for grades with other students, but that is good because it gives American students more incentive. Coming from other cultures, international students bring experiences and knowledge that can enrich the educational experience of their classmates. Many of them also stay in the United States and contribute to our society after they graduate. Colleges should welcome more students from abroad.

1. Identify the sentence that best sums up the thesis of this essay.
2. What opposing opinion does Reginald mention and respond to?
3. What do all three of his examples have in common?
4. What differences are there among them?
5. How is the concluding paragraph linked to the introduction?
6. What transition words does he use at the beginning of the third and fourth paragraphs?
7. How well does your experience match the examples in this essay?

Example by a Published Author: Enumerating Examples

Endangered Habitats

Edward O. Wilson

The cutting of primeval forest and other disasters, fueled by the demands of growing human populations, are the overriding threat to biological diversity everywhere. . . .

Not many habitats in the world covering a kilometer contain fewer than a thousand species of plants and animals. Patches of rain forest and coral reef harbor tens of thousands of species, even after they have declined to a remnant of the original wilderness. But when the *entire* habitat is destroyed, almost all of the species are destroyed. . . . And so to threatened and endangered species must be added a growing list of ecosystems, comprising masses of species. Here are several deserving immediate attention:

Usambara Mountain forests, Tanzania. Varying widely in elevation and rainfall, the Usambaras contain one of the richest biological communities in East Africa. They protect large numbers of plant and animal species found nowhere else, but their forest cover is declining drastically, having already been cut to half, some 450 square kilometers, between 1954 and 1978. Rapid growth of human populations, more extensive logging, and the takeover of land for agriculture are pressing the last remaining reserves and thousands of species toward extinction.

San Bruno Mountain, California. In this small refuge surrounded by the San Francisco metropolis live a number of federally protected vertebrates, plants, and insects. Some of the species are endemics of the San Francisco peninsula, including the San Bruno elfin butterfly and the San Francisco garter snake. The native fauna and flora are threatened by offroad vehicular traffic, expansion of a quarry, and invasion by eucalyptus, gorse, and other alien plant species. . . .

The Colombian Chocó. The forest of Colombia's coastal plain and low mountains extends the entire length of the country. The Chocó, as the region is called after the state it includes, is drenched with extreme rainfall and blessed with one of the richest but least explored floras in the world. At present, 3,500 plant species are known but as many as 10,000 may grow there, of which one fourth are estimated to be endemic and a smaller but still substantial fraction are new to science. Since the early 1970s, the Chocó has been relentlessly invaded by timber companies and, to a lesser extent, by poor Colombians hungry for land. The forests are already down to about three quarters of their original cover and are being destroyed at an accelerating rate. . . .

But the long-term danger from climatic change looms in the decades ahead, for most ecosystems. If even the more modest projections of global warming prove correct, the world's fauna and flora will be trapped in a vise. On one side they are being swiftly reduced by deforestation and other forms of direct habitat destruction. On the other side they are threatened by the greenhouse effect.

—Edward O. Wilson. From *The Diversity of Life.*

1. Give the definitions of the following words: *ecosystems, vertebrates, endemics, fauna, flora, global warming, greenhouse effect.* Consult a dictionary if necessary.
2. What is Wilson warning us about in all of these examples?
3. What do all three examples have in common?

4. What differences do you notice?

5. What processes does he describe taking place in these regions?

6. In his book, Wilson actually lists 18 places in the world where ecosystems are in danger. Why does he list 18 instead of giving just one or two examples?

7. What conclusions can you draw from these examples?

WRITING EXERCISES: Basic, Intermediate, Challenge

Basic Exercise: Illustration by Examples

Write an essay giving three or four examples of activities you like to do in your spare time. Use at least a paragraph to explain why you find each activity satisfying. Create transitions between paragraphs so that the essay doesn't read like a laundry list of items. Do a prewriting activity in order to identify a main point about your spare time activities, such as, "My hobbies are more important than my job" or "All of my spare-time activities are closely related to my career goals" or "All of my spare-time activities help me develop artistic skills."

Intermediate Exercise: Illustration by Examples

Write an essay giving three or four examples of people who achieved success by overcoming disabilities. These may be famous people or acquaintances of yours. Remember that there are many kinds of disabilities, so your essay should tie your examples together around a clear main point. For example, you could argue that people are sometimes challenged to succeed in the very area in which they experience a disability (such as a person with a speech disability who becomes an actor), or you could develop the idea that people who overcome disabilities inspire us all to have the courage to face our own difficulties.

Challenge Exercise: Illustration by Examples

Write an essay in which you give three or four examples of bias in the media. Explain how several newspapers, news magazines, or news programs on television or radio appear to you to slant the news in a particular way. Tie your essay together by making a point about how this kind of biased reporting can be recognized by the public. Before writing your first draft, spend some time looking over some news reports and watching or listening to programs that claim to be unbiased. Concentrate on three or four of these particular programs or articles, preferably on the same or similar topics. Do some brainstorming to identify a focused main point.

Essay Topics: Illustration by Examples

1. Write an essay giving three or four examples of films that send important messages.
2. Write an essay giving three or four examples of famous people who made surprising comebacks.
3. Write an essay giving three or four examples of violent television programs.
4. Write an essay giving three or four examples of jobs once called "men's jobs" now held by women.
5. Write an essay giving three or four examples of vacation sites that are particularly good for children.
6. Write an essay giving three or four examples of athletic activities that are good for older people.
7. Write an essay giving three or four examples of work that people do at home.

PEER REVIEW QUESTIONS: ENUMERATION

1. Here is my impression of what you are illustrating in your essay:

2. Your introduction is interesting. ☐ Yes ☐ No
   Your introduction makes the purpose of your essay clear. ☐ Yes ☐ No
   The sentence that most nearly expresses your main point is the following:

3. You offer the following three or four examples to support your point:

4. You use the following transitional words and phrases to connect your examples:

5. Your conclusion (is/is not) effective for the following reason:

6. What I like best about your essay is the following:

7. I recommend you make the following changes:

Proofreading Practice: Parallel Structure

Enumeration involves seeing parallel situations and writing parallel statements. Add rhythm to your writing occasionally by using parallel structure. In his famous Gettysburg Address, Abraham Lincoln turned a speech that might have been forgotten into a document for the ages by giving it poetic rhythm. He did this primarily by using two- and three-part parallel combinations of words and phrases. Here, for example, is a passage based on such parallel combinations:

> Fourscore and seven years ago our fathers brought forth on this continent, a new nation, conceived in Liberty, and dedicated to the proposition that all men are created equal.
>
> Now we are engaged in a great civil war, testing whether that nation or any nation so conceived and so dedicated, can long endure. We are met on a great battlefield of that war. We have come to dedicate a portion of that field, as a final resting place to those who here gave their lives that that nation might live. It is altogether fitting and proper that we should do this.
>
> But, in a larger sense, we cannot dedicate—we cannot consecrate—we cannot hallow—this ground. The brave men, living and dead, who struggled here, have consecrated it, far above our poor power to add or detract.

Notice that in each of the underlined combinations the words are in the same form: two verbs ("add or detract"), two adjectives ("fitting and proper"), and so on. Imagine how awkward the speech would be if it read, "We cannot dedicate, we cannot consecrate, to hallow is impossible. . . ." In using parallel form, Lincoln was careful to match all of the parts smoothly.

Sentences that contain two, three, or more elements in a series require parallel structure. Parallelism refers to the **forms** of the words, not their meaning. Do not try to match parts that do not fit, as in this example:

	adj	adj	adj	verb phrase
Incorrect:	My sister is nosy,	competitive,	stuck up, and	never lends me any money.

Be sure that all elements fit:

	adj	adj	adj	adj
Correct:	My sister is nosy,	competitive,	stuck up, and	stingy.

Or, if one element does not fit, you can take it out and put it in a separate sentence, as shown here:

Also Correct: My sister is nosy, competitive, and stuck up. Besides that, she never lends me any money.

TEST YOURSELF: Parallelism

Rewrite each sentence so that the parallel series is correct. One sentence is correct.

1. My friend Jessica looks good in everything she wears: formal dresses, pants, swimsuits, and even wearing old clothes from the flea market.
2. There are several things you should do during a fire: stay out of elevators, all doors closed, call the fire department, and do not panic.
3. The story tells about a young woman who is oppressed by her father, her boss harasses her, but paralyzed by her fear of leaving home.
4. Registering for college courses takes a lot of persistence, patient, and resourcefulness.
5. The United States benefits from immigrants because they take jobs others do not want, bring strong family values to American society, and an increased percentage of young people in an aging society.
6. In the emergency room Thomas saw patients waiting, EMT workers rushing in with patients on gurneys, and office assistants helping patients fill out forms.
7. The school requires that all children wear uniforms, arrive punctually, do their homework, and good behavior at all times.

Answers: 1. and even old clothes from the flea market 2. keep all doors closed
3. harassed by her boss 4. patience 5. and increase the percentage 6. correct
7. and behave well at all times

PROOFREADING EXERCISES: Basic, Intermediate, Challenge

Basic Exercise: Parallelism

Proofread the sentences below, underlining the words or phrases that do not match. Explain how they can be corrected to make them fit into parallel combinations.

1. Frank is lazy, resentful, and impatience.
2. The course stimulated my interest, gave me new ideas, and expanding my awareness.

3. Sports utility vehicles are durable in rugged terrain, convenient for camping, but they are wasteful on fuel.
4. Sam needs either a new job or he should get a raise.
5. To excel on this test, you should memorize the chapter headings, do all the exercises, and careful notes.
6. The surgeon worked carefully, swiftly, and professional.
7. Without money, brains, or untalented, he managed to succeed.

Intermediate Exercise: Parallelism

Write words or phrases in the blanks provided, being careful to match them with the other elements in the group.

Charlene knew she had many qualifications for the job. She was experienced, efficient, and _____. Her previous employer gave her a letter of recommendation that stated how well she shared tasks with others, came up with new ideas for the firm, and _____. Nevertheless, as the day came for the interview, she felt hesitant and _____. She realized that an unattractive mannerism, a careless gesture, or _____ might create a bad impression. So many others must be seeking this job, she thought, that only the most _____ and knowledgeable candidates would be taken seriously. After spending an afternoon researching the company and _____, she felt more confident. Three years ago, when she took her last interview, she was poised, _____, and confident, so she knew she could succeed this time as well.

Challenge Exercise: Parallelism

Correct the underlined words or phrases to make them match the rest of the sentence in parallel combinations.

Members of the state legislature decided to do something to reduce the number of traffic accidents in the state. They attributed the increased number of accidents to speeding, poorly maintained highways, and there are drunken drivers. Most of the legislators believed that more could be done to reduce traffic deaths and why there are so many injuries from accidents. Some members of the assembly believed that either more state police or by enforcing current laws better would help. However, others argued that passing new laws would help more than to enforce current laws more strictly. Some younger legislators pointed out some new problems. For example, they said that drivers were causing accidents when they used their cell phones to carry on conversations, send text messages, and business deals. These representatives proposed laws that would require the use of seat belts, would prohibit texting and talking on cell phones while driving, and severe penalties for drivers who cause accidents while using cell phones. There was considerable controversy over these proposals. A few members blamed older drivers for the problem and even proposed that the legislature deny seniors the right to drive, but they were interrupted, laughed at, and members of the other party silenced them.

Key Words from Chapter 8 for Review

enumeration, illustration, parallelism

CHAPTER 9

Defining a Term

STEPPING UP: WRITING TIP 9

Writing an essay in which you are defining a term challenges you to think clearly about the meaning of words and to think critically and creatively about ideas. Prewriting exercises like brainstorming, clustering, and cubing will help you explore the possible meanings of the term you are defining. If you can learn to write an effective definition essay, you will have a wonderful head start toward writing successful examination essays and academic papers.

Writing an Essay Based on the Definition of a Term

Dictionaries give us short definitions of a word when we are not sure of its meaning. Thesauruses, as well as essays, articles, and other books that define terms, do much more than that: They explain terms in greater depth for people who are already familiar with them. These additional reference materials help readers understand the concept embodied by a term from many perspectives. These sources genuinely *explain ideas* rather than simply *clarify the meaning* of a word.

For this reason, it is not usually effective, though it may be tempting, to begin a definition essay with a quotation from a dictionary. Doing so is the least original way to begin such an essay, in part because that beginning can be a dead end rather than a springboard to inspiration. If you decide to start your essay that way, be sure to explain to your reader that a dictionary definition alone is not adequate information to help us understand a term fully. In addition, you should provide your own short definition of the word as a foundation for building a broader explanation of the concept the word represents.

Student Essay: Defining a Term

Read Jocelyn Harkins's essay defining the term *friendship* and then respond to the questions that follow it.

The Meaning of Friendship

JOCELYN HARKINS

Most of us use the word *friendship* every day without thinking about what it really means. To many people, being a friend means only that two people spend time together, hang out at the same places, and get to know each other. But my definition of friendship is of two people deciding that they will be closely involved in each other's lives and support each other permanently, just like members of the same family. Sometimes they are more than family.

By my definition, many people who are called "friends" are just acquaintances. Relationships like that are convenient for a while until one of the people involved transfers to another college or moves to another city. Then they write to each other for a while until they forget about it. In other cases, people keep up long-term connections by writing or e-mailing but never really do anything to support each other or talk about what is really bothering them. Some people also consider their co-workers friends but forget that they see them only at work and don't know much about their personal lives. If one of them changes jobs, that's the end of their "friendship."

These kinds of relationships can't compare to a true friendship, which is based on a really close and supportive connection over many years, no matter if one of the parties moves away, changes jobs, or drops out of college. Real friends are there for each other, especially when they need each other because one of them is in the hospital or has a personal problem. In a poem called "The Death of the Hired Man" by Robert Frost, a homeless man who used to work for a couple on their farm is dying and he comes back to them. He doesn't have a home, but the wife says to her husband, "Home is the place where, when you have to go there,/They have to take you in." That's just the way a friend is: a person who will listen to you or help you when there is nobody else. To use computer language, a friend is the "default" person who can always be counted on and will always take you in.

One example in my life of a real friend is Sonya. We first met in middle school and became close friends. Then we went to the same high school for one year until she moved to Pittsburgh. We stayed in touch and visited each other for the next two years, and went to different colleges. I know we will continue to be friends for the rest of our lives, because we have stayed close even through experiences with boyfriends that didn't work out, changing jobs and going to different schools. I know we will be at each other's wedding and will be there if we have children and when either one of us has problems.

Using my definition, I would have to say there aren't many examples of true friends in the world. But everybody needs one or two true friends. Most people have a lot of co-workers, family members, and acquaintances, but sometimes they don't serve our needs like a true friend. Many families are dysfunctional and not supportive, and we can't count on acquaintances and co-workers to be there next year or the year after when we need them. Nothing can take the place of a true friend.

1. In your own words, explain what Jocelyn means by the words *a true friend*.
2. Identify the kinds of relationships she considers not true friendship.
3. Identify the thesis statement in this essay.
4. What is the difference in purpose between paragraphs 2 and 3?
5. What is the purpose of her quotation from Robert Frost's poem in paragraph 3?
6. What method does Jocelyn use to develop paragraph 4?
7. What opinions does Jocelyn express that might be explored and debated further?

Example by a Published Author: Definition Essay

Read the following passage defining the term *community* and answer the questions that follow it.

A Sociologist Defines the Term "Community"

Amitai Etzioni

A key concept I draw upon in the following characterization of a good society is the term "community." Given that it has been repeatedly argued that such a social entity cannot be defined, this matter is first addressed. Several critics have argued that the concept of community is so ill-defined that it has no identifiable designation. Robert Booth Fowler, in his book, *The Dance with Community*, shows that the term is used in six different and rather incompatible ways.[1] Colin Bell and Howard Newby write, "There has never been a theory of community, nor even a satisfactory definition of what community is."[2] In another text, Bell and Newby write, "But what is community? . . . It will be seen that over ninety definitions of community have been analyzed and that the one common element in them all was man!"[3] Margaret Stacey argues that the solution to this problem is to avoid the term altogether.[4]

As I see it, this "cannot be defined" is a tired gambit. We have difficulties in precisely defining even such a simple concept as a chair. Something to sit on? One can sit on a bench or bed. Something to sit on with four legs? Many chairs have three, or even just one, and so on. The same criticism has been leveled against rationality, democracy, and class, and yet nobody seriously suggests we stop using these concepts.

The following definition seems to me quite workable: "Community is a combination of two elements: (a) A web of affect-laden relationships among a group of individuals, relationships that often criss-cross and reinforce one another (rather than merely one-on-one or chainlike individual relationships). (b) A measure of commitment to a set of shared values, norms, and meanings, and a shared history and identity—in short, to a particular culture."[5]

---

[1] Robert Booth Fowler, *The Dance with Community* (Lawrence: University Press of Kansas, 1991), 142.
[2] Colin Bell and Howard Newby, *The Sociology of Community: A Selection of Readings* (London: Frank Cass, 1974), xiii.
[3] Colin Bell and Howard Newby, *Community Studies: An Introduction to the Sociology of the Local Community* (New York: Praeger, 1973), 15.
[4] Cited in Bell and Newby, *Community Studies*, 49.
[5] Amitai Etzioni, *The New Golden Rule: Community and Morality in a Democratic Society* (New York: Basic Books, 1996), 127.

The definition leaves open the amount of conflict that occurs within a given community, but does define it as a social entity that has the elements necessary (bonds and shared values) to contain conflict within sustainable boundaries. Moreover, the definition indicates that communities need not be territorial. Indeed, there are many ethnic, professional, gay, and other communities that are geographically dispersed; that is, the members of these communities reside among people who are not members. (Often, these communities are centered around particular institutions, such as places of worship, hiring halls, bars, or social clubs.)

—Amitai Etzioni. From *The Monochrome Society.*

1. Define or look up the following words: *entity, incompatible, gambit, affect-laden.*
2. According to Etzioni, are there a few, or many, definitions that have been offered for the word *community*? Do the sources he cites agree or disagree about the number of definitions that have been given?
3. What other common words does he mention that are difficult to define?
4. In your own words, explain the two parts of Etzioni's definition of *community*.
5. Does Etzioni believe that conflict can occur within a community without destroying its identity as a community?
6. What does he mean when he says that communities "need not be territorial"?
7. What examples does he give of communities that are not territorial? Give an example of one community that is territorial and one that is not.

Examples of Short Definitions

Here are several short definitions of terms that might be used to develop larger definitions of the accompanying concepts in the form of essays.

Attention Deficit Disorder (ADD) is a neurological disorder that causes people to have difficulty focusing on sustained tasks.

A social network is a Web service that allows members to post personal information, create a personal profile, and exchange messages, photographs, and Internet links with friends, acquaintances, or people who share a common interest.

String theory is a recent concept in physics that seeks to unify the four basic forces in the cosmos by explaining the behavior of particles much smaller than electrons.

Graphic novels are works of fiction designed in the form of cartoons but, unlike comic books, with realistic characters and serious plots.

Wikileaks is an organization with a Web site that publishes secret and classified information from anonymous sources around the world.

You may be expected to write a definition essay on familiar concepts such as *success, love, democracy, maturity, responsibility, courage, mother, father, liberty,* and so on. It is possible to compose original essays on such subjects, even though they have been written about for centuries. If you take on one of these topics, however, you will have to limit its scope. Instead of writing about love in general, for instance, you would probably do better to write about a specific type of love—romantic love, love for one's country, love of God, or love of humanity—and find your own way of defining it.

Limiting the Scope of Your Definition

Such broad topics must be focused before you write. The meaning of the term *success,* for example, is too large a topic for a cohesive essay if you do not limit it in some way. This may mean concentrating on your individual definition of *success.* For instance, to define the term effectively, you might want to explain what success is *not* (i.e., what people sometimes mistakenly think it means). Everything in your essay should then focus on and back up your unique definition without wandering off this purpose.

Examining Your Subject from Different Angles

Try doing a cubing exercise to explore the range of a broad topic. For discussion, let's stick with the term *success* as a subject for a definition essay. How can you describe success; to what can you compare it? What is it associated with? Can you analyze its causes and effects and divide it into parts? How is success used in the world? What can you say for or against striving for success? Try cubing or focused writing to gather perspectives on success. Obviously, you will have a lot to say, and there are plenty of examples of success you can include in your essay.

Giving Examples of the Concept

Let's say you have come up with an original definition of *success* that will allow you to create an effective essay. You have decided that success is getting the most out of every experience and learning from it, whether the experience is a victory or defeat, a triumph or disappointment. One of the best ways to make your essay believable and interesting is to think of several real-life examples of such success. Maybe you know a friend who kept failing in school and at work but ultimately succeeded by learning from his failures. Perhaps you could give an example from history of a person who, like Abraham Lincoln, failed many times but learned from his setbacks. Or perhaps you could mention Maya Angelou or another writer who used all she learned from her difficult experiences to compose meaningful books that positively influenced others.

An Important Grammatical Hint about Defining

In creating definitions, try to avoid the "is when" error. It is ungrammatical to write, "Success is when you reach an important goal." *Success* is a noun and should not be equated with a *when* clause: "when you reach an important goal" tells *when* something happened, not *what* something is. It is grammatically preferable to write, "Success is the achievement of an important goal" or "Success means reaching an important goal." You may also write, "A person succeeds when he or she reaches an important goal."

Correct these two sentences.

Wealth is when you have a lot of money.

Arbitration is when a third party is brought in to settle a dispute.

WRITING EXERCISES: Basic, Intermediate, Challenge

Basic Exercise: Definition Essays

Respond to the following.

1. Write a sentence giving your own definition of the term *hero*.
2. Identify two kinds of heroism.

3. Describe what you think is a false notion of heroism.
4. Name two people who fit your definition of *hero*.
5. In one sentence, explain why people admire heroes.
6. In one sentence, explain one good effect of heroes.
7. In one sentence, identify one kind of harm heroes can do.

Intermediate Exercise: Definition Essays

Choose one of the following terms and respond to the directives given:

love   courage   happiness   faith   beauty   intelligence

1. Write one sentence in which you give your definition of one of these terms.
2. Identify at least three types of this concept.
3. Identify two people who exemplify this concept, one whom you know from personal experience and one who is a public personality.
4. Identify one familiar definition of this term that you reject in favor of your own definition.
5. Describe the causes or effects of this concept.
6. Explain what this concept is associated with.
7. Explain what is the opposite of this concept.

Challenge Exercise: Definition Essays

Choose one of the following terms and respond to the directives given.

philosophy   economics   literature   science   art   psychology

1. Write one sentence in which you give your definition of one of these terms.
2. Identify at least three types of this concept.
3. Identify two examples of this concept, one from personal experience and one from the knowledge you gained about this discipline in a course.
4. Identify one familiar definition of this term that you reject in favor of your own definition.
5. Identify the goals and objectives of this field of knowledge.

6. Explain what benefits one gains from knowing about this discipline.
7. Explain what is the opposite of this concept.

Essay Topics: Definition

1. Write an essay based on one of the three preceding exercises.
2. Find three dictionary definitions of *morality* and write an essay in which you analyze these definitions and develop one of your own. Explain how people acquire their notions of moral and immoral behavior, and explain whether concepts of good and evil are the same everywhere or vary from one society to another and from one person to another. Include examples of people whose lives demonstrate moral or immoral behavior.
3. Write an essay defining the word *adult*. Explain what it means to be adult in attitudes, values, priorities, and behavior. Include several examples of adult behavior, as well as examples of several people who you think are adults and several who you think are not.
4. Write an essay defining the term *addiction*. Explain how a mere habit or preference for something becomes an addiction and the difference between a habit and an addiction. Include examples of addictive behavior and of different things people become addicted to.
5. Define the term *hip-hop*. Describe the music itself as well as the culture and attitudes from which it has emerged. Explain how the hip-hop culture developed and how it differs from previous popular music culture. Give examples of several hip-hop artists and explain why they are popular.
6. Write an essay defining *entertainment*. Explain the difference between entertainment and education, religion, politics, and journalism—all of which sometimes contain elements of entertainment. Give examples of some of these categories, showing the difference between pure entertainment and education, religion, and other social institutions.
7. Write an essay defining the term *pornography*. Explain the difference between pornography and genuine art, literature, film, theater, or research that features sex and violence. Give examples of pornography and of art that contains these elements.

PEER REVIEW QUESTIONS: DEFINITION

1. I think that your overall intention in this essay is to define the term _____ so that we understand the following about it:

2. Your introduction is interesting. ☐ Yes ☐ No
   Your introduction identifies the term you are defining.
   ☐ Yes ☐ No
   The sentence that most nearly states your definition of the term is the following:

3. You develop your definition by the following method:

4. You give the following examples of the concept you are defining:

5. Your conclusion (is/is not) effective for the following reason:

6. What I like best about your essay is the following:

7. I recommend you make the following changes:

Proofreading Practice: Use of Pronouns; *Who* and *Which* Clauses

Personal pronouns are words such as *I, you, he, she, it, we,* and *they* that take the place of nouns. Using pronouns correctly means choosing the right **case** of the pronoun. When the pronoun is the subject of a statement, use *I, he, she, we,* and *they*; when the pronoun is the object of a verb or preposition, use *me, him, her, us,* and *them.*

<u>She</u> and <u>I</u> met <u>them</u> in the hallway.
<u>They</u> knew what would happen to <u>him</u>, and <u>we</u> knew it too.

Notice that *it* and *you* have the same form in both subject and object position:

<u>You</u> will hear <u>it</u> when <u>it</u> comes closer to <u>you</u>.

Common mistakes occur most often when pronouns are used in combination.

Incorrect: <u>Me</u> and <u>him</u> went to the same high school.
Correct: <u>He</u> and <u>I</u> went to the same high school.

| **Incorrect:** | Between you and I there should not be any secrets. |
| **Correct:** | Between you and me there should be no secrets. |

In informal speech, we also hear statements such as this.

| **Informal:** | Me and my friends have been doing Pilates for six months. |
| **Standard:** | My friends and I have been doing Pilates for six months. |

If such combinations confuse you and you are not sure whether to use *I* or *me*, *we* or *us*, *he* or *him*, *she* or *her*, or *they* or *them*, eliminate one of the pronouns and read the sentence with only one. You will almost always know which is right.

Me and my friends often study in the cafeteria.

Eliminate *my friends*: You would not write, "Me often study in the cafeteria."

| **Correct:** | My friends and I like to study in the cafeteria. |

Relative pronouns—*who*, *which*, and *that*—introduce **relative clauses**, which are often used in definition essays. A clause beginning with *who*, *which*, or *that* is called a relative clause because it is relatedto some person or thing preceding it. Take, for example, the sentence that follows.

The Cooperative Education Department has arranged an internship for Melissa, who wants experience in a publishing firm.

The relative clause in this sentence gives useful information about Melissa relating to her desire for an internship. Because this clause only relates to the main clause, it will not stand alone as a whole sentence. One error to avoid is to leave a relative clause as a fragment by separating it from the main clause.

Avoiding Relative Clause Fragments

As a general rule, do not try to begin sentences with the words *who*, *which*, or *that*. These words usually begin relative clauses, not whole sentences. Doing so will almost certainly produce a fragment. The sentence above cannot be divided into two sentences.

Incorrect:	The Cooperative Education Department has arranged

fragment

an internship for Melissa. <u>Who wants experience in a publishing firm.</u>

Incorrect:	After completing the first part of the examination, students will have one hour to do the second part.

fragment

<u>Which will be given to them by the proctors.</u>

fragment

Incorrect:	Samantha is excited about a Web site. <u>That she discovered while doing research on South American music.</u>

Another error that occurs frequently with relative clauses is the lack of agreement between verbs and the words they represent, called **antecedents**. In our first sentence, we have the clause *who wants experience in a publishing firm*. In this clause, the verb *wants* has an s-ending. We cannot tell whether it should be *who want* or *who wants* until we identify the antecedent, which is *Melissa*. If we change the sentence to plural, with two antecedents, Melissa and Hector, the verb changes.

Relative clause (plural):	The Cooperative Education Department has arranged internships for Melissa and Hector, who <u>want</u> experience in publishing firms.

Restrictive and Nonrestrictive Clauses

Should you use a comma before *which* and *who*? Sometimes you should and sometimes you should not—it depends on whether the clause is **restrictive** or **nonrestrictive**. A **restrictive clause** is one that is necessary to the meaning of a sentence; a **nonrestrictive clause** is one that simply adds extra information to a sentence that can be understood without it. A nonrestrictive clause is a bit like a phrase you could put in parentheses—interesting, but not crucial. For instance, if you write, "George W. Bush, <u>who was in the White House from 2001 to 2008</u>," the *who* clause adds information that is not necessary for the reader to identify President Bush. However, if you write, "presidents <u>who complete two terms in office</u>," the reader cannot identify which presidents you are referring to without including the *who* clause. Note that clauses beginning with *that* are always restrictive; do not set them off with commas. Many stylists will also advise you to use *that* rather than *which* in restrictive clauses.

Preferred:	The books <u>that you ordered</u> have arrived.
Acceptable:	The books <u>which you ordered</u> have arrived.
Nonrestrictive	
Clause	Toni Morrison's *Sula,* <u>which is on the</u>
with Comma:	<u>reading list,</u> has been ordered by the bookstore.

Using Who *and* Whom

Whether to use *who* or *whom* depends on how the word is used within its clause, not on the rest of the sentence. For instance, write, "Give it to the person *who* needs it." *Whom* would not work here, because *who* is the subject of the verb *needs*. However, it would be correct to write, "Give it to *whomever* you choose." In this sentence, *whomever* is the object of the verb *choose*. In reverse form, the clause reads, "You choose *whomever*." Notice that the beginnings of the two sentences are the same: "Give it to. . . ." The function of *who* or *whom* in its own clause, then, is what tells you which form to use, not what the rest of the sentence says.

TEST YOURSELF: Pronouns and Relative Clauses

Correct the error in each sentence. One sentence is already correct.

1. The class watched a film called *The Experience of Childbirth*. Which was informative but not entirely up to date.
2. The winner of the recount was the incumbent mayor. Who was expected to win by a wide margin.
3. Ted took all of the psychology courses that was offered by the college.
4. E-mail responses came back from all the students who the club invited.
5. Kimberly often consults her academic adviser, who have helped her apply to graduate school.
6. The company designed its Web site for the younger customers whom it wished to attract.
7. Most of the assignments, that Robert missed can still be made up.

Answers: 1. *Childbirth*, which 2. mayor, who 3. courses that were offered 4. whom the club 5. who has helped 6. correct 7. assignments that

Basic Exercise:
Pronouns and Relative Clauses

Find the seven errors in this passage. Look for fragments, misuse or lack of commas, errors in verb forms, and wrong pronoun case.

To people like you and I, happiness means having your life the way you want it. Some people define happiness as just a feeling, that you have when you just had a wonderful meal or saw a great film. I prefer to define it as a situation. In which you have succeeded in arranging your personal life and your career in satisfying ways. Several things that is important to happiness are understanding your own needs, relating well to others, and setting realistic goals. Happiness can come to anyone, but it is most likely to be achieved by thoughtful persons. Who understand that they can reach many goals if they are willing to make the necessary sacrifices. In public life me and my friends see many examples of people, who have attained a level of happiness that we all might wish to attain.

Intermediate Exercise:
Pronouns and Relative Clauses

Find the seven errors in this passage. Look for fragments, misuse or lack of commas, errors in verb forms, and wrong pronoun case.

The word *democracy* is favored by most nations and is certainly important to we Americans. Many countries cannot truly be called democratic. A true democracy is a country, in which the government belongs to the people, not to a small elite group. Open and fair elections are necessary to any democracy. Elections that are free of corruption and control by rich and powerful groups or individuals. A system of checks and balances, which protects the integrity of the government and prevent one official or body from gaining absolute control, is also needed. A leader who the people legitimately elect will work within such a system better than a dictator. Who is accustomed to having no one question his opinions and orders. Although many countries have elements of democracy, none of them is likely to become a perfect democracy. Which is a utopian form of government not yet possible in the world of politics as we know it.

Challenge Exercise:
Pronouns and Relative Clauses

Write sentences of your own following the directives given.

1. Write a sentence beginning with a person's name followed by a comma and *who*.
2. Write a sentence beginning with the name of your college followed by a comma and *which*.
3. Write a sentence using the phrase *me and my classmates* correctly.
4. Write a sentence using the phrase *she and I* correctly.
5. Write a sentence using *that has* after a singular antecedent.
6. Write a sentence using *that have* after a plural antecedent.
7. Write a sentence using *whom* correctly.

Key Words from Chapter 9 for Review

antecedent, case of pronouns, pronoun, relative clauses, restrictive and nonrestrictive clauses

STEP THREE

Writing Essays Based on Your Reading and Research

Writing for Examinations

STEPPING UP: WRITING TIP 10

Like many students, you may dread essay examinations and believe that they do not allow you to show your full knowledge and ability. How, after all, can you be expected to plan, compose, and proofread in sixty minutes or so? Yes, such exams are stressful, but with practice you can overcome the anxiety they produce and become more confident of your ability to cope with them successfully. Confidence and effectiveness come from a positive attitude and from your genuine desire to gain the set of skills necessary. Remember that in learning to write effective exams you are also learning to organize material, think critically, and express yourself fluently under time constraints. Combining these skills will make you a more confident student, writer, worker, professional person, and citizen. Think of essay exams as necessary training for your career and your life.

Facing Essay Exams with Confidence

You may confront an essay test at the end of your writing course, possibly one that will have a big effect on your future in college. You will also have to pass a number of essay exams in advanced content courses, especially those in the humanities and social sciences. Most students find such tests stressful, especially if passing the test is the primary or even the only measure that determines whether you continue to the next English course. An examination that is supposed to demonstrate what you have learned throughout a whole semester may seem unfair, but such essay tests have always been a feature of college education. Such tests may include both long and short essays. For that reason, even if your course happens to allow alternative means of assessment such as portfolios of your work, or a final grade in which the exam is averaged with other grades earned in the course, you should develop the ability to do well on a timed writing exam.

Essay Exams and the Writing Process

The writing process for a timed examination essay has to be different from the one you have learned to use when you work on an essay over the course of a week or two. In an hour or two you will not have enough time to do a variety of prewriting activities, develop some focused writing on the topic, compose a draft of the essay, revise the draft, proofread, and make final corrections. Nor will you be allowed to read your work to classmates and receive feedback in the process of revising your ideas and wording. Although your mastery of these skills may not be sufficiently demonstrated and measured by a timed, pass-or-fail test, such exams will make you a more capable and confident writer and will help you do a better job with writing assignments and tests in the future.

The most important thing to remember in a timed writing test is that, despite the time restriction, you will have enough time to show how well you can write. To do that, though, you will have to use your time sensibly. Most students who fail timed writing tests do not run out of time, though they often panic and fail to use their time well. An hour or two can seem short, but you can write much more than you might expect even in fifteen minutes. Once you have your topic and have organized your ideas well, you will probably be so absorbed in your work that you will write a lot in a short time.

The trick in writing exam essays effectively is to do some prewriting, but do it quickly, and spend most of your time actually writing. Proof-reading afterward may be important, but if you write carefully and pay attention to your grammar, spelling, and punctuation as you write, you may be able to limit your proofreading to a quick once-over in which you look for careless mistakes that slipped by. If you are a headlong, rapid writer who leaves many careless mistakes, however, you may have to save a solid chunk of time for proofreading, preferably sounding the words to yourself as you reread your work.

Unless the test you are facing has special provisions for writing several drafts, it is almost never a good idea to write a whole draft and then try to rewrite it entirely, especially if you have a short time limit. Students who do that usually merely copy their work over in neater handwriting without doing much revising or correcting. In the worst cases, they run out of time before completing the second draft and are left with one rough draft and a half-completed revision.

While neatness and clear handwriting create a good impression, your readers are more likely to be looking for other elements, which you may not have taken time to improve. As with all writing, experiment with timed writing strategies and discover what works best for you.

Pointers for Taking Essay Examinations

Here are some guidelines for taking timed essay tests.

- **Read the directions patiently and carefully and try to do exactly what they say.** A common fault is to focus on a single word or phrase that catches your interest and to begin expressing your thoughts without bothering to answer the whole question. If the instructions call for five or six paragraphs, be sure you supply them; if they ask you to respond to a short reading, be sure to examine the reading several times.

- **When you have several topics to choose from, select a topic that you can easily develop with concrete examples and varied arguments.** Some topics may seem interesting but lead you to run out of ideas quickly, causing you to repeat yourself instead of developing your argument with subtopics.

- **Construct a quick outline.** State your main idea and make clear to yourself what your subtopics are. This is the most efficient prewriting activity for a timed exam.

- **Look at your work from the graders' point of view.** Make it easy for them to give you a high grade on the test by writing a well-developed and well-organized essay with full paragraphs, correct grammar, effective transitions, and a clearly stated main idea. If you like to employ slang, sarcasm, unusual experiments with grammar, or abbreviated spelling, save such experiments for text messaging and creative writing; they are not likely to help on a basic writing test. At best, they will leave the grader puzzled.

- **Don't confuse summary with analysis.** Some examinations may ask you to summarize part or all of a reading before writing an essay about it. Be sure to make a clear difference between summarizing, which means merely condensing what the reading says, and analyzing and discussing the reading, which requires you to think beyond what the reading says.
- **Don't confuse mere length with development.** Under the pressure of a time limit, you may feel the need to just keep writing in a hurry so that your essay will look impressive. Yes, it should *look* impressive, but it won't *be* impressive if you become wordy and repetitive. If you get stuck, look again at the writing prompt (the writing instructions) and your own outline to see what remains to be done.
- **Accept your own feelings of anxiety and pressure.** A certain amount of tension will help you concentrate and work hard. Many students do their best work on exams because they try hard, just as athletes outdo their own personal bests and set records in the Olympics, when the competition is most intense. Your anxiety will be harmful only if it is so intense that it makes you panic and freeze up.

Engaging the Assignment

Your college may have a standard format for the essay examination you must pass. This may be a test created by the institution itself or one supplied by a large testing company. If not, your instructor or your department may make up an exam tailored to your course. Either way, there are a number of typical assignments used for such exams. Most of them call for some kind of persuasive writing. You may be asked to defend your opinion on a familiar social issue of the kind discussed in Chapter 14. Some tests present students with an imaginary situation, either on campus or in their community, and ask them to write a letter to the person in charge, such as the dean of the college, proposing a solution to a problem and defending it.

Some tests of this kind encourage you to include examples from your own experience and that of others to support your position. However, others direct you to focus on the topic in a more impersonal way, avoiding reference to yourself. Most students find it easier to support their ideas with examples from their own lives, but before you use this method of development, make sure your exam allows doing so.

There are many kinds of writing examinations, some designed by a single department or college, some by a testing company, and some by a state department of higher education. They tend to follow a few major patterns, however, and you should become familiar with the exam you will face before you take it. Your instructor may coach the class in how to excel on the exam, or you may be encouraged to attend workshops to prepare you for taking it. The wise student takes advantage of every opportunity to be ready when examination day arrives.

Some writing proficiency exams are very specific in what they ask you to do, laying out exactly what you should include in your essay and explaining how many words or paragraphs you should write. Others are more open and free-form, calling on you to use your imagination and creative powers to use the assignment merely as a springboard to get started. Be sure you know what is expected of you before you begin!

Here are two typical but very different sets of instructions, which we call *writing prompts*, commonly used in writing examinations. Remember that there are many others, and that you should become an expert in the one your college or your course requires.

A. Your college is planning to add two new extracurricular programs that will benefit students. Write a letter to the dean identifying two programs that you believe will most enrich students' cultural knowledge and social lives. Develop your letter in four or five full paragraphs.

B. Mark Twain said, "I have never let my schooling interfere with my education." Explain what you think he meant by this remark, and write an essay of about 500 words in which you explain why you agree or disagree with his opinion. Include examples from your own experience and that of people you know to support your main point.

These are obviously very different topics that call for different writing strategies. Topic A requires you to focus on a given situation and to analyze it in a factual way. It calls for a carefully organized essay in which you enumerate the advantages of several activities and explain what beneficial effects they would have. To be effective, you will have to focus sharply on the facts of the situation. You would be wise to structure your essay on a simple form of enumeration in order not to repeat yourself. Note an important detail in the writing prompt: You are to explain why the two activities you suggest will "enrich students' cultural knowledge and social lives." Don't wander off the point by discussing other kinds of advantages, such as whether a volleyball team or a chorus would bring in money to the school. Follow the directions for writing closely.

Topic B is more philosophical and personal. It encourages more creative thinking and use of your own experiences. However, like Topic A, it has a sharp focus: In your response, you would need to be sure to explain what you think Mark Twain meant by his remark. In your essay you would make use of your own experience, but you would need to avoid letting your writing become simply the story of your life, or even of your schooling, rather than a defense or rebuttal of the opinion Twain expresses. Essays of this kind may also be based on a longer passage, even a whole article, rather than a one-line quip. You may even be asked to sum up the meaning of the reading before writing your response to it. As with any writing prompt in an examination, follow directions carefully.

Writing a Summary as Part of an Essay Examination

Some essay exams include a short exercise in which you are asked to summarize a reading excerpt before you write the main essay expressing your own point of view. When writing a summary, remember that you are supposed to capture in your own words the exact idea expressed in the reading. A summary, unlike your essay itself, should not include your opinions.

For practice, read the paragraph below and determine which summary, A or B, better captures the author's meaning.

In Athens, women had no more political or legal rights than slaves; throughout their lives they were subject to the absolute authority of their male next-of-kin. They received no formal education, were condemned to spend most of their time in the women's quarters of their home, and were subject to arranged marriages. A wife seldom dined with her husband—and never if he had guests—and on the rare occasions that she went out of doors, was invariably chaperoned; it was illegal for her to take with her more than three articles of clothing, an obol's worth of food and drink (in today's terms, a sandwich and a glass of milk), and if she went out after dark she had to go in a carriage with a lighted lantern.

—Reay Tannahill. From *Sex in History* (New York: Stein and Day, 1980): 94.

A. This paragraph is interesting because it includes details of life in ancient Greece such as schooling, dining habits, and the way men and women related to each other.

B. This paragraph explains that women in ancient Greece had almost no rights or freedom. They were not formally educated, they could not choose whom they wanted to marry, and they had to follow strict rules of dress and behavior.

Which of these two passages accurately states the paragraph's points in shorter form, and which one comments on the paragraph without summarizing its point?

Essay Examinations in Content Courses

When you take examinations in liberal arts courses such as history, psychology, sociology, and literature, you will sometimes be required to write essays. Such examinations are meant to test your grasp of a subject more than your writing proficiency. Because the instructor will expect you to demonstrate specific knowledge of course material, concentrate above all on answering the question or questions precisely and illustrating your points with specific facts. However, a fluently written and well-organized essay will always make the best impression, and many instructors include the quality of your writing as part of the exam grade.

Here are some typical essay assignments for courses in literature, history, and political science.

A. (Literature) Shakespeare's heroes are usually committed to a higher purpose and larger groups beyond themselves, whereas his villains tend to be individualists who are chiefly interested in their own gain and selfish advantages. Discuss whether this pattern is true of two plays we have read in this course. Use details from both plays to support your points.

B. (History) The Civil War was fought over slavery but was also about two opposing visions of the future of the United States. Explain how important the conflict over slavery was in causing the war, and compare the Confederate vision of U.S. society of the future with the vision held by the Union—the North. Explain the extent to which the Reconstruction brought about one or the other of these social visions.

C. (Political Science) The U.S. system of government is based on fundamental democratic principles, on belief in rule by the people. However, many elements in the system set it apart from a pure democracy, in which the people as a whole make all important decisions. Explain what elements in the three branches of government could be described as democratic and what elements limit the direct power of the people.

In each of these essay assignments, the instructor is looking for particular responses, sometimes even specific facts that she or he wants you to include in your essay. For example, Topic A asks you to identify a number of heroes and villains from two plays read in the course. To receive a high grade on the essay, you would have to discuss these characters in detail, explaining whether they do or do not fit the pattern mentioned in the topic statement.

Topic B contains two important aspects, both of which you would have to discuss in detail to earn a high grade: One is the importance of slavery in the prewar South and the debate over slavery in the new territories; the other is the clash between the Confederate vision of an agricultural society ruled by a propertied upper class and the Northern vision of an urban industrial society based more on upward mobility. A third follow-up topic (don't forget to look back at the topic statement as you write to be sure you don't omit something) is whether the North, by winning the war, created a nation close to its vision.

Topic C calls for the writer to show knowledge of the three branches of government, with enough detail to demonstrate ways in which such elements as the electoral college, the selection of Supreme Court justices for lifetime appointments, and the equal number of senators for every state regardless of population provide a check on absolute rule by the people.

To do well on any of these essays, you would have to organize your ideas and provide plenty of facts asked for in the question. The instructor will be looking for you to provide abundant details from all the reading, discussing, listening, and note-taking you have done in the course. Above all, follow directions carefully and present an adequate number of supporting details to illustrate your points.

Unlike personal essays based partly on your own experience, essays of this type require previous knowledge from textbooks, class discussions, and lectures. To do well on them, you must study hard and review your notes before the examination. As with personal essays, however, you will make a strong impression if you write correctly, fluently, and in an organized way. Nearly all professors are favorably impressed by fluent, correct, and concise writing, even if they tell you that they care more about the content. Although writing well will not be an adequate substitute for content, it will signal to your instructor that you are a careful, intelligent student. First impressions always matter.

TEST YOURSELF: True or False?

Determine whether the following statements are true or false.

1. In essay examinations, grammar is always the most important factor in determining grades.
2. It is not important to read and follow directions carefully on an essay examination because creativity is what really matters.
3. When writing with a time limit, you should choose a topic that you can develop easily with significant ideas and interesting examples.
4. Even with a time limit, you should spend at least a few minutes planning your essay and constructing a simple outline.
5. If you are afraid of running out of time, it is a good idea to keep writing rapidly to fill up several pages, as the graders probably won't notice if you repeat yourself or wander off the topic.
6. When writing an essay in a content course such as history, economics, or literature, it is more important to impress the grader by using terminology from the textbook than to demonstrate knowledge of facts and ideas.
7. The added stress of a timed examination always causes students to write far less well than when they are not under pressure.

Answers: 1. F 2. F 3. T 4. T 5. F 6. F 7. F

Basic Exercise: Essay Examinations

Respond to the following items.

1. Explain what prewriting strategies you have used or expect to use before writing a timed essay examination.
2. Describe how you cope with stress during a timed essay examination.
3. How can someone who has performed less well on an examination essay than he or she had hoped improve his or her writing strategy for future essay exams?
4. Which of the following is a good strategy for writing an examination essay? A. Spend at least half of the allotted time doing prewriting

activities. B. Begin writing immediately without wasting time planning your essay. C. Spend a short amount of time designing a clear, general plan; spend most of the time writing the essay.

5. Which of the following statements is true? A. After writing a timed essay examination, you should spend a few minutes proofreading your work carefully. B. Proofreading a timed essay is not important because you are not likely to find any errors that you will be able to correct anyway. C. Proofreading is the most important part of an essay examination, and therefore you should spend more time on it than on planning and composing.

6. When writing an essay for an examination in a content course, you should discuss only general concepts and omit factual details. Is the preceding statement true or false?

7. Explain what an essay examination in a content course is designed to test. What is it trying to assess that is not measured in a short answer, multiple choice, or true/false test?

Intermediate Exercise: Essay Examinations

Explain how you would go about planning a timed essay responding to either Topic A or Topic B.

Topic A: Imagine that you are on a hiring committee that is charged with the task of choosing a technology supervisor for an advertising company. After interviewing ten candidates, you have narrowed down your choices to two. One is a thirty-year-old woman who does not have a college degree but has excelled as a technology director for a real estate company. The other is a thirty-five-year-old man who has a bachelor of science degree in computer science and experience in computer sales and service, but who has served two years in jail for a burglary he committed in his early twenties. Write a letter to the committee explaining which candidate, in your opinion, is the stronger of the two.

Topic B: Your college collects student activity fees from all students when they register. As a member of the student senate, you have to vote on whether the fees should be spent on one large project to improve recreational facilities in the student union or on separate funds to support cultural activities for each student group throughout the year. Write a letter to the student newspaper explaining your preference.

Challenge Exercise: Essay Examinations

Imagine that you are the instructor in a content course you are currently taking or have taken, either in college or in high school. Design an essay assignment that will demonstrate how well students understand the material of the course. Explain what you would expect students to include in the essay to earn an A. What must they do to pass with a grade of C?

Key Words from Chapter 10 for Review

analysis, multiple choice, short answer, summary, writing prompt

Making a Comparison

STEPPING UP: WRITING TIP 11:
MAKING COMPARISON

Writing a **comparison** essay presents a challenge because you must keep two subjects in your mind at the same time. To succeed, remember that you are writing not two essays but one essay exploring the similarities and differences between these two subjects. To make your comparison valuable and interesting, keep your eye on gaining new insights into the two subjects you are comparing and into the overall concepts involved. If you compare two actresses or presidents, you hope not only to learn a lot of facts about both but also to gain a better understanding of how to evaluate an actress's or a president's career. If you compare two short stories, you should notice details in both that you might otherwise have missed, and you should come away knowing more about how to analyze fiction.

Responding to Ideas in Your Writing

When you are writing essays that require you to read or conduct research using books and articles, you will have to reach beyond the opinions you have developed as a result of personal experience. You will have to respond to ideas you find in the materials you read. This process involves a kind of conversation or dialogue between you and another writer. You will have to make your own opinions clear to the reader and to explain how you agree and disagree with points made in the articles or books you are using. When writing an essay for an examination in a content course, for example (see Chapter 10), you may respond to ideas expressed in the books assigned in your course. You may also make use of facts you find in other reading materials, especially if you are writing a research paper (see Chapter 15). If you are writing about a work of literature such as a poem, play, or short story (see Chapter 16), you will not only have to make your own opinions clear but also find meanings in the work that may not be stated openly—that is, you may have to *interpret* the work.

Writing an essay in which you make a comparison is one of the ways you can make use of material beyond your personal knowledge in order to develop your ideas. Except in comparisons based entirely on people or experiences in your personal life, you will have to find out some facts about the two subjects you are comparing, such as two famous people, two kinds of jobs, two places, or two institutions. When you make use of materials beyond your own knowledge, which we call **secondary sources**, you will be expected to summarize, quote, and paraphrase them correctly, using MLA, APA, or some other format, as explained in Chapter 15.

Comparing and Contrasting as a Way of Knowing

Making comparisons is something we begin doing as children. It is a fundamental way of understanding our world, from the time we compare toys and favorite games as toddlers to the time we write comparison essays in college. Writing an insightful, well-organized comparison on any subject is a way of understanding the subject better. You will probably be asked to write comparison/contrast essays on term papers and exams, so it is a good idea to learn about this mode of composition.

Types of Comparison

Creating essays that compare people, places, experiences, or concepts is a challenge. It requires you to juggle language, content, and organization; therefore, you should learn to work with a clear plan. Above all, remember what a comparison is for: to understand your subject better. The best way to do that is to discuss the subjects together. Begin your essay with an introduction that mentions *both* persons or things, not just one. This way, you will avoid the trap of discussing one, then the other, and leaving the reader to figure out how the subjects are similar or different. Which of these two sentences makes a better starting point for a comparison?

1. Making a film is more complicated than making a CD album.
2. Making a film is very expensive.

Either sentence might make a good introductory statement for an essay, but only sentence 1 contains a comparison. We expect the writer to give several reasons why making films is more complicated than making CD albums. In the process, we expect to learn a lot about both filmmaking and music recording.

These are the three general types of comparison.

Categories of Comparison

Parallels:	Pointing out similarities between two people, things, or concepts
Contrasts:	Pointing out differences between two people, things, or concepts
Comparison/ Contrast:	Pointing out both similarities and differences between two people, things, or concepts

The following three paragraphs illustrate the three main kinds of comparison. The first paragraph discusses the similarities between two activities, the second contrasts the differences between two experiences, and the third explores both the similarities and the differences between two U.S. presidents. Notice that all three passages begin with sentences that mention both subjects.

Paragraph A

Comparing Two Similar Activities

Thomas realized that his two favorite activities, reading and shopping, have a lot in common. First, he spends a lot of time doing both, even though both take a lot of effort. Sometimes when he shops, he drives to a large wholesale store where he has a membership, and he stocks up on a large number of supplies at low cost. He also has a membership in a bookstore chain and sometimes picks up a large number of books at once, and he often buys books for his e-reader online. When he visits a bookstore, he likes to browse through books to pick out something that suits his mood, just as he browses in the supermarket to select something that suits his taste buds at the moment. He likes to compare favorite writers the way he compares groceries. In his reading, he tries to balance some informative, high quality selections with some that he reads for entertainment. Likewise, when he shops, he can't resist some junk food and cheap clothes just because he feels the impulse to buy them. These, too, he balances with purchases that show more long-range judgment. And in both shopping and reading, he alternates between short spurts of activity and multi-hour marathons of patient concentration. Thomas prides himself on being the best shopper and the best reader in his family.

Paragraph B

Contrasting Two Opposite Experiences

Wanda's experiences in high school and college were totally different. In the large urban high school she attended, she often felt overwhelmed by the crowds of students she didn't know, and she didn't have the confidence to join athletic teams or participate in extracurricular activities. She had the opportunity to choose from many available courses, but the classes were often crowded. By contrast, in the small liberal arts college she attended, she felt more at home because she developed many friendships and joined the drama club. The small seminars encouraged her to be active in class, and even though she was now far away from home, she was able to adjust to the new environment with the help of a counselor. On the other hand, she sometimes missed the energy of the city and the variety of students around her in her high school.

Paragraph C

Comparing and Contrasting Two Presidents

Presidents William Jefferson Clinton and George W. Bush may resemble each other on the surface, but to their supporters they are very different. Both men were governors of Southern states before being elected president, and both speak with a slight Southern accent. Both were elected at a fairly young age and were more athletic than most political leaders. Both came from Protestant backgrounds and appealed to churchgoers. Both were first elected with less than 50% of the votes cast, and both had exhibited imperfect behavior in the past, which their supporters considered irrelevant but their *opponents frequently criticized. However, these resemblances are superficial, and as their supporters will tell you, the two men represent different political philosophies. President Clinton favored government policies to help the poor and a foreign policy based on negotiation, whereas President Bush favored stimulating business through tax cuts and an aggressive foreign policy based on military action. President Clinton appointed mostly liberal judges, whereas President Bush appointed very conservative ones. Whatever similarities the public may have seen in their styles, they tried to point the country in different directions.*

As you might guess, there are not many pairs of things that are totally different or completely similar. Consequently, there are not many essays of the first two types, and you are more likely to be asked to write a comparison/contrast essay. This is a more interesting intellectual task, but also a more challenging one. It helps us see the complex nature of reality.

Gathering Facts on Both Subjects

Writing an interesting and meaningful comparison requires facts. Usually this means looking up information on the Web, reading books and magazines, or interviewing people who know a lot about your subject. Writers who succeed in their efforts to compare often have done a lot of research and preliminary thinking, and they start writing with a wealth of facts in front of them. To create a better comparison/contrast essay, begin by gathering your facts, concentrating on similarities and differences as you obtain information. Brainstorm to explore the range of facts you can assemble on each subject. Then do a cluster to identify the categories you are using to make the comparison. Following that, make lists of similarities and differences in each category. Your essay will be much richer as a result of this prewriting work.

Exploring Similarities and Differences: A Student Writer at Work

Andrea Johnson had to write a comparison essay. She decided to use the assignment as an opportunity to look into two careers she was considering—pediatric nursing and elementary education. Before writing her essay, Andrea gathered information on both careers, partly from what she and her friends already knew about both professions, and partly from reading, talking with relatives in both fields, and doing Web searches. Here is a list of similarities and differences she compiled, grouped into categories she wanted to know more about.

Andrea's Brainstorming Notes about Two Career Options

Nursing vs. Teaching: Preparation and Training

Similarities

Both careers require college degrees and training on the job.
Requirements for both careers are set by state and professional regulations that change frequently.
Some use of computer technology is required in both.
Courses in child psychology are required in both.
High academic averages are needed, and both nurses and teachers have to pass state licensing examinations that measure general and specialized knowledge.

Differences

Nursing training is more specialized and technical—less general education is necessary.
Nurses in some states can practice with a two-year degree and an R.N., but teachers must have a bachelor's degree and many even have master's degrees.
Nurses are required to update their technical knowledge in many states to be relicensed. Teachers often are expected to actively work on their professional development, but this does not necessarily involve learning new technical skills.
Teachers and nurses both have to use information technology, but teachers don't need advanced science unless they're science teachers.

Personal Characteristics Needed

Similarities

Both careers involve working with children, so both take a lot of patience, energy, and caring.
Nurses and teachers both have to relate to all children without bias and need plenty of insight into children's feelings. They also must be mature themselves so that they can help and guide children.

Differences

Nurses mostly help children one at a time; they must be good at one-on-one relationships with many kinds of children who have many kinds of physical problems. Teachers have to control and guide whole classrooms and project a strong personality and enough authority to teach many students at once.

Nurses often have to help children suffering from illness or pain, but teachers have to inspire and lead students mostly when they're healthy. Nurses have to be good in times of crisis and able to stay calm in emergencies. Teachers have to be able to create a positive group feeling and maintain a sense of purpose all day long as group leaders.

Teachers often earn tenure and stay at the same school in the same job for years, sometimes even for their whole career. Nurses often can change from one kind of job to another and from one kind of institution to another.

Pay and Opportunities

Similarities

Both careers often offer good salaries and benefits, but these vary according to state and locality. Both careers offer opportunities for advancement, especially for those who obtain advanced certification or degrees. Some administrative posts are available in both fields.

Differences

Nursing pays more at the beginning. Teachers can earn quite a lot in the long run, especially if they have an advanced degree.

Teachers may be able to become principals or superintendents with even higher salaries if they get further certification; nurses, however, can't become doctors or hospital administrators without extensive further education.

Teachers mostly work in schools; nurses work in many kinds of situations, including clinics, hospitals, and even schools.

Satisfactions and Difficulties

Similarities

Both jobs require many hours of hard work and involve repetitive tasks.

Both jobs offer security to experienced professionals because teachers can usually earn tenure and nurses are very much in demand. Both

nurses and teachers usually feel that the work they do is very im-
portant and can sometimes make an enormous difference in
children's lives.
Both nurses and teachers have to cope with children who are unruly
or difficult.

Differences

Teachers may have two or three months off during the summer,
whereas nurses work year round with shorter vacations.
Teachers have tenure and nurses don't, but nurses can usually change
jobs easily and find a new job if they lose one.
The satisfaction nurses get sometimes involves saving a child's life or
restoring him or her to health. Teachers' satisfaction is more general
and comes from knowing that they may have made a positive
difference in the overall development of children's knowledge and
values. Teachers work with students for whole semesters or whole
years. Nurses sometimes see children once or twice to give them a shot
or help them during a stay in the hospital and never see them again.
Nurses may work with individual children for long periods of time
if they have long-term illnesses or disabilities.
Teachers have to deal with behavioral problems of students in large
groups; nurses have to cope with individual children when they refuse
to take medicine, are afraid, or are uncooperative.

Organizing Your Material

Once Andrea gathered enough material to compose a successful,
meaningful comparison, she was faced with the decision about how
to organize it. Unlike narratives, in which one event follows another
chronologically, comparisons do not organize themselves, so planning
is crucial. At first, Andrea thought she would use the block pattern of
organization, first writing about nursing, then writing about teaching.
This is the easiest way to organize a comparison, and the one most
writers fall back on if they do not plan ahead.

The Block Method of Organizing

1. Introduction
2. A body paragraph or two on the first subject (nursing)
3. Transition

4. A body paragraph or two on the second subject (teaching)
5. Transition
6. Several paragraphs analyzing similarities and differences between the subjects (be sure to include this part)
7. Conclusion

The **block method** can be effective, and it looks easy. But inexperienced writers who use it often write two flimsily connected descriptions and leave it to the reader to analyze the two subjects' similarities and differences. If you use the block form, keep both subjects in mind at all times, mentioning similarities and differences between them in every part of your essay. Begin your introduction by mentioning both topics, make a transition that clearly shows their connection, and continue with a full discussion of their similarities and differences. Remember that it is your job, as the writer, to analyze your topics' similarities and differences—do not leave the work to your reader.

The Similarities/Differences Method of Organization

Andrea considered two other possible patterns of organization. The second is to write first about all the similarities between the two subjects, then about the differences. An outline of this method would look something like the following.

1. Introduction
2. Several paragraphs discussing similarities between the two subjects (nursing and teaching)
3. Transition
4. Several paragraphs discussing differences between the two subjects (nursing and teaching)
5. Conclusion

You can reverse this plan and discuss the differences first. Either method is effective when you want to show readers that what most people think about your two subjects is untrue. For example, let's say that your readers believe two presidents or two actresses are just alike. To address this perspective, discuss the similarities between the subjects first, but then use the rest of the essay to contrast them by showing that they are actually different. Or, you can surprise your readers by showing that two subjects that most people think of as widely different really have a lot in common. In that case, you discuss the differences first, and then the similarities.

Organizing by Categories

Andrea considered a third, more complicated type of comparison essay—the kind that provides a running analysis of similarities and differences by moving from one category to another, as Andrea did in her brainstorming. For instance, a comparison of short stories might move from a discussion of settings to one of plots and then one of themes. This kind of approach may seem difficult at first, but it can result in impressive essays. (This is especially true when you use this method on an essay examination.)

Picture the method of organizing by categories as follows.

1. Introduction
2. A paragraph on the similarities/differences in category #1
3. Transition
4. A paragraph on the similarities/differences in category #2
5. Transition
6. A paragraph on the similarities/differences in category #3
7. Conclusion

Student Essay: Exploring Similarities and Differences

Andrea's brainstorming notes grouped her ideas into categories using the last method described. During brainstorming, however, she decided that her thesis—the idea she wanted to argue about the two careers—would be stronger if she used a different method of organization than grouping by categories. Read her essay and identify which method of organization she used.

Becoming a Nurse or a Teacher

ANDREA JOHNSON

What kind of person should become a nurse or a teacher? Most people probably think the same kind of person could be either one. But there are nurses who want to quit and become teachers and teachers with master's degrees who have entered nursing programs. Students who are considering becoming pediatric nurses or elementary school teachers should realize that these two professions, which used to be linked together in people's minds as "women's work," require different skills and different personalities. To outsiders, they may seem similar, but those on the inside know how different they are.

It's true that, superficially, nursing and teaching seem to have a lot in common. Pediatric nurses can save children's lives and restore them to health. Elementary teachers sometimes inspire children to great achievements and turn around lives that might have been thrown away. Both work with children every day, and both need to know a lot about child psychology. Both have to be caring, patient, and firm in the way they treat children, and both must have a sense of humor as well as the ability to see and appreciate all the differences between children of different backgrounds.

In addition to working with children, nurses and teachers both have to have a lot of education and must pass licensing tests in order to practice their profession. Nurses can have a two-year degree or a bachelor's degree, and some even have a master's or Ph.D. Teachers need at least a bachelor's degree, and in many states they have to earn a master's. Both jobs pay in the $40,000 to $60,000 range for people with experience, and both are pretty secure. Good teachers usually earn tenure after a number of years, and nurses are so much in demand that if they are well qualified they can almost always get a job. In both professions, however, nurses and teachers have to earn licenses by passing tests and may have to renew their licenses after several years. In many states this means taking additional courses or doing other kinds of professional development to keep up with current trends in the field.

Although people who choose nursing and teaching are usually not ambitious in the same sense that politicians and business executives are, both careers offer possibilities for advancement. Nursing has a number of specialties and administrative posts, and teachers can, with extra certification, become assistant principals or principals, or even superintendents, just as some nurses return to medical school and become doctors.

If these careers are so similar, wouldn't the same people be good at both? It turns out that if you talk to people inside these professions, they really aren't much alike. Both work with children, but nurses mostly see children one at a time, children who suffer illness or accidents, or have other health problems. Teachers have to manage whole classrooms of children, and they rarely have time to relate closely to individual children. That means that nurses and teachers need different skills and maybe even different personalities. Although both have to be caring and patient, teachers have to spend most of their day projecting a strong sense of authority, purpose, and direction so that all their students learn. They have to be good organizers and planners but do not have to be ready to face life-or-death emergencies, suffering, and even death. Nurses have to maintain empathy for all of the children they help, and they need a lot of skill in relating to children who are afraid or in pain. They can't be too sensitive about the sight of blood or broken bones, and they shouldn't expect to have much long-term impact on children's attitudes or values.

Although both jobs require hard work, teachers have summer vacations that last two or three months, while nurses have less time off. Nurses have to work year round, but they don't have to take home endless papers, exams, and lab reports to grade or to plan lessons. Teachers always work in schools, but nurses may work in hospitals, clinics, or even schools and take on a variety of responsibilities. This means that a teacher should be someone who can imagine herself or himself doing almost the same work for many years and who prefers stability, while a nurse may change from one kind of work to another or even from one kind of institution to another.

Teachers could be described as "long-term" people. The satisfactions they get usually come from knowing that they have made a difference in a child's life that may be evident years later. We've all heard of celebrities who attribute their success to an elementary teacher whom they never forgot. Nurses are more "high adrenalin" people who gain satisfaction from intervening in children's lives in ways that may save them from dying or restore them to health. They may not have to work as frantically as characters on *ER* and other hospital programs on television, but they have to be strong, alert, savvy people who can deal with any emergency.

When asked why they want to be nurses or teachers, people often say that it's because they love children. But teaching and nursing are two different ways of loving children and call for different types of people. Maybe not much attention was paid years ago to the differences between them because the jobs were lumped together as "women's work." Now that more men are going into both professions, however—even though the majority of nurses and elementary teachers are still women—the public is beginning to realize that these distinct careers demand two different sets of skills and character traits. For those considering them, the question is not which is better, but which is better for you?

1. Which plan of organization did Andrea use?
2. Is this essay primarily a comparison of similarities, of differences, or both?
3. What is the thesis, or main point, of Andrea's comparison? Which sentence could be considered a thesis statement?
4. How are the introductory and concluding paragraphs linked?
5. Identify the topic of each body paragraph.
6. What factual information helps you understand the point of Andrea's comparison?
7. What kind of additional information would strengthen the essay and help Andrea make her career decision?

Example by a Published Author: Comparing and Contrasting

Read the passage below, in which Howard Gardner compares and contrasts two famous psychologists, Sigmund Freud and William James, one European and the other American. Answer the questions after the passage.

Two Great Psychologists

Howard Gardner

Freud and James represented different historical movements, different philosophical traditions, different programs for psychology. Freud, the pessimistic European intellectual, had chosen to focus on the development of the individual psyche, its battles within the individual's immediate family, the struggle for independence, the manifold anxieties and defenses that attend the human condition. For Freud the key to health was self-knowledge and a willingness to confront the inevitable pains and paradoxes of human existence.

James had considerable sympathy with this analysis, for his own life had featured many of the strains and tensions that Freud graphically described. Yet James also sensed a difference in the emphasis in their respective world views. While praising Freud, he had also pointed out to a confidant, "I hope that Freud and his pupils will push their ideas to the utmost limits, so that we can learn what they are. . . . It reveals an entirely unsuspected peculiarity in the constitution of human nature." James, in fact, had chosen to embrace a more positively oriented form of psychology, one less circumscribed by the biological imperatives of behavior, more open to the possibilities of change and growth. More so than his Austrian counterpart, the American thinker stressed the importance of relationships with other individuals, as a means of gaining ends, of effecting progress, and of knowing oneself. In a famous phrase, he had commented, "A man has as many social selves as there are individuals who recognize him and carry an image around of him in their mind." Perhaps most important, James was a potent influence on the succeeding generation of social scientists, including James Mark Baldwin and George Herbert Mead, who came to focus on the social origins of knowledge and on the interpersonal nature of an individual's sense of self.

But what united Freud and James, and what set them apart from the mainstream of psychology both on the Continent and in the United States, was a belief in the importance, the centrality, of the individual self—a conviction that psychology must be built around the concept of the person, his personality, his growth, his fate. Moreover, both scholars deemed the capacity for self-growth to be an important one, upon which depended the possibility of coping with one's surroundings. While neither would have used the phrase, I find it reasonable to say that both of these redoubtable psychologists were sympathetic to the idea of "personal intelligences." At the same time, however, their orientations toward such intelligences would have differed. Freud was interested in the self as located in the individual and, as a clinician, was preoccupied with an individual's own knowledge of himself; given this bias, a person's interest in other individuals was justified chiefly as a better means of gaining further understanding of one's own problems, wishes, and anxieties and, ultimately, of achieving one's goals. In contrast, James's interest, and even more so, the interests of the American social psychologists who succeeded him, fell much more on the individual's relationship to the outside community. Not only did one's knowledge of self come largely from an ever-increasing appreciation of how others thought about the

individual; but the purpose of self-knowledge was less to promote
one's personal agenda, more to ensure the smooth functioning of
the community.

—Howard Gardner, from *Frames of Mind*.

1. Define these words, using a dictionary if necessary: *psyche, graphically, manifold, defenses, confidant, circumscribed, redoubtable, agenda.*
2. Which of the two psychologists does the author describe as more optimistic?
3. Which of the two was more interested in social relationships?
4. What similarities between Freud and James does the author describe?
5. What differences does he describe?
6. Describe the structure on which this comparison is based.
7. According to the author, what made both psychologists different from others of their time?

WRITING EXERCISES: Basic, Intermediate, Challenge

The following exercises provide practice in developing comparisons by using many supporting details.

Basic Exercise: Comparison and Contrast

Rewrite the passage below, filling in details that show similarities and differences between living in a city and living in a small community. Write two or three sentences in each blank, supplying observations from your own experience or from what you have seen in films or television programs or learned from your reading or conversations with other people.

The physical surroundings in a small community are different from those of a city. A small town is quiet; you hear mostly

_____.
_____
_____.

A large city is noisy; you hear _____.
_____
_____.

A small town also looks different than a city. For instance, you see _____.

_____

_____.

In a metropolis, on the other hand, you are surrounded by

_____.

_____

_____.

The way people spend their time in a small community is also different from the pastimes city people engage in. In a small town, people mostly _____.

_____

_____.

Urban people, however, like to _____.

_____

_____.

However, there are some similarities between life in a small town and in a city. Certain kinds of shopping are almost the same in either place. For example, you can buy _____ anywhere. In addition, there are some things that people spend their time doing that are the same in both places. For instance, people in small towns and big cities all like to. _____

_____

_____.

With all their differences and similarities, I prefer to live in _____ because _____.

_____

_____.

Intermediate Exercise: Comparison and Contrast

In this brainstorming exercise, list as many facts as you can in each category that would help create body paragraphs for an interesting comparative essay.

Main Idea: Doing research in the library and doing research on the Internet require some different skills but have many similarities.

Different skills required:

Using the Internet:

1. _____

2. _____

3. _____

Using the library:

1. _____

2. _____

3. _____

Similarities:

1. _____

2. _____

3. _____

Challenge Exercise:
Comparison and Contrast

This poem, written by Dudley Randall, is an imaginary conversation in verse between two famous African American leaders of the early twentieth century, Booker T. Washington and W.E.B. DuBois. They have different points of view on how to deal with racism in their time. Read the poem and answer the questions that follow it.

Booker T. and W.E.B.

"It seems to me," said Booker T.,
"It shows a mighty lot of cheek
To study chemistry and Greek
When Mister Charlie needs a hand
To hoe the cotton on his land,
And when Miss Ann looks for a cook,
Why stick your nose inside a book?"
"I don't agree," said W.E.B.,
"If I should have the drive to seek
Knowledge of chemistry or Greek,
I'll do it. Charles and Miss can look

Another place for hand or cook.
Some men rejoice in skill of hand
And some in cultivating land,
But there are others who maintain
The right to cultivate the brain."
"It seems to me," said Booker T.,
"That all you folks have missed the boat
Who shout about the right to vote,
And spend vain days and sleepless nights
In uproar over civil rights.
Just keep your mouths shut, do not grouse,
But work, and save, and buy house."
"I don't agree," said W.E.B.,
"For what can property avail
If dignity and justice fail?
Unless you help to make the laws,
They'll steal your house with trumped-up clause.
A rope's as tight, a fire as hot,
No matter how much cash you've got.
Speak soft, and try your little plan,
But as for me, I'll be a man."
"It seems to me," said Booker T.—
"I don't agree,"
Said W.E.B.

1. This poem employs the point-by-point method of comparison. What are the two main topics about which the two leaders disagree in this poem?
2. How does each leader want his followers to behave?
3. What does each man assume about racism in U.S. society?
4. These men were leaders of civil rights movements during the Reconstruction Period not long after the Civil War, when people remembered the days of slavery. Do a Web search on both men and read summaries of their careers. How can their argument be applied to our society today?
5. What differences can you detect between the two men's personalities?
6. Does the poem show a preference for one speaker or the other?
7. You probably side with one speaker or the other. How do the other speaker's points help you understand the problem of racism more clearly?

Essay Topics: Comparison/Contrast

1. Compare your attitudes toward marriage and family with those of your parents.
2. Compare your high school courses and college courses.
3. Compare two employers you have worked for.
4. Compare two television programs you watch frequently.
5. Compare two musical groups or athletic teams.
6. Compare attitudes toward family in the United States and in another country.
7. Compare two short stories or poems you have read.

PEER REVIEW QUESTIONS: COMPARISON/CONTRAST

1. I think that your overall purpose in comparing these two subjects is to make the following point:

2. Your introduction is interesting. ☐ Yes ☐ No
   Your introduction identifies the two subjects you are comparing. ☐ Yes ☐ No
   Your introduction and conclusion clearly express the thesis you are supporting in your comparison. ☐ Yes ☐ No

3. You analyze the following similarities between the two subjects:

4. You analyze the following differences between the two subjects:

5. You use the following method of organizing your comparison:

6. What I like best about your essay is the following:

7. I recommend that you make the following changes:

Proofreading Practice: Modifiers in Comparisons

Adjectives in Comparisons

Besides their simple forms, adjectives have two forms that are used in comparisons. The **comparative form** is used to compare two unequal things, and the **superlative form** is used to set one thing off from all the others.

Simple Form	Comparative Form	Superlative Form
good	better	best
young	younger	youngest
strong	stronger	strongest
easy	easier	easiest
happy	happier	happiest

Adjectives with three or more syllables always take *more* and *most* rather than the -*er* and -*est* endings.

beautiful	more beautiful	most beautiful
exciting	more exciting	most exciting

Your dictionary will show that some two-syllable words take -*er* and -*est*, while others take *more* and *most*.

heavy	heavier	heaviest
friendly	friendlier	friendliest
subtle	subtler	subtlest
cheerful	more cheerful	most cheerful
precise	more precise	most precise

Use the comparative form when comparing two things or people.

> She is <u>wealthier</u> than her sister.
> She is the <u>wealthier</u> of the two sisters.

(Remember to use *than*, not *then*, in making comparisons.)

> Use the superlative form to set off one from a whole group.

She is the <u>wealthiest</u> woman in the group.
She is the <u>wealthiest</u> of the three sisters.

Adverbs in Comparisons

Adverbs also have comparative and superlative forms. Nearly all adverbs take *more* and *most*. The only exceptions are the few that serve as both adjectives and adverbs—*early, late, hard, fast, low,* and *straight.* These take -*er* and -*est*: *earlier, earliest.*

Simple Form	Comparative Form	Superlative Form
easily	more easily	most easily
violently	more violently	most violently
recently	more recently	most recently
happily	more happily	most happily

We also make negative comparisons, using adjectives and adverbs in combination with *less* or *least*.

expensive	less expensive	least expensive
difficult	less difficult	least difficult
safely	less safely	least safely
forcefully	less forcefully	least forcefully

Do not use both the *-er* or *-est* ending and the helping words *more*, *most*, *less*, or *least*.

Incorrect: You are more better than the last shortstop.
They are less healthier than they should be.
Correct: You are better than the last shortstop.
They are less healthy than they should be.
Incorrect: This was the most saddest film I have seen.
This was the least richest pastry on the menu.
Correct: This was the saddest film I have seen.
This was the least rich pastry on the menu.

TEST YOURSELF: Adjectives and Adverbs in Comparisons

Correct the errors in the passage below.

Harold has gained and lost weight many times. This has happened partly because he is an actor and some roles require him to be more heavier than others. He once had to play a protestor who went on a hunger strike, so he had to look much more skinnier than you usually does. He found it difficulter than he expected to lose thirty pounds for the role. Another time he played the role of a fat man and had to get much more bigger. To do this, he stuffed himself with pasta, pastries, and other foods with lots of fat and sugar. He had to do this more rapid than he wanted to because of a deadline. After he lost the extra weight he worked out until he was in the most fittest condition of his life. Then he got a role playing a soccer star and couldn't have been cast perfecter.

Answers: 1. to be heavier than others 2. look much skinnier 3. found it more difficult 4. to get much bigger 5. more rapidly than he wanted 6. in the fittest condition 7. more perfectly

---

PROOFREADING EXERCISES: Basic, Intermediate, Challenge

Basic Exercise:
Adjectives and Adverbs in Comparisons

Correct the seven errors in this passage.

Yolanda is very different from her sister. Yolanda is a more better student than Sonya, but Sonya is more sociable and popular. Although Yolanda is more young than Sonya, she has always been considered just as mature. Sonya, however, often takes the lead in social situations because she converses easier with others than her sister, especially with older people. In school Yolanda often helps her older sister with homework because she can read and memorize rapider than Sonya. They support each other in many ways and are the dependablest of friends in times of trouble. They also share all their secrets with each other, and no sisters could ever be more honester with each other then they are.

Intermediate Exercise:
Adjectives and Adverbs in Comparisons

Correct the seven errors in this passage.

Attitudes of teenagers today toward dating and relationships are very different from those of their parents. Today's adolescents are less likelier to go on formal dates then their parents did. Instead they usually hang out with groups of friends and wait a longer time before getting married. They talk more easier about sex and gender roles than their parents did, and they are toleranter about questions of sexual preference. Their parents had more stronger beliefs about having children outside wedlock and were less readier to accept relationships between people of different religions and races. Today's teenagers are also used to women competing more confident with men than in the past.

Challenge Exercise:
Adjectives and Adverbs in Comparisons

Correct the seven errors in this passage.

Experts debate whether medication or therapy is the effectiver way of treating depression. Before today's antidepressant drugs were discovered, all treatment had to be talk therapy, which sometimes produced recovery and sometimes did not. With the advent of Prozac and more recent developed drugs, claims were made that medications worked faster and with more greater effect. As combinations of therapy and medication achieved increasingly more higher levels of success with many patients, new studies were done to compare the methods of talk therapy and the use of medications. Although the results of such studies so far are less clearer than we might wish, some consensus is emerging that certain combinations of drugs and therapy are powerfuler modes of cure then either drugs or therapy alone.

Key Words from Chapter 11 for Review

block pattern, comparative form of modifiers, comparison, contrast, organizing by categories, secondary sources, superlative form of modifiers

Explaining a Process or Procedure

STEPPING UP: WRITING TIP 12

Giving clear directions is not easy, as we all know from having taken a wrong turn while trying to remember a stranger's directions before the days of GPS. The challenge you will face in writing a process essay is to be sure that your reader follows every step in your explanation. To this end, it is a very good idea to read your draft aloud to a number of people separately. Find out if there is anything that confuses them, and don't be satisfied until several readers are able to rephrase your instructions accurately. Some employers, before sending out a memo, try it out on a few employees, having them explain the content in their own words. We live in a visual culture; people want to *see* procedures and processes. They become impatient with written instructions. Make yours crisp and reader-friendly.

"How-To" Writing: Giving Clear Instructions

Clarity and thoroughness are the key principles to **process writing** and **procedural writing**. When you explain how something happens or give instructions about how to do something, every step must be easy to follow. Achieving this means using clear language and a reader-friendly method of organizing your material. Imagine that you are the reader relying on your essay to provide you with complete information on a topic. Does your essay do that? Or, are there gaps where information is missing and passages where the meaning is ambiguous? Double meanings can enrich a poem, but they only confuse the reader of procedural writing. Use topic sentences at the beginning of every paragraph to signal each stage in the process or procedure you are describing. In explanatory writing, it is better to lean in the direction of being too mechanical and obvious than to risk being unclear.

If procedural writing is to succeed at guiding a reader through a process, it must be thorough. Procedural essays usually follow a **step-by-step plan** of organization and leave nothing out. An instruction manual that tells you how to hook up a desktop computer, for instance, cannot contain confusing statements or omit anything you need to know; if it does, the computer will not work.

Most of us are used to giving instructions aloud and being able to rely on the aid of gestures, tone of voice, and listener feedback to help us navigate the process. As a writer, you cannot use these aids. You can get feedback while drafting your essay, but once you have completed your final version, your words alone have to say it all. The reader cannot ask you to explain what he or she does not understand.

A crucial step in ensuring that your reader understands what you are saying is making sure that she or he can understand your terminology. It is appropriate to use specialized terms when you are writing for experts on your topic, but if you are writing for general readers, use vocabulary only as technical as necessary and explain the meaning of all technical terms the first time you use them. Remember whom you are writing for: You will not write the same paragraph for general readers that you would for specialists.

Student Essay: Explaining a Procedure

Read the following student essay and answer the questions that follow it.

How to Get the Most Out of a Course

EDGAR SIMMS

Most of the students I know approach a course with the attitude, "How can I get an A in this course?" They need high grade-point averages to be admitted to competitive programs and graduate schools, and all they care about is their grades. But they are missing out on another side of college education. They should ask themselves the question, "What can I get out of this course?" That includes a high grade, but there is much more to it. I have some advice on how to get the most out of any course you take.

First, figure out why you are taking the course and what you hope to learn from it. In some cases, you don't have a choice because the course is required. In a mandatory course, ask yourself what you really can learn that will be worthwhile to you, either as part of your major or as knowledge that will help you in your career. Then focus on that part of the course and relate everything else to it. For instance, if there is a term paper, do it on a topic that matters to you. And ask questions in class about your special interests. For instance, if you're taking a required economics course but you want to be a nurse or a doctor, ask questions about the economic problems in health care and write a term paper about medical malpractice.

When you choose elective courses, pick the ones that will really matter to you, not just courses taught by "hot" professors or ones that have a reputation for being easy. Sometimes a course that's too easy will bore you, and you end up not doing as well as you expected. If you take a more difficult course in astronomy, and you are really fascinated by what's being discovered about the possibility of life on other planets, you will probably earn a good grade because you'll work hard without realizing it. Let your real interests guide you, and you'll do better.

There are also some pointers I can give about behavior that will help you do well in any class. Most students head for the back of the room and never say anything. They often make fun of students who sit at the front, wave their hands in the teacher's face, and do all the talking. Maybe you don't want to look like the "teacher's pet," but you should sit near the front and join all the class discussions. This isn't just to impress the teacher but to keep yourself interested in the course material and remember it better. When you talk a lot, and when other students disagree with you, you will remember what went on much better than if you just sit at the back and pretend to take a few notes.

Another thing you should do, which you may avoid at first, is to go see your professors during their office hours. This isn't to earn a higher grade (although it may help sometimes) but to make the course part of your identity and remember what you learned in it. And, of course, if you're having trouble understanding anything in the course, it's even more important that you communicate with the professor and with a tutor, if one is available.

One last suggestion is to form a study group. Students in some cultures do this all the time, but most students in the United States aren't used to doing it. Try to find three or four other students in your class and meet once every week or two to discuss what's going on in the course. This will help you be interested in, understand, and remember the subject of the course.

All of these methods work. Use them. You'll get more out of every course you take. Remember that you're paying a lot of money for your education and putting a lot of time into it. Don't waste it. Besides, by using these methods, chances are you will earn a higher grade-point average than the students who spend all their time trying to find easy courses, professors who give high grades, and methods of cheating on exams.

1. In your own words, identify the procedure Edgar explains in this essay.
2. How does he distinguish his approach from that of many other students?
3. In his opening paragraph, how does he seek to arouse interest in his subject?
4. How many parts does the body of his essay contain?
5. What are the two categories of courses he identifies?
6. What advice does he give for each separately? For all courses?
7. How clear are his points of advice? Could you follow them easily?

Analyzing a Process: Making the Connections

Organizing your material in a process essay can be easy. Follow a step-by-step plan or one that groups your explanation into a few categories, and do not wander from your main purpose. To make your explanation easy to follow, guide the reader by using **transition words** such as *before, next, then, afterward, however,* and *therefore* between paragraphs and occasionally between sentences within paragraphs. Help the reader to visualize the procedure by imagining yourself as the reader and mentally putting yourself through the process. Try to anticipate and prevent the reader's likely errors and misunderstandings by identifying and explaining the points where readers might take the wrong step or become confused. Include a few FAQs—frequently asked questions—to highlight the problem spots that most people run into as they become involved in whatever process you are explaining.

It is important to include sufficient information in procedural writing, but keep in mind one caution: avoid clutter. Do not editorialize or digress; include only information that will keep the reader on track. No matter how interesting irrelevant details may be, they distract readers by interrupting their trains of thought. When giving directions to a driver, for example, it is wise to avoid making a statement like, "When you pass the church, you'll see a turnoff on the right; don't take that." It is more precise—and easier—to say, "Take the second right."

Researching the Facts of the Process

To write a successful essay explaining a process or procedure, you must have correct information. A simple procedural essay based on personal experience will not require much research, but one involving technical details, sociological ideas, or scientific facts requires you to do some reading. Obviously, an essay explaining how the Federal Reserve System affects the economy requires specialized knowledge, as does an essay explaining how to acquire a patent on a new invention. Students usually write essays about subjects they are familiar with, but even when you feel confident about your grasp of a process, do some preliminary reading and research to make sure that you have enough facts and that your facts are correct. And when you use other sources of information, you *must* cite them properly. (Procedures for quoting, paraphrasing, and preparing a bibliography are explained in Chapter 15.)

Example by Published Author: Explaining a Process

Process analysis gives a step-by-step account of how something develops. It is similar to procedural writing, but instead of giving someone instructions, in process analysis you are describing a social phenomenon or an institutional structure. For example, read the following explanation by Jane Jacobs from her well-known book on American cities, *The Death and Life of Great American Cities*, and answer the questions that follow it.

The Kind of Problem a City Is

Jane Jacobs

Big cities and countrysides can get along well together. Big cities need countryside close by. And countryside—from man's point of view—needs big cities, with all their diverse opportunities and productivity, so human beings can be in a position to appreciate the rest of the natural world instead of to curse it.

Being human is itself difficult, and therefore all kinds of settlements (except dream cities) have problems. Big cities have difficulties in abundance. But vital cities are not helpless to combat even the most difficult of problems. They are not passive victims of chains of circumstances, any more than they are the malignant opposite of nature.

Vital cities have marvelous innate abilities for understanding, communicating, contriving, and inventing what is required to combat their difficulties. Perhaps the most striking example of this ability is the effect that big cities have had on disease. Cities were once the most helpless and devastated victims of disease, but they became great disease conquerors. All the apparatus of surgery, hygiene, microbiology, chemistry, telecommunications, public health measures, teaching and research hospitals, ambulances and the like, which people not only in cities but also outside them depend upon for the unending war against premature mortality, are fundamentally products of big cities and would be inconceivable without big cities. The surplus wealth, the productivity, the close-grained juxtaposition of talents that permit society to support advances such as these are themselves products of our organization into cities, and especially into big and dense cities.

It may be romantic to search for the salves of society's ills in slow-moving, rustic surroundings, or among innocent, unspoiled provincials, if such exist, but it is a waste of time. Does anyone suppose that, in real life, answers to any of the great questions that worry us today are going to come out of homogeneous settlements?

Dull, inert cities, it is true, do contain the seeds of their own destruction and little else. But lively, diverse, intense cities contain the seeds of their own regeneration, with energy enough to carry over for problems and needs outside themselves.

—Jane Jacobs. From *The Death and Life of Great American Cities.*

1. Define these words and phrases, using a dictionary if necessary: *malignant, innate, premature mortality, juxtaposition, provincials, homogeneous settlements, inert.*

2. How does Jane Jacobs explain the ability of cities to overcome problems?

3. What specific problem does she mention that cities overcame?

4. How does she describe the relationship between cities and the countryside?

5. What kind of cities does she believe have the power to overcome serious problems?

6. What quality do cities have that tend toward self-destruction?

7. What kinds of communities are not likely to provide solutions to the big social problems?

WRITING EXERCISES: Basic, Intermediate, Challenge

Basic Exercise: Procedural Writing

Below is a plan for an essay explaining how to prepare for and execute a successful job interview. Answer the questions that follow the plan.

Essay Plan

Introduction: What Makes an Effective Interview
  I. Planning
  II. Creating a Favorable First Impression
  III. Successful Strategies for the Interview

IV. Some Things to Avoid

V. Following Up

VI. Conclusion: Final Thoughts

1. What do you think are the most important elements of interviewing to stress in your introduction?

2. What kind of planning do you think will strengthen an interview?

3. In Section II, how can a prospective employee enhance his or her first impression?

4. In Section III, name some of the most important strategies to remember in the interview itself.

5. In Section IV, what do you think are the two or three things to avoid that could ruin a good interview?

6. In Section V, what do you recommend that a prospective employee should do to follow up after an interview?

7. In your conclusion, what overall attitude toward effective interviewing do you want the reader to gain from your essay?

Intermediate Exercise: Procedural Writing

Read the following explanation from Dr. Spock's famous book, *Baby and Child Care*, and answer the questions that follow it.

Helping Children with Their Lessons

BENJAMIN SPOCK, M.D., AND STEVEN J. PARKER, M.D.

Sometimes a teacher will advise parents that their child is falling behind and needs tutoring in a subject. Sometimes the parents have the idea themselves. This is something to be careful about. If the school can recommend a good tutor whom you can afford, go ahead and hire him. Too often parents make poor tutors, not because they don't know enough, not because they don't try hard enough, but because they care too much and become too upset when their child doesn't understand. I learned that as a seven-year-old. If a child is already mixed up in his lessons, an impatient parent may be the last straw. Another trouble is that the parents' method may be different from that being used in class. If the child is already baffled by the subject as presented in school, the chances are that he will be even more baffled when it's presented in a different way at home.

I don't want to go so far as to say that a parent should never tutor a child, because in some cases it works very well. I'd only advise a parent to talk it over thoroughly with the teacher first, and then quit right away if it isn't going well. Whoever is tutoring the child should keep in touch with the teacher, at regular intervals.

What should you do if children ask for help with their homework? If they are puzzled and turn to you for clarification, there's no harm in straightening them out. (Nothing pleases parents more than to have a chance occasionally to prove to a child that they really know something.) But if your children are asking you to do their work for them because they don't understand it, you'd better consult the teacher. A good teacher prefers to help children understand and then let them rely on themselves. If the teacher is too busy to give your child some extra time, you may have to lend a hand; but even then you should just help him to understand his work; you should not do it for him. Your child can have many teachers but only one mother and father. Your role as parent is more important.

Relations between Parent and Teacher

It's easy to get along with the teacher if your son is the teacher's pride and joy and doing well in class. But if your child is having trouble, the situation is more delicate. The best parents and the best teachers are all very human. All take pride in the work they are doing and have possessive feelings toward the child. Each, no matter how reasonable, secretly feels that the child would be doing better if the other would only handle him a little differently. It's helpful to the parents to realize at the start that the teacher is just as sensitive as they are, and that they will get further in a conference by being friendly and cooperative.

Some parents are afraid of facing a teacher, but they forget that just as often the teacher is afraid of them. The parents' main job is to give a clear history of the child's past, what his interests are, and what he responds to well or badly, and then to work with the teacher on how best to apply this information in school. Don't forget to compliment the teacher on those parts of the class program that are a great success with the child.

Occasionally a child and teacher just don't "fit" temperamentally, no matter how hard they both work at it. In these cases, the principal can be involved in the question of whether to move the child to another class.

Parents should avoid blaming the teacher if their child is unsuccessful in class. If the child hears the parents bad-mouthing the teacher, he will learn to blame others and to avoid taking responsibility for his contribution to his problems. You can still be sympathetic: "I know how hard you are trying," or "I know how unhappy it makes you when your teacher is dissatisfied."

—Benjamin Spock, M.D., and Steven J. Parker, M.D.
From *Dr. Spock's Baby and Child Care.*

1. Identify the categories Dr. Spock uses to organize the material in this passage.
2. What's the first thing he says parents should do if their child has trouble in school?
3. What are two reasons parents sometimes do not make good tutors?
4. What does Dr. Spock recommend if your child asks for help with homework?
5. What does he caution against doing when a child asks for help?
6. What attitude does he say parents and teachers often have toward one another?
7. According to Dr. Spock, what is the difference between the roles of parents and teachers?

Challenge Exercise: Procedural Writing

Choose a procedure you know how to do, such as parking a car, buying a dress, ordering a product online, preparing and giving a speech, planning a wedding, planning a trip, or doing a workout at the gym. Write answers to the following questions.

1. What are four or five steps or categories you could use in writing an explanation of this procedure?
   What is the most effective order in which these steps or categories can be arranged?
2. What are two problem spots in the procedure—places where things might go wrong or the reader might make a mistake?
   Why is it important for the reader to avoid making errors at these junctures?
3. In what part of your writing could you use your personal experience to enliven your explanation?
4. What are several transitional words and phrases you might use in moving from one section of your explanation to the next?
5. What are the underlying assumptions you have about your subject that you would want your reader to share?

Essay Topics: Procedural Writing

Choose one of the following topics and write a "how-to" or procedural essay. Begin with a concise, clear statement of purpose and develop your discussion step by step, using transitional words. Be sure to obtain and fact-check the necessary information, either by doing Internet research or by reading articles or books on the subject.

1. How to design a Web page
2. How to eat what you like but stay thin
3. How to prepare for a career in _____
4. How a baby develops in the first year
5. How popular music has changed in the last decade
6. How the demographics of your state or city have changed in the last decade
7. How to choose the right subject for an academic major

PEER REVIEW QUESTIONS: PROCEDURAL AND PROCESS WRITING

1. Here is my impression of what you are explaining in your essay:

2. Your introduction is interesting. ☐ Yes ☐ No
   Your introduction makes the purpose of your essay clear. ☐ Yes ☐ No
   The sentence that most nearly expresses your main point is the following:

3. You explain the process or procedure in a clear, step-by-step sequence. ☐ Yes ☐ No

4. Your explanation is thorough and leaves nothing out. ☐ Yes ☐ No

5. Your conclusion (is/is not) effective for the following reason:

6. What I like best about your essay is the following:

7. I recommend you make the following changes:

Proofreading Practice: Present and Progressive Tenses

Writing about a process or procedure mostly involves the **present tense**: You are explaining how something occurs in general rather than describing a single event that happened in the past. Using the present tense, of course, requires you to watch your –s and –es endings carefully: Use –s and –es endings for singular (she *writes*); do not use the ending for plural (they *write*). For non native speakers of English, the present tense is often hard to distinguish from the **progressive tense**, which is the form created by adding –*ing* to the verb in combination with a form of *be* (*am, is, are*).

What is the difference between the two phrases below?

Susan <u>writes</u>.
Susan <u>is writing</u>.

Both are in the present tense, but the second is called the **present progressive**. This form refers to an action caught in the moment when it is happening, whereas the **simple present** refers to general actions that take place repeatedly. For instance, we can say:

Susan <u>writes</u> to her sister every week.
Susan <u>is writing</u> at this very moment.

When explaining a process, you will use mostly the **simple present**, but you might need the **present progressive** to tell about one procedure while something else is happening. For example, "Don't disconnect the set while the battery <u>is charging</u>" or "While you <u>are compiling</u> the guest list, don't forget to include the groom's friends."

TEST YOURSELF: Present and Present Progressive Tenses

Correct the errors in the verb forms below. One sentence is correct.

1. Alice always do Pilates or yoga on Fridays.
2. Some of the money is belonging to Fred's uncle.
3. This difficult step in the procedure require preparation.
4. The instruction manual is explaining how to install the program.
5. Prolonged wars usually causes inflation.
6. A bridge is being constructed over the bay.
7. The cookbook suggest preheating the oven for 10 minutes.

Answers: 1. does 2. belongs 3. requires 4. explains 5. cause 6. correct 7. suggests

---

Basic Exercise:
Present and Present Progressive Tenses

Correct the verb errors in the sentences below. One sentence is correct.

1. Every Saturday Jeremy attend a physics class.
2. Carla should be the parliamentarian because she is knowing *Robert's Rules of Order.*
3. Stage acting demand both physical and emotional effort.
4. John liked the film because it is ending with a hilarious twist.
5. Global warming cause the polar ice cap to melt.
6. The population of the Southwest is increasing.
7. Opening the package require a pair of scissors.

Intermediate Exercise:
Present and Present Progressive Tenses

Correct the seven errors in this passage.

In February 2011, the people in Egypt turned out in the streets of Cairo for many days to demand a change of government. Such demonstrations in most countries are usually causing a crackdown by the authorities, often a violent one. The people who take part in such demonstrations always runs the risk of being injured or arrested, and the journalists and photographers who try to cover the action are often being attacked as well. When the demonstration is large enough, it is forcing the government to respond in a big way, either by making real changes or by using large-scale force and violence. In Egypt, despite the huge size of the demonstration, the government did not react with large-scale violence, which is showing that sometimes nonviolent demonstrations can be effective. Although some people are doubting the principles of nonviolence preached by Gandhi and Dr. Martin Luther King, Jr., it is clear that there are situations in which a large, disciplined movement, committed to nonviolence, can create change more effectively than the use of force or terrorism is doing.

Challenge Exercise:
Present and Present Progressive Tenses

Correct the seven errors in this passage.

The first telescopes used to study the stars and planets were refracting telescopes, which uses two main lenses to magnify images. An important step in astronomy occurred when Sir Isaac Newton built the first reflecting telescope, which use two mirrors instead of lenses. Mirrors improve magnification and light gathering power in several ways. First, mirrors can be made larger than the largest lenses and thus gathers more light. In addition, mirrors do not have the problem of bending different colors of light at different angles as lenses are doing, and thus can focus images more sharply. A reflecting telescope has a large mirror at the back, which gathers the incoming light and is focusing it through a smaller mirror at the front, which reflects it through a magnifying eyepiece. The light is traveling twice the length of the tube, thus allowing for twice as much magnification as a refracting telescope of the same length. The large telescopes built in the twentieth century, such as the Hale Telescope on Mt. Palomar in California, are modeled on a reflecting design, but are containing many modern improvements over Isaac Newton's simple instrument.

Key Words from Chapter 12 for Review

present progressive tense, present tense, procedural writing, process writing, step-by-step plan, transition words

Analyzing Cause and Effect

STEPPING UP: WRITING TIP 13

Writing about causes or effects is one of the most interesting modes of composition. However, it is far too easy to lose your objectivity and become obsessed with a single cause or effect. In discussions of nearly all topics, personal or social, many factors are at play. Try to examine the problem with patience and openness. Of course, your essay will express your strong point of view, but try not to arrive at your conclusions before you have considered a whole range of possible causes or effects. This extra intellectual effort will make your essay stronger and more convincing. Do some thoughtful prewriting.

Analyzing Cause and Effect to Explore an Issue

Analyzing causes and effects can be simple or complicated and intellectually profound. At any level of difficulty, your intention when examining cause and effect is to reveal something to readers that they might not see—for example, the causes of teenage rebellion or high dropout rates, the benefits of exercise, or the effects of video games on children. College assignments often involve analysis of cause and effect because exploring either why something happens or what results from something exercises your brain in many ways at once. You have to think logically, remain open to complexities, search out the facts, and organize your material clearly. **Analyzing causes** requires you to think backward from a point in time and explain what caused a known situation. **Analyzing effects** means thinking ahead from a point in time, looking at a known situation and explaining what resulted or will result from that situation. The two examples below explore the causes of two social phenomena. The student essay looks at a well-known fact—the existence of community colleges—and figures out why there are so many of them. The reading by a published author (a well-known economist) analyzes the causes of the financial crisis of 2008.

Student Essay: Analyzing Causes
Where Community Colleges Came From

MICHAEL CAPELLA

A hundred years ago in the United States, there were elementary schools, high schools, and colleges, but no community colleges. Only in the last half of the twentieth century were community colleges beginning to appear in most states across the country. Now there are so many that a large percentage of college students, probably about one-third, attend community colleges. Why, we may ask, did this new kind of institution spring up, and why did it catch on? There are three main reasons.

One reason why community colleges are popular and necessary is that there are so many nontraditional students. These are students who are different from the students of the past who came from well-off families, lived in dormitories or sorority or fraternity houses, spent time going to football games and parties, and graduated in four years at the age of 21 or 22. Nontraditional students may be older, have families to support, hold down jobs, take courses part-time, commute to campus, and speak first languages other than English. They may come from other countries, and their parents may not speak English at all. Also, they may not come to college with a good knowledge of math and science, either because they studied them years ago in high school, or because they dropped out of high school and earned a G.E.D.

These nontraditional students usually can't afford to attend traditional four-year colleges, even if they are admitted to them. They fit in much better at community colleges, where they can take longer to graduate by going part-time and may be able to take remedial courses in subjects in which they are weak. The older students, such as women who didn't have a chance to go to college after high school and want a college degree after they have raised their children, may feel out of place on campuses full of 18-year-olds.

Another reason why community colleges are appearing everywhere is that they often have courses and degree programs connected to nearby job opportunities. In states with many insurance companies, they may offer special courses that train students to work in the insurance field. In communities with many job opportunities in banking or hotel management, they may offer career training in those areas. Since many of the students at community colleges need well-paying jobs that won't take them many years to obtain, they often choose career training like nursing, computer science, and finance.

The most important reason why community colleges are so numerous is that the job market has changed. Jobs that used to require a high school diploma now demand at least an associate's degree. Years ago, every student had the opportunity to get a free high school education; nowadays, every student who graduates from high school in most states has a chance to get a community college education that is not very expensive. More skills and knowledge are required for almost any decent-paying job than in the past, so community colleges are necessary to give everyone a chance. And many students who aren't sure whether they can make it in college turn out to be top students and go on to earn higher degrees. Some even become teachers, doctors, and lawyers.

Anybody who has gone to a community college can see why community colleges were necessary to fill a big gap in American education. If only teenage students from well-to-do families who earned top grades in high school were allowed to attend college, most of today's undergraduates would be out of luck. Community colleges came along to give everybody a chance to pursue their dreams—and they still do that.

1. Identify the thesis of this essay and the thesis statement.
2. How many causes does Michael name for the proliferation of community colleges?
3. Identify each cause. Which one seems most important to Michael? Where does he put it in the essay, and why?
4. Explain the difference between a traditional and nontraditional student.
5. What details does Michael bring in to describe traditional and nontraditional students?
6. How does he support his point that community colleges help students get jobs?
7. Name one or two additional reasons why community colleges have become important.

Example by a Published Author: Analyzing Causes

The following passage explains some causes of the financial crisis that occurred in 2008. Read the selection and answer the questions that follow it.

The Causes of the Financial Crisis of 2008

Joseph Stiglitz

The basic outlines of the story are well known and often told. The United States had a housing bubble. When that bubble broke and housing prices fell from their stratospheric levels, more and more homeowners found themselves "underwater." They owed more on their mortgages than what their homes were valued. As they lost their homes, many also lost their life savings and their dreams for a future—a college education for their children, a retirement in comfort. Americans had, in a sense, been living in a dream.

The richest country in the world was living beyond its means, and the strength of the U.S. economy, and the world's, depended on it. The global economy needed ever-increasing consumption to grow; but how could this continue when the incomes of many Americans had been stagnating for so long? Americans came up with an ingenious solution: borrow and consume as if their incomes *were* growing. And borrow they did. Average savings rates fell to zero—and with many rich Americans saving substantial amounts, that meant poor Americans had a large negative savings rate. In other words, they were going deeply into debt. Both they and their lenders could feel good about what was happening: they were able to continue their consumption binge, not having to face up to the reality of stagnating and declining incomes, and lenders could enjoy record profits based on ever-mounting fees. . . . It was unsustainable—and it wasn't sustained. The breaking of the bubble at first affected the worst mortgages (the subprime mortgages lent to low-income individuals), but soon affected all residential real estate.

When the bubble popped, the effects were amplified because banks had created complex products resting on top of the mortgages. Worse still, they had engaged in multibillion-dollar bets with each other and with others around the world. This complexity, combined with the rapidity with which the situation was deteriorating and the banks' high leverage (they, like households, had financed their investments by heavy borrowing), meant that the banks didn't know whether what they owed to their depositors and bondholders exceeded the value of their assets. And they realized accordingly that they couldn't know the position of any other bank. The trust and confidence that underlie the banking system evaporated. Banks refused to lend to each other—or demanded high interest rates to compensate for bearing the risk. Global credit markets began to melt down.

At that point, America and the world were faced with both a financial crisis and an economic crisis.

—Joseph Stiglitz. From *Freefall: America, Free Markets, and the Sinking of the World Economy* (New York: 2010): 1-3.

---

1. Define these words, using a dictionary if necessary: *stratospheric, mortgage, stagnating, amplified, leverage, compensate.*
2. What does the author mean by the term *housing bubble?*
3. According to Stieglitz, how were Americans "living beyond their means"?
4. What were the savings patterns of ordinary people before the crisis? How did this differ from the savings patterns of rich people?

5. What does it mean for homeowners to be "underwater"?
6. Which homeowners' mortgages were affected first when the bubble burst? What behavior by the large banks made problems worse after the bubble burst?
7. In your opinion, based on what Stieglitz says, what could banks and ordinary people do differently to prevent such a disaster in the future?

Being Logical: Causes vs. Coincidences

The Latin phrase *post hoc ergo propter hoc* translates to *after something, therefore because of something.* This familiar mistake in logic means that you cannot assume one event causes another simply because the second event comes after the first. For instance, if someone wore a yellow tie in the morning and it rained in the afternoon, and believed the yellow tie had caused the rain, he would be guilty of making this mistake. Most of us engage in this kind of superstitious thinking once in a while, but we should avoid it when writing a cause and effect analysis.

How can you tell whether something really is a cause or effect, and not just a **coincidence**? Consider these examples; which would you say are logically connected?

- Poverty and terrorism
- Video games and students' performance in school
- Cell phones and automobile accidents
- Signs of the zodiac and world events
- Immigration and unemployment
- Players' salaries and winning teams
- The number 13 and bad luck
- Hollywood films and teenage behavior

Several of these pairs can be shown by evidence to be connected. Which ones cannot? What seems obvious and logical to one person may not seem that way to someone else. However, when you write an essay analyzing causes or effects, it is your job to explain connections convincingly. It is not enough to claim, for example, that the crime rate in a particular city dropped when a particular mayor was in office and therefore he or she necessarily caused the drop. What additional information would you need to decide whether the mayor helped reduce the rate of crime? What if other cities whose mayors used different methods of policing experienced equal drops in crime? How can we determine what causes crime to go up or down?

Identifying All the Causes and Effects

Whether discussing the crime rate, education, or a personal situation, you are usually better off assuming that there is more than one cause or effect for any given situation. Keep your mind open to all the possibilities. If most problems were so simple that one obvious cause or effect could be identified easily, sociologists, economists, psychologists, and historians would not be busy writing books arguing about causes and effects of such subjects as the causes of the two World Wars and the Great Depression, the results of global warming, and the future of the economy. Obviously, these are complex and controversial questions.

Finding the Necessary Information

To write a convincing analysis of cause and effect, you need factual information. Even in essays that are not primarily research papers, you should strengthen your analysis with factual information whenever you can. Rather than simply giving your opinion on whether capital punishment does or does not reduce the murder rate, do a Web search and look up an article or two that will provide statistics on the subject. If you are explaining why so many high school students drop out of school, gather information on dropout rates and what the experts have said on the subject. If you limit your analysis to your own school and your own observations, you still can write a valuable essay, but it will not clarify the larger problem as well as an essay in which you begin with your own observations but move on to analyze the problem using reliable data.

Basic Exercise: Cause and Effect

Practice identifying several causes and effects for every topic. For each of the topics below, list at least three causes or effects. Underline the one that you believe to be most important.

1. Name three reasons why you are attending college.
2. Name three reasons why your neighborhood has gotten better or worse.
3. Name three reasons why hip-hop has been become popular outside the United States.
4. Name three causes of happiness in your life.
5. Name three ways technology has changed your life.
6. Name three ways having a baby has affected the life of someone you know.
7. Name three ways your college degree will improve your life.

Intermediate Exercise: Cause and Effect

Practice identifying several causes and effects for every topic. Brainstorm each of the topics below and list at least three causes or effects. Underline the one that you believe to be most important.

1. Name three causes of high dropout rates in public schools.
2. Name three reasons why young people marry later in life than previous generations.
3. Name three reasons why students take online courses.
4. Name three reasons why immigrants come to the United States.
5. Name three effects of divorce on children.
6. Name three effects of sports teams on college campuses.
7. Name three effects of computer technology on jobs.

Challenge Exercise: Cause and Effect

Analyze the cause and effect statements below and identify mistakes in logical reasoning. Improve each statement so that it contains a more logical connection between cause and effect.

1. The scientists who tell us about global warming must be right. It was much warmer this month in my home state than it was a year ago.
2. Men must be smarter at science than women because there are three times as many men as there are women earning Ph.D.s in physics in the United States.
3. If children continue to spend time playing video games, the rate of violence in schools will certainly increase rapidly.
4. The sources of Jason's information must be reliable because he found all of them in the library rather than on the Internet.
5. All of today's Olympic athletes must be using steroids because they keep breaking the records of earlier athletes.
6. People who live in the suburbs are happier than people who live in small towns because suburbanites earn larger incomes.
7. If all countries spoke the same language there would be no wars because wars are always between nations that speak different languages.

Essay Topics: Cause and Effect

Write an essay on one of the following topics. Do some preliminary thinking and prewriting activities. Base your analysis on both your own observation and information you can find about the topic on the Internet.

1. Explain what is causing the problem of obesity in America.
2. Explain why reality television shows are popular.
3. Explain why many young people do not vote in the United States.
4. Explain what causes eating disorders in many young women and men.
5. Analyze how cell phones and e-mail affect the behavior of young people.
6. Analyze how speaking English as a second language affects a student's college experience.
7. Analyze how blogs are influencing journalism and politics.

PEER REVIEW QUESTIONS:
CAUSE AND EFFECT

1. My impression of your essay is that you are explaining the cause or effect (circle which) of _____.

2. Your introduction is interesting. ☐ Yes ☐ No
Your introduction makes the purpose of your essay clear. ☐ Yes ☐ No
The sentence that most nearly expresses your main point is the following:

3. You identify the following causes (or effects):

4. Your analysis is logical and not oversimplified. ☐ Yes ☐ No

5. Your conclusion (is/is not) effective for the following reason:

6. What I like best about your essay is the following:

7. I recommend you make the following changes:

Proofreading Practice: Compound and Complex Sentences

When you write a cause and effect analysis, you will often use transition words such as *if, so, whenever, because, therefore, as a result,* and *consequently* to connect the parts of your analysis. Using these transitions, however, requires a mastery of certain kinds of **compound** and **complex sentences**. Remember that sentences beginning with *if, whenever, when,* and *because* (called **subordinate conjunctions**) are **complex sentences**. That means that the first part is a **dependent clause** that should be followed by a comma. Examples of complex sentences follow.

If it rains on Wednesday, we will have the party inside.
Because the customers prefer ATMs, the bank reduced the number of tellers.

However, sentences connected by *therefore, as a result, as a consequence, consequently,* and *hence* are **compound sentences** that require semicolons. The short connective word *so,* on the other hand, is preceded by a comma. Examples follow.

The first paychecks were late; as a result, many workers were angry.
The college changed its financial aid policy; therefore, many students were unable to attend.
The combination of music and cinematography was perfect, so the film won many awards.

TEST YOURSELF: Compound and Complex Sentences

Be careful to distinguish between compound sentences that require semicolons and complex sentences that require commas. Identify the correct sentences in the following group and correct the ones that contain errors.

1. The second floor is closed this week, consequently, we will hold the meeting in a classroom on the third floor.
2. Because the music was not difficult to read; Ted was able to recognize the melody.
3. Stricter immigration laws were passed, so it became harder to get a visa.
4. Sales figures dropped during March; therefore, analysts expected a decline in stock prices.
5. Whenever medication is combined with therapy. Patients with this condition tend to improve quickly.
6. Short stories usually focus on brief periods of time, as a result, the reader cannot see characters develop as they do in novels.
7. If you follow these instructions and use the map, your trip should take only three hours.

Answers: 1. ; consequently 2. read, Ted 3. correct 4. correct 5. therapy, patients 6. ; as a result 7. correct

---

PROOFREADING EXERCISES: Basic, Intermediate, Challenge

Basic Exercise:
Compound and Complex Sentences

Three of the sentences below are correct; identify them and correct the other four.

1. Whenever Jennifer has a cold. She takes echinacea and vitamin C.
2. Samuel prepared well for the test, so he felt confident.
3. Species adapt differently to changes in climate, therefore some thrive better than others.
4. Too many accidents occurred at the intersection consequently the city installed a traffic light.
5. Because illegal immigrants often work for low wages. Some employers prefer to hire them.
6. The book was difficult to read; hence many students left the assignment incomplete.
7. If the city pays part of the cost, the stadium will probably be built.

Intermediate Exercise: Compound and Complex Sentences

Compose sentences on the following models. Be sure to use correct punctuation.

1. Because the company's network was down, the work schedule had to be revised.
   Your sentence:
   Because _____, _____.
2. Whenever the registration period begins, students hurry to sign up for the best courses.
   Your sentence:
   Whenever _____, _____.
3. If the bill passes in the state senate, the governor will probably veto it.
   Your sentence:
   If _____, _____.
4. A writing section was added to the test; consequently, the tutors changed their methods.
   Your sentence:
   _____; consequently, _____.
5. The first CD sold five million copies; as a result, the company put out a second one immediately.
   Your sentence:
   _____; as a result, _____.

6. Jobs in computer science declined sharply; therefore, fewer students chose that major.
   Your sentence:
   _____; therefore, _____.
7. Elsie grew up among farm animals, so she decided to become a veterinarian.
   Your sentence:
   _____, so _____.

Challenge Exercise: Compound and Complex Sentences

In the paragraph below, find and correct the seven errors in sentence structure.

Many arguments have been put forward to explain the drop in violent crimes in large cities. Because the decline has been steady over a number of years; experts assume there must be identifiable reasons for it. If improved police work has been one of the causes. City mayors should be aware of that fact. However, other causes have been considered, therefore, it is a good idea to recognize the complexities of the problem. The crack epidemic has abated somewhat hence the crimes resulting from it have declined. Furthermore, the population of young men in the cities—at least those not already incarcerated—has dipped steadily as well, this, too, has contributed to the reduction of crime. Some sociologists have also argued that there have been fewer unwanted pregnancies in recent years, particularly among teenage women, as a result, fewer children grow up to be dysfunctional adults. Among all these possible causes, experts cannot reach a consensus on the chief reason why crime has gone down, therefore, they are still doing studies about it.

Key Words from Chapter 13 for Review

coincidence, compound and complex sentences, dependent clause, subordinate conjunctions

Arguing Persuasively

STEPPING UP: WRITING TIP 14

In the media nowadays, many people see and hear commentators who spout dogmatic opinions primarily for audiences who already agree with them. However, effective argumentative writers—political columnists, book reviewers, movie reviewers, sports analysts—are adroit, informed, and flexible. They are persuasive analysts rather than bullies with clubs. Bellowing in a bigoted manner will often silence dissent but not persuade anyone who is open-minded. To improve your persuasive skills, try writing an essay from the other side: make as strong a case as you can for a position with which you disagree. You may learn something in the process, and isn't that what writing is all about?

Writing Persuasively to Convince Your Readers

Writing that explains why the reader should believe or do something is called **persuasive** or **argumentative writing**. In this kind of writing you are trying to reinforce or change someone's opinion. Persuasive writing is everywhere: in political speeches and debates, in newspapers and broadcast news editorials, in lawyers' courtroom speeches, in sales promotions, and in books advocating change in domestic and foreign policies.

Nearly every attempt at persuasion is based on an idea that can be expressed in one thesis statement. The speaker or writer argues that something *should* or *ought* to be done. Persuasive writing frequently uses words such as *should, ought, might, must, have to, could, probably, likely, possibly, certainly,* and *undoubtedly.* Learn to use them correctly in your own essays. Such words measure what the writer thinks should be changed in people's attitudes or actions. These words signal *why* relationships—and they usually end with a call to action.

The essay below takes a position on capital punishment, a topic that has been debated for centuries and continues to provoke us through high-profile criminal cases and changes in the law. Read the essay and answer the questions that follow it.

Student Essay

Why the Death Penalty Is a Bad Idea

MELISSA O'BRIAN

In many states, the death penalty is still practiced, and many voters favor it. In most countries outside the United States, however, it has been ended. Countries that have the death penalty, in fact, cannot be members of the European Union, and Pope John Paul II spoke out against it. Why is it that so many people in this country still favor the death penalty, even though most of the world disagrees? I think it is because many criminals who commit horrible crimes deserve an extreme punishment, and people react emotionally to these crimes, ignoring the reasons why it is wrong for society to practice capital punishment. But the fact remains, the death penalty is wrong in principle as well as in practice.

We all know about crimes that are so cruel and vicious that we want the perpetrators to get what they deserve. And we also read about criminals such as predators of children who get out of jail and repeat their terrible crimes. To some people these examples prove that the death penalty is justified. I agree that it is hard to claim that such wrongdoers do not deserve to die, but the question is, should society try to give them what they deserve out of revenge? Law courts are not intended to take revenge on criminals but to carry out justice. In many cases, we know how awful the crime was, but we often can't be one hundred percent sure that the person convicted is the one who did it. Justice requires that a punishment that cannot be reversed such as the death penalty should never be given to someone when there is even a slight chance that the wrong person has been sentenced.

There have been many cases overturned by using DNA analysis, so we now know that it is possible to execute innocent people—and probably some states already have done so. Many prisoners on death row have been released who were already sentenced for crimes they did not commit. And what about criminals who may have committed the crimes but maybe acted out of self-defense, insanity, or other factors that might deserve some other penalty? And should we execute criminals who can serve society behind bars? When the former gang leader Tookie Williams was executed in California in 2005, many of his supporters believed he had set a good example by writing children's books that warned young people to stay out of gangs. Since then, many other people convicted of murder have been put to death, and many of them may have deserved lesser sentences but did not have effective lawyers. Some may even have been innocent. How many people on death row might be in some of these categories? It is against the principles of a democratic society to execute people under these circumstances where there is any doubt about their crimes or when rehabilitation is possible.

In practice, the death penalty does not work very well. Some juries are biased against groups of people they do not like and apply the death penalty unfairly. It also costs too much to execute criminals. Some people imagine that all society has to do is catch murderers and rapists and execute them right away, but that is not what happens. It takes millions of dollars in court costs and legal fees to convict someone and put them on death row. And after that there are many appeals that can take years and cost much more. It may be true that it costs a lot of money to keep inmates in prison but not as much as the expense of death penalty trials.

One of the main arguments for capital punishment is that it is supposed to make other criminals think twice before they commit murder. But most studies show that there is not much of a connection between states that have the death penalty and a drop in violent crimes. People who commit murder usually do not expect to get caught, or they are so desperate or insane that they do not care whether they are caught. Many people who commit crimes of passion, for instance, kill themselves afterward; obviously the death penalty would not stop them from doing the crime.

People who favor the death penalty should realize that they are reacting out of emotion, not reason and common sense. They want to get back at someone who commits the worst of crimes. They may be right in their feelings, but in principle capital punishment is wrong and uncivilized, and in practice it costs society and taxpayers too much to be worth the emotional satisfaction some people get from it.

1. Identify the thesis statement in this essay.
2. Explain what Melissa is trying to do in her introductory paragraph.
3. Explain what similarities you see between the introductory and concluding paragraphs.
4. How many points does Melissa make against the death penalty? What are they?
5. What counter arguments does she bring up? How does she answer them?
6. Which is her strongest argument? Which is her weakest?
7. How could she strengthen her arguments by doing research?

Example by a Published Author

Is Cloning Wrong?

Lee M. Silver

Some object to cloning because of the process that it entails. The view of the Vatican, in particular, is that human embryos should be treated like human beings and should not be tampered with in any way. However, the cloning protocol does *not* tamper with embryos, it tampers only with *unfertilized* eggs and adult cells like those we scratch off our arms without a second thought. Only after the fact does an embryo emerge (which could be treated with the utmost respect if one so chooses).

There is a sense among some who are religious that cloning leaves God out of the process of human creation, and that man is venturing into places he does not belong. This same concern has been, and will continue to be, raised as each new reprogenetic technology is incorporated into our culture, from in vitro fertilization twenty years ago to genetic engineering of embryos—sure to happen in the near future. It is impossible to counter this theological claim with scientific arguments. . . .

Finally, there are those who argue against cloning based on the perception that it will harm society at large in some way. The *New York Times* columnist William Safire expresses the opinion of many others when he says, "cloning's identicality would restrict evolution." This is bad, he argues, because "the continued interplay of genes . . . is central to humankind's progress." But Mr. Safire is wrong on both practical and theoretical grounds. On practical grounds, even if human cloning became efficient, legal, and popular among those in the moneyed classes (which is itself highly unlikely), it would still only account for a fraction of a percent of all the children born onto this earth. Furthermore, each of the children born by cloning to different families would be different from one another, so where does the identicality come from?

On theoretical grounds, Safire is wrong because humankind's progress has nothing to do with unfettered evolution, which is always unpredictable and not necessarily upward bound. H. G. Wells recognized this principle in his 1895 novel *The Time Machine*, which portrays the natural evolution of humankind into weak and dimwitted, but cuddly little creatures. And Kurt Vonnegut follows this same theme in *Galápagos*, where he suggests that our "big brains" will be the cause of our downfall, and future humans with smaller brains and powerful flippers will be the only remnants of a once great species, a million years hence.

Although most politicians professed outrage at the prospect of human cloning when Dolly [the cloned sheep] was first announced, Senator Tom Harkin of Iowa was the one lone voice in opposition. "What nonsense, what utter nonsense, to think that we can hold up our hands and say, 'Stop,'" Mr. Harkin said. "Human cloning will take place, and it will take place in my lifetime. I don't fear it at all. I welcome it". . . .

Those who want to clone themselves or their children will not be impeded by governmental laws or regulations. The marketplace—not government or society—will control cloning. And if cloning is banned in one place, it will be made available somewhere else—perhaps on an underdeveloped island country happy to receive the tax revenue. Indeed, within two weeks of Dolly's announcement, a group of investors formed a Bahamas-based company called Clonaid (under the direction of a French scientist named Dr. Brigitte Boisselier) with the intention of building a clinic where cloning services would be offered to individuals for a fee of $200,000. According to the description provided on their web page (http://www.clonaid.com), they plan to offer "a fantastic opportunity to parents with fertility problems or homosexual couples to have a child cloned from one of them."

Irrespective of whether this particular venture actually succeeds, others will certainly follow. For in the end, international borders can do little to impede the reproductive practices of couples and individuals.

—Lee M. Silver. From *Remaking Eden: How Genetic Engineering and Cloning Will Transform the American Family.*

1. Define these words, using a dictionary if necessary: *the Vatican, protocol, embryo, reprogenetic, theological, unfettered, impeded.*
2. Is Silver for or against human cloning? Explain.
3. What objections to cloning from religious people does he mention?
4. How does he answer them?
5. What objection does he mention that is based on the good of society? How does he answer it?
6. What authors does he cite to advance his opinion? Why does he include two novelists in an argument about science and technology?
7. In his opinion, what will make it impossible for laws and governments to stop cloning and similar reproductive technology?

Guidelines for Persuasive Writing

When you attempt persuasive writing, keep the following guidelines in mind.

- **Be logical and fair.** Do not **overgeneralize, oversimplify,** or exaggerate. If you level with your readers, they will respect you and are more likely to be persuaded.

- **Support your thesis.** You will not convince anyone if you just keep restating your opinion. Do your homework: give facts, reasons, examples, testimony (other people's opinions), and personal experience to make a strong case.
- **Respect your readers.** They have the right to disagree and are not necessarily stupid or wrong if they do, so do not insult them. Consider the objections they might have to your position and try to answer those objections.

Which statement is more persuasive?

A. Sidney must be on a low-carbohydrate diet because he lost 20 pounds.

B. Low-carbohydrate diets help some people lose weight in a hurry; Sidney told me he lost 20 pounds in three weeks by cutting his carbohydrate intake in half.

Without evidence, Sentence A isn't a logical statement. There are many ways to lose weight. Sentence B is logical and focused, although one example is only support, not proof, of the general statement.

Which statement is more persuasive?

A. *Spider Man* is a great film; it set records at the box office during its first week.

B. *Spider Man* is a great film. The acting of Kirsten Dunst and Tobey Maguire is outstanding, the special effects are thrilling, and the plot has exciting twists.

Sentence A lacks support. Box office sales the first week do not indicate how good a film is, only that it is popular. Sentence B makes a claim, then backs it up with supporting reasons, so it is more persuasive.

Which statement is more persuasive?

A. Although a new sports arena will bring jobs and profits to neighborhood businesses, taxpayers' money would be better spent on improving the public schools.

B. Anyone who supports spending taxpayers' money for a sports stadium is irresponsible and stupid.

Sentence B offers an insult rather than an argument. Sentence A makes a more careful, though debatable, claim and backs it up.

Stressing the Argument, Not the Personalities

The Latin phrase *ad hominem*, meaning "to the person," refers to the gimmick of sidestepping an argument by criticizing the person making it. In political campaigns, this technique unfortunately works far too well, especially when it comes in the form of negative advertising about the opposing candidate's character. Such attacks, however, do nothing to weaken the *arguments* of the candidate, only his or her attractiveness to voters.

In argumentative writing, by contrast, we appeal to the reasonableness and good judgment of the reader, trusting that, in an academic exchange, evidence and logic will win out over personal attacks. Our goal is to guide readers to see the correctness of our position, not to vote for a candidate.

It is true that the way we respond to an argument is often influenced by what we know about the writer. That response, however, has more to do with whether we think the author believes what he or she says than with the validity of the arguments themselves. If reliable evidence shows that capital punishment does (or does not) deter serious crime, it should not matter who presents that evidence. What does matter, however, is how well it is presented—well-presented evidence is tight, clear, and without logical contradictions. A well-reasoned argument, unlike an election campaign, cannot be defeated by a verbal assault on the personality of the writer.

Approaching the Argument from Several Angles

An argumentative (persuasive) essay is different from a mathematical proof. Most argumentative writing involves social issues, political policy, academic questions, or psychological or medical controversies. Such matters are complicated and can be seen from different perspectives and supported with diverse kinds of evidence. Reasoning is crucial in argument, but logic alone is not sufficient to make a persuasive case in controversies over human problems. A debate about capital punishment, for example, may involve legal, sociological, economic, philosophical, and political arguments. If you can combine several of these approaches, you will make a more convincing case than if you rest your case entirely on one approach and ignore others. It helps to do some brainstorming, clustering, or cubing to explore the range of the topic and see it from different perspectives.

Researching and Presenting Supporting Materials

Researching your subject will always improve an argumentative essay. No matter how convinced you may be of the rightness of your opinion, research will probably turn up facts that either strengthen or complicate (or, on occasion, even disprove) your argument. Also, research will make you aware of opposing facts and arguments that you should not ignore. It is not always necessary to bring the **counterargument** into a persuasive essay, but doing so effectively strengthens your own position: Winning against a strong defense is more impressive than sinking baskets on an empty court. If you favor capital punishment, for example, how do you answer religious objections to taking a life? If you oppose capital punishment, how do you respond to the argument that the death penalty is the one sure way to prevent a killer from taking more lives?

When you find material in books, in articles, or on Web sites that helps make your case, be sure to present it properly. Chapter 15 covers how to use MLA procedures for quoting, paraphrasing, and constructing a bibliography. Never present material from a source by pretending that it is yours. If you use language from the source, use quotation marks and cite the source. If you use the facts and ideas but not the language, you still must identify and cite the source. Only general material that can be found in many sources can be presented without an identified source.

When you incorporate facts and arguments from secondary sources, use critical judgment. Statistics, for instance, can be very convincing but also very misleading. Be sure that the statistics you use are reliable and represent the situation authentically. They should be up-to-date, comprehensive enough to be convincing, and significant in what they reveal. If you quote authorities, try to choose ones with relevant credentials and an unbiased viewpoint. If you cite sociological theories or historical trends, avoid overgeneralizations and half-baked opinions. Irresponsible, immature arguments are seldom persuasive to informed readers.

Basic Exercise: Argumentation

Decide which of the two statements in each pair is more convincing and defend your choice.

1. A. The drinking age should be lowered to 16 because all college students drink already.

   B. The drinking age should be lowered to 16 because the chief harm isn't from drinking itself but from drunken driving and binge drinking by a small percentage of teenagers.

2. A. All use of text messaging, cell phones, iPads, and other electronic devices should be strictly prohibited from college classrooms because they distract from learning.

   B. Some forms of technology, such as iPads and text messaging, can be used to enhance learning in the classroom if done the right way.

3. A. Professional athletes should not be allowed to strike because they are not worth the money they are paid.

   B. Professional athletes should use strikes as a very last resort because strikes can shut down a whole season and harm the sport for years to come.

4. A. Young adults should never use medications such as antidepressants or birth control pills because these medications sometimes have side effects.

   B. Young adults should consult a doctor before using medications that have possible side effects.

5. A. Penny's instructor graded her unfairly because she received a B while two other students with the same grades on their papers and exams received As.

   B. Penny's instructor graded her unfairly because she received a B even though she was never absent or late.

6. A. Weight Losers must be a better program than Scale Down because Hector used Weight Losers and lost five pounds while Donald used Scale Down and gained three.

   B. Weight Losers seems to be a more effective program than Scale Down because three studies show that 60% of Weight Losers members lost at least 10 pounds and kept the weight off for two years, whereas only 10% of Scale Down members lost any weight after two years.

7. A. You can tell that the defendant is guilty because he looked shifty-eyed and nervous when he was interviewed on television.
   B. The defendant is probably guilty because he has no alibi, the gun was found in his possession, and samples of his DNA were found at the scene of the crime.

Intermediate Exercise: Argumentation

Read the following passage and answer the questions that follow it.

There are good reasons to oppose mandatory testing for drugs at the workplace and in schools. For one thing, it would violate the rights of citizens, because the Fourth Amendment to the U.S. Constitution protects people against "unreasonable searches and seizures." In places of employment, it would be an invasion of privacy for workers to be forced to take drug tests, and in educational institutions it would create a frightening atmosphere for students who should have a positive, trusting attitude toward their schools. Furthermore, testing is not foolproof and could create false accusations against workers or students, who in some cases could sue companies and school systems for millions of dollars. The cost of administering reliable drug tests would be exorbitant to begin with. In addition, the argument that drug use is widespread and is causing harm to businesses and schools is not entirely adequate, since there are many other patterns of behavior, including petty crime, abuse of legal substances, bullying, and sexual harassment that occur. For these equally harmful practices no one is proposing that all workers and students, most of whom are innocent of such behavior, must be tested or investigated in some way because of the bad actions of a few.

1. Identify an example of citing an authority in this passage.
2. Identify an example of an argument discussing consequences of the proposed action.
3. Identify an argument made by the opposing side that this writer rebuts.
4. Explain an economic argument used in this passage.
5. Explain which argument you find to be strongest and which you find to be weakest.
6. Explain what kind of personal example could be used to support the argument made in this passage.
7. State an argument that you think would further strengthen this passage.

Challenge Exercise: Argumentation

Write responses to the following directives.

1. Give two arguments in favor of capital punishment and two against it.
2. Give one economic reason and one medical reason for (or against) legalizing marijuana.
3. Explain what kind of statistics would be useful in supporting or opposing the construction of a large sports stadium in your city or town.
4. Explain what kinds of experts could be quoted to support or oppose legal abortion.
5. Identify which part or parts of the U.S. Constitution are relevant to an argument for or against holding suspected terrorists without trial.
6. Identify what examples you might use to argue for or against changing the method of voting in United States elections.
7. Describe a personal experience of your own you might use to support or oppose increased testing of school children throughout the United States.

Essay Topics: Argumentation

Write an essay in which you agree or disagree with one of the following statements. Base your argument not only on your own analysis and opinions but also on support from material found on the Web and in the library. Narrow the topic if necessary.

1. The threat of terrorism requires Americans to give up some of our civil liberties.
2. Social networks such as Facebook are having a beneficial effect on young people's lives.
3. Nationwide testing is having a beneficial effect on American education.
4. Films based on novels are usually not as good as the books.
5. Marriage should be redefined to include gay couples.
6. Home schooling is providing better education than public schools.
7. The use of performance-enhancing substances should be made legal in sports.

PEER REVIEW QUESTIONS: ARGUMENTATION

1. In your essay, you are trying to convince me that:
2. Your introduction is interesting. ☐ Yes ☐ No
   Your introduction makes the purpose of your essay clear. ☐ Yes ☐ No
   The sentence that most nearly expresses your main point is the following:
3. You offer the following supporting arguments to back up your main point:
4. Your method of argument seems fair, logical, and persuasive, and you use more than one way to support your point. ☐ Yes ☐ No
5. Your conclusion (is/is not) effective for the following reason:
6. What I like best about your essay is the following:
7. I recommend you make the following changes:

Proofreading Practice: Sentence Combining

Argumentative or persuasive writing often requires you to construct complicated sentences. To improve your sentence-forming skills, practice **sentence combining**. To develop variety in the kinds of sentences you write, practice combining shorter statements into more complex sentences. You can combine short elements of sentences in various ways. For example, we can combine the following basic sentences in several ways.

Rosa woke up.
She got out of bed.

She got dressed quickly.
She ate breakfast.
She left for work.

One way is to write this as a single sentence:

After waking up and getting out of bed, Rosa got dressed quickly, ate breakfast, and left for work.

Here is another:

Rosa woke up, got out of bed and dressed quickly; then she ate breakfast and left for work.

And a third:

Rosa, after waking up, got out of bed, dressed quickly, and ate breakfast; then she left for work.

Can you think of another way?

After you have written a complete draft of any essay, but especially an argumentative essay, revise some of your sentences to avoid monotonous repetition of patterns. If one sentence after another follows the subject-verb-object pattern, try varying the beginnings of your sentences as well as their overall structure.

TEST YOURSELF: Sentence Combining

Combine the following basic sentence elements into no more than two well-shaped sentences. Do the exercise in two different ways.

1. Helen lost her watch.
2. She looked for it in the car.
3. She looked for it in her purse.
4. She looked for it in her apartment.
5. She finally gave up looking.
6. She bought a new watch.
7. Then she found the old one in her desk.

Answers: (two possibilities; try your own): 1. Helen lost her watch and looked for it in the car, in her purse, and in her apartment. Finally, she gave up looking and bought a new watch; then she found the old one in her desk. 2. Having lost her watch, Helen looked for it in the car, in her purse, and in her apartment. After giving up looking, she bought a new watch, only to find the old one in her desk.

Basic Exercise: Sentence Combining

Combine the following basic sentence elements into no more than two well-shaped sentences. Try to do the exercise in two different ways.

1. Rafael wanted a job.
2. The job would be in sales.
3. He looked in the want ads.
4. He stopped at the placement office.
5. He did a Web search.
6. He found six openings.
7. He applied for two of them.

Intermediate Exercise: Sentence Combining

Combine the following basic sentence elements into no more than two well-shaped sentences. Try to do the exercise in two different ways.

1. The first year of college is exciting.
2. It forces you to schedule your time.
3. You meet new classmates.
4. You try new activities.
5. You explore new subjects.
6. You make major decisions.
7. It causes you to become a new person.

Challenge Exercise: Sentence Combining

Combine the following basic sentence elements into no more than two well-shaped sentences. Try to do the exercise in two different ways.

1. Learning a new language requires patience.
2. It takes time.
3. You learn new grammatical concepts.
4. You learn new kinds of pronunciation.
5. You acquire aspects of a different culture.
6. It improves your memory.
7. It also helps you to understand English.

Key Words from Chapter 14 for Review

ad hominem argument, counterargument, overgeneralizing, oversimplifying, persuasive writing, sentence combining

Writing a Research Paper

STEPPING UP: WRITING TIP 15

When you have an assignment to write a research paper, avoid saying to yourself, "I'll do that later." Students who achieve success in writing research papers develop a plan and work through each step carefully as they progress. If you find a useful fact or quotation, keep a record of the complete information—Web site, author, title, and page numbers. Trying to find a source or a particular piece of information after you have accessed it a first time will increase your work enormously. If you are permitted to choose your own topic, make your choice early (some prewriting work will help) and leave time for your research and revision. Advancing from a handwritten draft to the keyboard is much more complicated with a research paper than with other essays. Although using MLA or APA format is not particularly difficult, the technical details of these styles require careful attention and usually extensive revision. Do every step carefully, and you'll save yourself much time and effort in the long run.

Choosing a Topic

In some classes, your research topic may be assigned, but if you are allowed to choose, select a topic that is of interest to you and that is specific enough that you can do meaningful research on it. Instead of it being a heavy chore, your research project will become an exciting piece of detective work. Choosing a subject you really want to research might mean focusing on a personal matter that affects your life, such as a career that you intend to pursue or a problem you have encountered. It might also mean investigating a famous person or historical event you have read about and in which you have a special interest.

However, personal interest is only one aspect to consider when choosing a topic. You should also be realistic and choose a topic that will not require far more time and difficult research than you can manage in the time you have available. A topic suitable for a master's thesis would be too demanding for a research essay in most undergraduate courses, certainly for a short paper in a composition course. If you have any doubts about whether a topic you are considering would be appropriate for the research task you have undetaken, be sure to discuss your concerns with your instructor *before* you do a lot of reading and writing.

Making Sense of Sources

Writing about academic subjects often requires you to do research using library and Internet sources and to make intelligent and correct use of material from books, articles, and Web sites. Your professors will tell you whether they want an assignment to be entirely your own analysis and opinions or whether they want you to use researched information to augment your views. Essays about literature, for example, are done both ways. Often instructors want students to do as much of their own thinking about a play, poem, or story as possible and prefer that they not use secondary sources. Some papers on literature, however, are greatly enriched by the use of biographical, historical, and critical sources; therefore, in advanced courses, professors may assign topics requiring research.

Using Sources Effectively

Planning and organizing an essay using research materials is similar in many ways to writing a persuasive essay without research. As in any effective essay, your examples should support your main idea. In a research essay, your examples will be quotations, facts, and summarized or paraphrased passages from articles, books, and Web sources. When you select these secondary materials, be sure they not only are interesting but also lend support to your main point. Sometimes you will be tempted to include interesting material that wanders away from your point. For example, if you are trying to prove that capital punishment does not reduce crime, you may find articles discussing different methods of execution, all of which are interesting but not related to your point. You should resist the temptation to include such irrelevant facts even if you find them fascinating. As in any persuasive essay, stick closely to your main argument.

Being Aware of the Different Research Formats

To use researched material effectively, find out about the different formats for research papers in different disciplines. The two most common are Modern Language Association **(MLA) format,** used in the humanities, and American Psychological Association **(APA) format**, used in the social sciences. The Modern Language Association's style book is the *MLA Handbook for Writers of Research Papers, Seventh Edition;* information about MLA format also can be found at the MLA's Web site, www.mla.org, or at university Web sites such as the Purdue University OWL (Online Writing Lab) site, http://owl .english.purdue.edu/handouts/research/r_mla.html. The American Psychological Association's style guide is titled the *Publication Manual of the American Psychological Association, Sixth Edition;* you can get online information about this format from the APA's site at www .apastyle.org/ or the Purdue OWL APA site at htttp://owl.english .purdue.edu/handouts/research/r_apa.html.

One note of caution about borrowing information from sources: Do not hide behind material someone else has written. If you are good at finding interesting material on the Web or in the library, you will be tempted to just download it and dump it on the page. But that will not produce an interesting paper, at least not a cohesive one. Imagine yourself as a courtroom attorney presenting a case. Your source material is your evidence—the facts and testimony that support the conclusion you want your "jury," the readers, to reach. It is your case to win or lose; the factual evidence and what your witnesses say are crucial, but you are the lawyer directing the case. You have the first and last word.

Learning to Paraphrase, Summarize, and Quote Sources

Paraphrasing

Familiarize yourself with the three chief ways of presenting source material: **paraphrasing**, **summarizing**, and **quoting**. Paraphrasing a passage from an article or book means restating *in your own words* what the passage says. Summarizing means stating in shorter form the main facts and ideas of the original text, again using your own words. *In your own words* means *entirely* in your own words, not a few of your own words, then seven or eight words from the article, then a few more of yours, and so on. You may have to practice to be able to paraphrase without using the author's own words and without changing the meaning. Here is an example of a paraphrased passage.

Original

Of the numerous achievements that distinguish Richard Wright's place in the history of American literature, perhaps none is more important than the fact that he was the first African-American writer to sustain himself professionally from his writings alone.

—Henry Louis Gates, Jr. From *Richard Wright: Critical Perspectives Past and Present.*

Paraphrase

According to Henry Louis Gates, Jr., one memorable fact about Richard Wright is that he made enough money just by his writing to support himself, and that he became the first African-American author to do so (xi).

Notice that the paraphrased passage says essentially the same thing as the original *but uses entirely different words.*

Why do you need to paraphrase? When writing research papers in some disciplines, especially the social sciences, you will use many kinds of sources written in many styles. Using too many varied quotations might drown out your own voice. And, quoting too many passages word for word can be boring, especially when all you need is some of the facts presented in them.

Summarizing

Summarizing allows you to shorten the source material so that you can reduce several pages' worth of source material into a paragraph or several paragraphs into a few sentences. When you paraphrase, you convert a short passage from the book or article into your own words. When you summarize, you condense a larger amount of factual material into a shorter passage that is entirely in your own words. In the process of shortening the material, however, be sure not to oversimplify or distort what the author is saying.

Here is an example of a summary:

Original

The best college and university teachers create what we might call a natural critical learning environment in which they embed the skills and information they wish to teach in assignments (questions and tasks) students will find fascinating—authentic tasks that will arouse curiosity, challenging students to rethink their assumptions and examine their mental models of reality. They create a safe environment in which students can try, come up short, receive feedback, and try again. Students understand and remember what they have learned because they master and use the reasoning abilities necessary to integrate it with larger concepts. They become aware of the implications and applications of the ideas and information.

—Ken Bain. From *What the Best College Teachers Do* (Cambridge, Mass.: Harvard University Press 2004): 47.

Summary

Ken Bain writes that the most successful professors create a classroom environment where students engage in interesting work that challenges their assumptions and where they feel safe to experiment, fail, and try again. The knowledge they acquire that way stays with them because they can relate it to larger contexts (47).

Quoting: The Long and Short of It

Everyone knows how to quote short statements: Put the words in quotation marks. Here is an example of a short quotation (whole sentence):

> One critic writes, "This story should have ended before the last paragraph" (Smith 117).

Be sure to introduce quotations as this example does, with a comma before the quotation, and be sure to close the quotation at the end. Then cite the last name of the author of the source from which you borrowed the quoted matter and the page number on which the quotation is found in parentheses, followed by a period.

Sometimes you might include only a phrase from a sentence in your source. Here is an example:

> One critic argues that the author should have "ended before the last paragraph" (Smith 117).

Notice that the phrase fits into the sentence smoothly and grammatically, with no comma before it or capital letter at the beginning of it. However, the source is still cited the same way at the end.

Parenthetical Citation

You must end each direct quotation, summary, or paraphrased passage in the body of your paper—which is called your *text*—with a set of parentheses enclosing the author's name and a page number. When citing Web sites in text, you may not have an author's name, or there may be no pages. When no author is listed for a Web source, which is common, you may instead list a shortened form of the title in quotation marks. Keep in mind that for in-text citations you do not need to cite the author's name if you have mentioned it in the text before the quotation, paraphrase, or summary.

Common Mistakes in Short Quotations

Probably the most common error in presenting short quotations is forgetting to close the quotation with a second set of quotation marks. Another is to begin a quote without introducing it with a phrase such as "One critic writes . . ." or "Smith argues . . ." or "According to Taylor . . ." Always introduce your quotations: Without this lead-in to the quotation, sometimes called an *attributive tag* or *signal phrase*, the reader is left wondering whom or what sort of person you are quoting. Still another common error is the failure to use the correct method of **parenthetical citation**. Notice that *the period comes after the final parenthesis*, and nothing but the author's last name and page number is put inside the parentheses.

Long quotations, that is, quotations of five lines or more, are set off from the rest of the text and are not set in quotation marks. After introducing the quotation (using a colon), indent the entire left margin of the quotation 10 spaces (indent twice as far as the normal indentation at the beginning of a paragraph). Place the period at the end of the quotation, then a space, and then the parenthetical citation. The following example shows how a long quotation can be effectively incorporated into a writer's text.

One well-known critic praises Richard Wright's work as follows:

> *Of the numerous achievements that distinguish Richard Wright's place in the history of American literature, perhaps none is more important than the fact that he was the first African-American writer to sustain himself professionally from his writings alone. Primarily through the success of* Native Son *and* Black Boy, *Wright was able to support, for two decades, a comfortable life for himself and his family in Paris. (Gates xi)*

Common Mistakes in Long Quotations

A very common mistake made with long quotes is using quotation marks. Another is not separating the parenthetical citation from the end of the quotation. A third common mistake is not indenting 10 spaces from the left margin (the right margin should be at the normal setting).

Using the Library and Internet

The Internet and the library are not totally separate sources of research material. In fact, a very large part of what is found in libraries is available *somewhere* on the Web—if you can find it. In coming years, more and more of the vast stores of printed material in libraries will be available in databases, so that, according to some, libraries with paper copies of material will become increasingly obsolete as research centers will be transformed into centers used primarily for accessing electronic materials.

But for older materials, especially those on topics that have been written about for 50 years or more, that day is still a long way off. For that reason, if you are researching a paper in a course involving historical materials, expect to use a university library or another substantial library. Although many articles are available online, you may not be able to access full-text electronic copies of books. In addition, when you find a section of the library devoted to books on your topic, you may enjoy looking through what could be several shelves of volumes devoted to your subject. This experience is a bit like scrolling through several screens of Web links on your subject, but can be richer and more substantial. For example, look at the library stacks in the section on Shakespeare, the Bible, Mark Twain, or the Civil War. You will find a multitude of outstanding sources that have maintained their relevance over time and that may not be available online.

Searching the Web and using a library are both similar and different. Both require persistence and patience, as well as know-how. Libraries have their own computerized catalog of holdings grouped by author, title, and subject. Once you identify them, you have to go get them in the stacks or have the librarian get them for you. Web sites, of course, require searches by author, keyword, or title. They have the advantage of not being physically removable by a single user, like books that are checked out; on the other hand, Web sites can be unavailable for a variety of reasons, and some of them frequently change addresses and content. Books and articles can be photocopied, whereas Web materials can be downloaded or printed for your immediate use.

Analyzing Source Material; Evaluating Web Sites

Know the difference between electronic versions of printed materials collected in online databases and independently created Web pages. Many Web sources exist in large electronic collections that amount to online libraries containing newspapers, magazines, and journal articles from printed sources. These online collections, often called *full-text databases*, may be available to you through your college library or city library. If they are, you can rely on them the way you would print materials from the library. Material from independent Web sites, however, must be evaluated differently.

When looking for sources on the Internet, bear in mind a few general guidelines.

■ Check the source of Web pages: Is there an author or institutional sponsor? If an author, does that person mention qualifications or credentials? Can you contact that person? If an institution, is it qualified to give information on this subject, and does it have its own Web site? To check the source, read the Web address and look for a tilde sign (~) with a personal name after it. That indicates a personal Web site. If the domain of the URL is .com, it is a commercial site; if the domain is .gov, it is a government site. Other domains are .edu, for colleges and schools, and .org, for nonprofit organizations. Foreign countries also have their own domains, such as .uk for United Kingdom and .de for Germany (Deutschland). Such information will help you determine how valuable and reliable the material is.

■ Assess the purpose of the Web page. Is it trying to sell you something, persuading you to support a cause or contribute money, or merely supplying information?

■ Is the Web page up-to-date? Having current information is important for some topics, such as foreign policy, health issues (e.g., AIDS and flu immunization), and government programs. A page on AIDS that was set up in 1992 and never updated would be far less useful than a page that was updated last year.

■ Try to detect bias in the information you are accessing. Many Web pages pretend to give you nothing but the facts but actually have a strong prejudice. Check facts against other sources to see whether any of them are in error or whether important facts have been left out. Remember that many Web pages have not been scrutinized and approved by authoritative experts or groups. Check to see whether links are mentioned on the site and whether the links are still accessible. Do they also seem reliable and unbiased?

■ Look at sites that can help you become an experienced evaluator of Internet sites, such as the following:

www.lib.berkeley.edu/TeachingLib/Guides/Internet/Evaluate
.html
http://guides.library.jhu.edu/evaluatinginformationhttp://lib
.nmsu.edu/instruction/evalcrit.html
www.library.cornell.edu/olinuris/ref/research/webcrit.html

Avoiding Plagiarism

Plagiarism means using the words, ideas, music, or art (what the legal profession refers to as **intellectual property**) of someone else as your own. In writing a research paper you'll make use of many sources, and you must present and identify any material you borrow as belonging to someone else, using the correct form for doing so. If you do not cite your sources appropriately, whether you summarize, paraphrase, or quote directly, you can be charged with plagiarism even if you do not plagiarize on purpose. When you cut and paste materials from Internet sites, for instance, it is easy to put them into your paper without identifying them correctly, in which case you are plagiarizing just as much as if you deliberately stole the material and tried to pass it off as your own.

Remember that all material in your essay that you borrow from a source must be documented. This means, as discussed earlier, that quotations of fewer than five lines must be put in quotation marks and followed by a set of parentheses containing the author's last name and page number. Again, long quotations do not require quotation marks but must be indented 10 spaces and also be followed by parentheses containing the source citation. Paraphrased material—that is, facts and ideas from a source put into your own words—must also be followed by a set of parentheses with the author and page.

Is there anything in your research paper that does not require **documentation** (a source reference in parentheses)? Yes: Any parts of the paper that express your own opinions, conclusions, or analysis will not need a source reference because *you* are the source. Also, information that is so general it can be found in many sources—such as when the Civil War ended, where the World's Fair took place in 1964, or how many plays Shakespeare wrote—need not be documented. If you are in doubt about facts that seem rather general but more specific than these examples, cite your source. It is better to overdo your source documentation than commit plagiarism.

Writing a Bibliography

These carefully noted in-text references are meaningless, however, unless you list the works—each book, article, and Internet source—from which they were taken. This list of works cited is called a **bibliography** (or *reference list*), and it's a crucial component of your research paper.

The works cited list should be on a separate page (or separate pages, if your list is lengthy) at the end of your paper, and the entries must be in alphabetical order so that any reader who wants to find the source that you cite can easily locate it. The word that appears in parentheses after your documented material must be the first word in an alphabetized entry in your list of works cited.

Research papers in the various disciplines follow particular bibliographic formats. As mentioned earlier in this chapter, two of the most common formats used at the college level are MLA and APA. The sample paper presented here uses MLA format.

Ultimately, the organization, presentation of material, and development of ideas in your paper are more important than the technicalities of form. Nonetheless, whether you are using MLA or APA format, you are expected to use it correctly. You do not need to memorize all the rules of these formats, but consult the appropriate handbook or Web site, listed at the beginning of the chapter, to ensure that you understand the rules and apply them without error.

Sample Research Paper in MLA Format

Read the research paper below and notice how the writer makes use of her sources, presenting them according to MLA guidelines. Notice, too, how she has narrowed her topic: Starting with the general subject of police informants, which includes their use in fighting organized crime, infiltrating political groups, combating terrorism, coping with gang violence, and reducing street crime, she has concentrated on the specific problem of "snitching" as an issue among young people in urban neighborhoods.

```
Justine Williams
Professor Lee
English 101
November 15, 2011


      Snitching: An Aid to Law Enforcement or a Menace?

     Among young people in many urban neighbor-
hoods, one of the worst labels that can be applied
to someone is "snitch." What is a snitch, and why
is there so much controversy about snitching? If
```

we look into what has been written on the subject, we find that the use of police informants, or snitches, is very common, and it often speeds up the arrest and conviction of criminals. However, no young adult in an urban neighborhood wants to be accused of being a snitch. For one thing, it may make him or her a target of violence, and for another, it makes him or her seem disloyal to peers. To understand the phenomenon of snitching, why it exists and whether anything should be done to change how it is being used in criminal cases, we need to look at some of the research that has been done on the subject.

As Alexandra Natapoff writes in a book called *Snitching: Criminal Informants and the Erosion of American Justice*, the use of snitches is common everywhere:

> Although it rarely comes to light, criminal informant use is everywhere in the American legal system. From warrants to surveillance to arrests, police routinely rely on criminal suspects to get information and to shape investigations. From charging decisions all the way through sentencing, prosecutors negotiate with defendants for cooperation in exchange for dropped or reduced charges and lighter punishment. Especially in the expansive arena of drug enforcement, turning suspects into so-called snitches has become a central feature of the way America manages crime, while the secretive practice of trading lenience for information quietly shapes major aspects of our penal process.(1)

Sociologists have noted how a climate of fear has made it difficult for the justice system to function properly (Simon 6). In large cities, along with the fear and distrust of the police, there is also a fear of gang violence against anyone who reports a crime. In the age of the Internet, informants can now be identified on Web sites such as Whosarat.com. The fear of being harassed or attacked increases as information becomes more accessible. This is both good, in cases where legitimate witnesses can be found to aid prosecution, and bad, when criminals want to frighten or attack witnesses. In many urban neighborhoods, the problem is two-sided. On one hand, the contempt for snitching has become so intense that many young people are afraid to provide legitimate information about any act of crime or violence they see. On the other hand, the justice system relies so heavily on the use of informants that it would be very difficult to reduce crime without the use of "snitches" (Thornburgh). The problem is made worse by the fact that many informants, especially those who have committed crimes and are promised lighter sentences in return for providing information, are often unreliable. In addition, their use has caused increased violence and led to false convictions, thus animosity toward anyone who provides information to the police. In neighborhoods where gangs are active, people who witness crimes or even accidents may be fearful of gang retaliation if they offer information of any kind to the authorities. In fact, gangs have been known to attack and kill people whom the police have turned into informants.

The problems caused by snitching affect minority communities disproportionately. Police informants are used frequently in cases involving drug arrests and gang activity in urban neighborhoods with a high percentage of Black and Latino populations. The violence, false arrests, and intimidation connected with the widespread use of informants thus affects nonwhite and working class people more than others and increases the hostility to police and distrust of the justice system which already exists in many of those neighborhoods. Furthermore, people begin to distrust one another, sometimes even within families. Students in school are intimidated into never speaking up when any wrongdoing occurs, and the social fabric of communities begins to unravel, despite the recent efforts in some communities to combat the kind of bullying that makes young people afraid to report any wrongdoings (Rivera). In summing up the social problems caused by the overuse of police informants, one writer states, "The potential implications of informant use for socially disadvantaged, crime-ridden communities are formidable: more snitches, more crime, more violence, more police-community dysfunction, and more distrust" (Natapoff 118).

Controversial "Stop Snitching" campaigns have occurred in several cities involving T shirts, DVDs, and rap stars refusing to "rat" on people who committed acts of violence. Rap artist Lil' Kim was sentenced to prison for lying about a shooting, and the anti-snitching movement received major coverage on television. NBA superstar Carmelo Anthony appeared in a "Stop Snitching" DVD made in Baltimore in 2006, and, even though he later expressed doubts about the "stop snitching" idea, in an ESPN interview he later stated, "I would never testify on anything. That's just the street code. If you snitch, you're talking about someone's life" (qtd. in Natapoff 127).

Unfortunately, "Stop snitching" as a motto did not distinguish clearly for many young people in urban neighborhoods the difference between legitimate testimony by bystanders who witness shootings and other crimes and the kind of police informants who often give information, sometimes false, to allow them to continue selling drugs or receive reduced sentences to crimes they have committed. Thus the overuse and misuse of police informants has made worse the problem that has long existed in many cities: the failure of people to help one another in emergencies and to report problems to the police or fire departments. This problem has plagued cities for several generations. As far back as the 1960s, there have been reports of accidents or crimes that were not prevented or prosecuted effectively because people were afraid to serve as witnesses. A famous case in 1964 involved the murder of a young woman named Catherine "Kitty" Genovese in the borough of Queens in New York City, in which thirty-eight residents witnessed a murder but no one even called the police (Gansberg). When the all-too-familiar tendency to avoid getting involved is increased by a fear of snitching, fighting crime becomes more difficult than ever. In 2009, the difficulty of controlling the violence in Baltimore became so bad that Mayor Sheila Dixon declared that she was "fed up" with the "stop snitching code of silence" that once was limited to gang members but had begun to affect "everyday citizens—grandmothers, girlfriends, children." "Our communities," she said, have to respect themselves first to demand respect" (qtd. in Fenton).

In addition to the unwillingness to risk the possibility of endangering one's own life or that of relatives or friends, snitching for some Americans, African-Americans in particular, carries with it strong historical associations. Because the police and the FBI have used informants for generations to spy on political activists, dissenters, ethnic power groups, and almost any organization suspected of threatening established authority, hostility to informers has been passed along for years within many urban communities. As recently as 2011, evidence emerged that one of the most respected civil rights workers, the famous photographer Ernest Withers, may have been an FBI informant (Mirkinson). Such revelations make it difficult for authorities to overcome the distrust they face within urban communities. However, it is possible for community leaders and the police to join forces in combating both crime and police misconduct. In 2010, for example Reverend Al Sharpton and Police Commissioner Raymond Kelly spoke out together against the lack of gun control in New York City (Zraick).

It is impossible and perhaps undesirable to eliminate all use of police and government informants, since their service is in such heavy demand and makes possible the conviction of hardcore criminals and mobsters in some cases. On the other hand, "snitching" will continue to carry a bad name until measures are taken to correct the misuse of informants who are tempted or coerced into providing false information that often leads to convictions of innocent persons. The public, especially in urban communities, needs to understand the difference between such "snitches" and those who supply eye-witness accounts of accidents and crimes.

Works Cited

Fenton, Justin. "Man Charged in Fatal Shooting: Police Explore Ties to Shooting of 12 Last Weekend." *Baltimore Sun*. Baltimore Sun, 1 Aug. 2009. Web. 18 Feb. 2011.

Gansberg, Martin. "Thirty-Eight Who Saw the Murder Didn't Call the Police." *New York Times* March 27, 1964.

Mirkinson, Jack. "Soledad O'Brien's 'Pictures Don't Lie' Looks at Civil Rights Photographer Ernest Withers' FBI Files." *Huffington Post*. 19 Feb. 2011. Web. 20 Feb. 2011.

Natapoff, Alexandra. *Snitching: Criminal Informants and the Erosion of American Justice*. New York and London: New York University Press, 2009. Print.

Rivera, Carla. "L.A. School Devotes a Day to the Battle Against Bullying." *L.A.Times*. L.A. Times, 9 Feb. 2011. Web. 18 Feb. 2011.

Simon, Jonathan. *Governing through Crime: How the War on Crime Transformed American Democracy and Created a Culture of Fear*. New York: Oxford University Press, 2007. Print.

Thornburgh, Nathan. "Crime: Looking for a Few Good Snitches." *Time, in Partnership with CNN*. Time, 19 Feb. 2006. Web. 18 Feb. 2011.

Zraick, Karen. "Sharpton and Kelly Are One Against Guns." *New York Times*. New York Times, 19 Nov. 2010. Web. 19 Feb. 2011.

Research Paper Checklist

Before submitting your paper, be sure you can answer "yes" to each of the following questions.

☐ Is your entire paper double-spaced, with no single-spacing or extra spacing between paragraphs?

- [ ] Is your thesis stated clearly near the beginning of your paper?
- [ ] Did you make transitions between paragraphs, especially between major parts of your paper?
- [ ] Are your long quotations at least five lines and indented ten spaces with proper parenthetical documentation at the end? Are all of your short quotations in quotation marks and do they all have parenthetical documentation after them?
- [ ] Is your paraphrased or summarized material entirely in your own words but true to the meaning and facts of the sources?
- [ ] Does every parenthetical citation begin with an author's last name or short title? Is each name (or title) followed, when possible, by a page number? Does that same name or title appear in the appropriate alphabetical position in your bibliography?
- [ ] Does your bibliography have the heading Works Cited, and are the entries double-spaced and in alphabetical order?

WRITING EXERCISES: Basic, Intermediate, Challenge

Basic Exercise: Writing with Sources

Complete this true/false quiz.

- [ ] true [ ] false   1. A short quotation must always be enclosed in quotation marks.
- [ ] true [ ] false   2. A paraphrased passage should not be followed by a source reference in parentheses.
- [ ] true [ ] false   3. APA stands for Association of Political Activists and is the name for a research form used only for political research.
- [ ] true [ ] false   4. A quotation of five lines or more should be indented ten spaces.
- [ ] true [ ] false   5. The entries in a Works Cited page should be in alphabetical order.
- [ ] true [ ] false   6. MLA and APA forms are the same for bibliographies.
- [ ] true [ ] false   7. Plagiarism is acceptable with sources that are not covered by copyright laws.

Intermediate Exercise: Writing with Sources

Read the following passage and complete the exercises that follow it.

How shall we know the past, and how date it? What aids to our vision will help us peer into theatres of ancient life and reconstruct the scenes and the players, their exits and their entrances, of long ago? Conventional human history has three main methods, and we shall find their counterparts on the larger timescale of evolution. First there is archaeology, the study of bones, arrowheads, fragments of pots, oystershell middens, figurines and other relics that survive as hard evidence from the past. In evolutionary history, the most obvious hard relics are bones and teeth, and the fossils that they eventually become. Second, there are *renewed relics*, records that are not themselves old but which contain or embody a copy or representation of what is old. In human history these are written or spoken accounts, handed down, repeated, reprinted or otherwise duplicated from the past to the present. In evolution, I shall propose DNA as the main renewed relic, equivalent to a written and recopied record. Third, there is *triangulation*. This name comes from a method of judging distances by measuring angles. Take a bearing on a target. Now walk a measured distance sideways and take another. From the intercept of the two angles, calculate the distance of the target. Some camera rangefinders use the principle, and map surveyors traditionally relied upon it. Evolutionists can be said to "triangulate" an ancestor by comparing two (or more) of its surviving descendants. I shall take the three kinds of evidence in order, beginning with hard relics and, in particular, fossils.

–Richard Dawkins. From *The Ancestor's Tale*
(New York: Houghton Mifflin, 2004): 12.

1. Identify three terms Dawkins uses to explain methods used to study the past.
2. Paraphrase his explanation of one of these methods, using only your own wording.
3. Write a sentence in which you quote a whole sentence from the passage in which he explains this method.
4. Write a sentence in which you quote a three- or four-word phrase from anywhere in this passage.
5. Imagine you are writing a research paper in which you use at least five lines from this passage in a long quotation. Write an introduction using an attribution tag (signal phrase) and set up the quotation in proper MLA format.

6. Imagine you are writing a research paper in which you summarize this entire paragraph in only three or four lines. Write this summarized passage with proper MLA citation.
7. Write a bibliography entry for Dawkins's book using proper MLA format.

Challenge Exercise: Writing with Sources

Using a page from a textbook in your field of study, respond to the following directives.

1. Summarize the page using only your own words but accurately conveying the main ideas of the source. Use a correct parenthetical citation at the end of your paraphrase.
2. Write a sentence in which you present information from the text, being careful not to quote directly. Use correct parenthetical citation at the end of your sentence.
3. Set up a long quotation of at least five lines from this page, introducing the quotation properly and using correct MLA form for a long indented quotation followed by parenthetical citation.
4. Write a sentence in which you quote a whole statement from the book, using correct MLA format for a short quotation: quotation marks and parenthetical citation afterward.
5. Write a sentence using a three- or four-word phrase from the book, using correct parenthetical citation.
6. Write a sentence in which you agree or disagree with an idea stated in the book, being sure to either paraphrase or quote the opinion stated in the book and separate it clearly from your own statement of your opinion.
7. Write a correct bibliographic entry for the book to which you have been referring.

Essay Topics: Writing with Sources

1. Research the day you were born. Find newspapers from that day and learn what was happening in the world. Identify one issue of the time and write a short essay about it.
2. Choose a film based on an actual historical event. Watch the DVD of the film and do research to find out how accurately the film presents the historical facts. Or choose a film based on the life of a real person. Watch the DVD of the film and do research to find out how accurately the film presents the biographical facts.
3. Research the controversy over voting machines. How reliable are ATM voting machines, and what problems might arise from

using them? Are other methods more useful? Should online voting from home computers be allowed?

4. Research the requirements for a career in which you are interested. Find out exactly what educational qualifications and skills you will need to acquire and what demands are placed on persons in this profession. Explore current controversies regarding the training for people in this field.

5. Research an important event that your family or ancestors were involved in—an immigration movement, a war, a great storm or earthquake, an accident, the building of a famous structure, an event in the Civil Rights Movement, or the overthrow of a government. Try to determine how your family's experience has affected your perspectives on the event.

6. Choose a story or poem assigned in your class and read two or three more works by the same author. Look up comments by critics on these works and gather information about the author's life. Write a paper exploring a common theme in these works. (See Chapter 16 for more on writing about literature.)

7. Explore the controversies surrounding a historical event such as the assassination of President Kennedy, the attack on Pearl Harbor, the White Sox baseball scandal in 1919, the Florida vote count in 2000, the impeachment of President Clinton, the Watergate scandal, the attack on the World Trade Center, or the government response to either Hurricane Katrina, the oil spill in the Gulf of Mexico, or the earthquake in Japan. Watch out for Web sites making irresponsible claims.

PEER REVIEW QUESTIONS: WRITING WITH SOURCES

1. In your essay, you are using sources to find out the following:

2. Your introduction is interesting. ☐ yes ☐ no
   Your introduction makes the purpose of your essay clear. ☐ yes ☐ no

continued

continued

> The sentence that most nearly expresses your main point is the following:
>
> 3. I am (am not) impressed with the way you use your sources for the following reasons:
>
> 4. I am (am not) impressed with your choice of sources for the following reasons:
>
> 5. Your conclusion (is/is not) effective for the following reason:
>
> 6. What I like best about your essay is the following:
>
> 7. I recommend you make the following changes:

Proofreading Practice: MLA Form

TEST YOURSELF: Using MLA Form

Correct the errors in these sentences. One sentence is correct.

1. One critic writes, "The theme of this poem is reality and illusion (Smith 46)."
2. Dr. Shirley Montgomery writes that "she has done three studies of this problem" (38).
3. Harold Smith states, "The history of that event remains vague" (Jones 139).
4. "The novel ends weakly," writes one critic, but it is worth reading" (Miller 227).
5. One biographer tells us that Shakespeare's father sold many properties (Greenblatt 61).
6. One sociologist asks, "Where can we find data to prove this" (Martinez 22)?
7. Most patients who took this medication, according to one source, improved (17).

Answers: 1. illusion" (Smith 46) 2. writes, "I have done . . . 3. (139)—wrong author's name 4. critic, "but it . . . 5. correct 6. this?" (Martinez 22) 7. name of author is missing

Basic Exercise: Using MLA Form

Which four statements use correct MLA form? What is wrong with the others?

1. Jason Miller writes, "The film fails to capture the style of the story" (26).
2. One critic says the book has a "fascinating but implausible plot" (p. 103).
3. Baroque music, according to one historian, emphasized structure (Callandra 59).
4. Jessica Smith writes, "Such a poem could not be written today" (34).
5. One economist predicted a major recession in 2007 (McDonald 83).
6. A standard reference work of the time failed to mention his name (449).
7. "Most of this poem is unintelligible, wrote one famous critic." (p. 77)

Intermediate Exercise: Using MLA Form

Correct the errors in these sentences. One sentence is correct.

1. One reviewer called the film "an unequaled masterpiece (Smith 246)".
2. Harrison McTwiggle reports that "he found the book enchanting" (38).
3. Simon Carruthers writes, "That day she found her true career" (Simon 321).
4. "Reading a poem," the editor writes, requires imagination and precision" (Smith 13).
5. In John Adams' day, Harvard University had one hundred students (McCullough 35).
6. "Where do we find her equal today" one biographer asks (Ferguson 44)?
7. One newspaper editor complained that not enough aid had been pledged (p. A19).

Challenge Exercise: Using MLA Form

Correct the seven errors in this passage.

Ernest Hemingway's story, *"A Clean, Well-Lighted Place,"* portrays two waiters observing a drunken old man lingering in their café, not wanting to go home. The younger waiter is impatient to leave to go home to his wife. His more mature co-worker, who lives alone, identifies more with the emptiness the old man must feel. He describes himself as one of "those who do not want to go to bed. (32)" After the man leaves and they close the café, he stops at a bar, feeling empty and afraid, with the word *nada* running through his mind. Although this story, unlike several others which Hemingway also published in "Scribner's Magazine" in 1933, is not directly autobiographical, it does, according to one biographer, express the "underside of Ernest's spiritual world" (Baker 238). The story was well liked by Hemingway's editor, Maxwell Perkins (Carlos Baker, p. 241) at the time and remains one of his best known works. Later critics have continued to respond to the power of the story. Warren Bennett in 1970, for example, finds it "superbly charged with dramatic as well as verbal irony (79). And David Kerner in 1992 finds the story to be a symbolic comment on the human need for a refuge, a theme explored somewhat differently in a story called The Gambler, the Nun, and the Radio," which was published in *Scribner's* the same year (pp. 573–4). The enduring relevance of "A Clean, Well-Lighted Place" is evident in the fact that it is often included in literary anthologies intended for study in college classrooms.

Key Words from Chapter 15 for Review

APA and MLA format, bibliography, documentation, intellectual property, paraphrasing, parenthetical citation, plagiarism, quoting, summarizing

CHAPTER 16

Writing about Literature

STEPPING UP: WRITING TIP 16

Writing about literature requires a kind of balance. At one extreme is the idea that every text has one meaning only and that you must find that meaning like an answer to a problem in mathematics. At the other extreme is the notion that any opinion is equally valid, and that anything interesting you can say about a poem, story, or play is just as good as any other opinion. To interpret and write about literature effectively, you should stay somewhere between these extremes. Most works of literature have a few dominant ideas, or themes. A poet may express love, admire courage, lament the loss of life in war, or convey nostalgia over past experiences. Missing these predominant ideas and feelings does a disservice to your reader, but overlooking other meanings and reducing the work to one idea is just as unhelpful. A poem may express love and hate at the same time, or admire heroism in war but lament the loss of life, and so on. A good reader is open to a literary work's complex ideas and feelings while remaining true to its text.

Methods of Interpreting a Story, Play, or Poem

Writing about different categories, or **genres**, of literature—stories, novels, plays, and poems—requires creative and critical thinking at the same time. If you are not an English major and do not have much experience in writing about literature, you may feel incompetent the first time you are asked to interpret a short story or poem. Do not be dismayed—a successful essay on literature does not require specialized knowledge or technical training. Unlike other academic disciplines, the **interpretation** of literature involves us as whole human beings; when you write about literature, you are responding to it as a whole person with life experience. We call writing about literature **literary criticism**. Professional literary critics may be more familiar than you are with other works of literature and with terminology that is new to you, but what matters most about literature, its vision of life, applies to all of us, whether or not we are well read.

This means that your essay should come more from your genuine response to the story or poem than from an attempt to sound intellectual or sophisticated. You will impress readers more with your keen insights and authentic responses than by borrowing ideas and phrases from critics. We call literary works themselves **primary sources**, and the writings of critics **secondary sources**. When you do include the ideas of other critics in your essay, you must respond to their ideas clearly, explaining what you agree and disagree with. And because literature is one of the humanities, you must use MLA format whenever you quote or paraphrase from secondary sources.

Student Essay: Writing about a Story

The following essay, like many written in composition courses, takes an approach that is sometimes called "reader response," that is, analyzing the thoughts, feelings, and associations brought up in the reader's mind when he or she fully experiences a work of **fiction**. This essay is a response to a short story titled "Eveline" by James Joyce.

A Trap or a Home?

JESSICA STEVENS

James Joyce's story entitled "Eveline" is about a young woman who is unhappy with her family life and her boring job and wants to escape.

She lives in Dublin, where she works in a store and brings home money that she gives to her father. Her mother is dead, and she is looking after two younger siblings. All these responsibilities add up to a heavy burden for her at her age, and she feels trapped by her situation. The story portrays her facing the biggest crisis of her life—a chance to elope with a sailor named Frank, who wants to take her to Buenos Ayres and marry her. The way she reacts in this moment of crisis would make any reader feel torn between opposite feelings: I want her to run away with Frank and have a life of her own, but I also want her to stay and fulfill her family responsibilities. The author succeeds in making a reader feel intense ambivalence and think about what it means to make a life decision.

Eveline's situation is a sort of trap that she can't get out of. She has taken on family duties that there is no one else to pick up if she leaves. Her father, even though he threatens her and bosses her around, is getting older and needs her help more and more. She is looking after younger siblings, and more than that, she promised her mother before she died that she would try to hold the family together as long as she was able to. And with all of that, she seems to be a traditional Irish Catholic girl who must have grown up with old-fashioned ideas about her role as a woman. The idea of running away from all that would be frightening and make her feel guilty, but the idea of staying is also terrifying, because she imagines ending up just like her mother, who sacrificed her own happiness and ended up demented.

Eloping to Buenos Ayres seems necessary if she is ever going to get away from the trap she is in. She is nineteen, which in those days meant she might be considered an "old maid" if she didn't get married soon. She isn't sure she is in love with Frank, but she likes being with him, and he really wants to marry her. She feels that this is her one big chance, and any reader would feel that too: if she doesn't do something now, she probably never will. At one moment in the story, I could feel her panic. Joyce writes, "She stood up in a sudden impulse of terror. Escape! She must escape! Frank would save her. He would give her life, perhaps love, too. But she wanted to live. Why should she be unhappy? She had a right to happiness." (31). At this moment in the story, I wanted to stand up and cheer for her to take off and go with Frank.

But she doesn't go with him. She can't, because she is over-whelmed by her responsibilities and the fear of taking such a drastic step. What would people think of her? What would happen to her? James Joyce shows how people can be trapped by their fears and by the way they are conditioned by their upbringing. Some scholars have pointed out that Eveline's fears of emigrating to Argentina are justified, since Buenos Ayres in the author's time was thought to be the global center of the "white slave trade," into which Frank might abandon her (Norris 288). On the other hand, as one critic writes, "'Eveline' was written as Joyce was preparing to elope with a twenty-year-old woman who barely knew him, and to whom he had little to offer, except—like Frank—a love of music and a promise to enfold her in his arms" (Norris 296). It is not possible to be sure whether James Joyce wants the reader to approve or disapprove of Eveline's choice. He apparently wanted his readers to decide for themselves. Most readers are probably sad when they realize that she can't break away from her dead-end job and boring life. Eveline's home has become a trap that she can never escape from. But her trap is the only home she knows, and she has some good feelings about her family. Some readers would probably say she does the right thing, or the only thing she can do. The ending of the story makes you feel sorry for Eveline but you accept her for who she is.

Works Cited

Joyce, James. "Eveline." *Dubliners*. Ed. Sean
    Latham. New York: A Longman Cultural Edition,
    Pearson, 2011: 26–32.
Norris, Margaret. "The Perils of 'Eveline.'"
    James Joyce, *Dubliners: A Norton Critical
    Edition*.Ed. Margaret Norris. New York:
    W.W. Norton, 2006: 283–298.

1. What does Jessica like about this story?
2. What feelings does she say it calls up in the reader? What does *ambivalence* mean?
3. What is the thesis statement of the essay? How is it reinforced in the conclusion?
4. What verb tense does Jessica use in discussing the story? Why is this correct?
5. What is the purpose of the quotation from the story in paragraph three?
6. What's the significance of the title of Jessica's essay?
7. Does Jessica give a balanced or biased view of the conflict between individual happiness and social responsibility?

Example by a Published Author: Writing about Poetry

Published literary critics usually analyze fiction and poetry using a critical method or theory and a wide knowledge of both the writer's work and the work of hundreds of other authors and critics. Always read stories and poems and experience them for yourself before reading the commentaries of critics. Literature is to be experienced, and your interpretation of it should grow out of your direct experience of reading it for yourself. Afterward, it can be extremely valuable to read what well-informed critics say about it. They will often point out things you missed and provide information about the author's life and work that you may not know.

The analysis below is by critic Paula Bennett, who is writing about a poem by Emily Dickinson. Bennett brings to her analysis both feminist theory and a wide knowledge of Dickinson's life and works, as well as the writings of many other poets. This passage is from Bennett's book, which takes its title, *My Life a Loaded Gun*, from one of Dickinson's poems.

Emily Dickinson's "My Life had stood—a Loaded Gun"

PAULA BENNETT

Lacking the male poet's long-established tradition of self-exploration and self-validation, women poets in our culture have been torn between restrictive definitions of what a woman is and their own fears of being or seeming unwomanly. As a result, they have been unable to allow the full truth of their experience to empower their speaking voice. Without predecessors to whom they might appeal or upon whom they might model themselves, they have either fit into the existing masculinist tradition, or they have worked within a subcultural tradition of their own—the literature of the "poetess." In either case, they have inevitably been led *to dissociate the concept of creative power from their woman selves.* Though often possessed, as in Bishop's case, of extraordinary gifts, they have rarely felt these gifts as inherently theirs.

For the woman to exercise her creativity to the fullest, she must first be able to heal the internal divisions that have historically distorted and controlled her relationship to her craft. The acceptance of the self, whatever that self is, is the base upon which the woman poet must work, the source of her greatest authority and strength. But for her to arrive at this self-acceptance, she must possess a definition of her womanhood that is broad enough, flexible enough, to encompass all that she actually is. Without such a definition, she can never fully own her powers or achieve in her poetry the depth and scope of which her experience might otherwise make her capable. Burdened with ambivalence and self-doubt, like too many creative women in every field, she will remain a stranger to herself and to other women.

No poem written by a woman poet more perfectly captures the nature, the difficulties, and the risks involved in this task of self-redefinition and self-empowerment than the poem that stands at the center of this book, Emily Dickinson's brilliant and enigmatic "My Life had stood—a Loaded Gun":

> My Life had stood—a Loaded Gun—
> In Corners—till a Day
> The owner passed—identified—
> And carried Me away—
> And now We roam in Sovereign Woods—
> And now We hunt the Doe—
> And every time I speak for Him—
> The Mountains straight reply—
> And do I smile, such cordial light
> Upon the Valley glow—
> It is as a Vesuvian face
> Had let it's pleasure through—
> And when at Night—Our good Day done—
> I guard My Master's Head—
> 'Tis better than the Eider-Duck's
> Deep Pillow—to have shared—
> To foe of His—I'm deadly foe—
> None stir the second time—
> On whom I lay a Yellow Eye—
> Or an emphatic Thumb—

Though I than He—may longer live
He longer must—than I—
For I have but the power to kill,
Without—the power to die—

(no. 754; p. 574)

Composed during the period when Dickinson had reached the height of her poetic prowess, "My Life had stood" represents the poet's most extreme attempt to characterize the Vesuvian nature of the power or art which she believed was hers. Speaking through the voice of a gun, Dickinson presents herself in this poem as everything "woman" is not: cruel not pleasant, hard not soft, emphatic not weak, one who kills not one who nurtures.

—Paula Bennett. From *My Life, A Loaded Gun.*

1. Define these words, using a dictionary if necessary: *predecessors, subcultural, ambivalence, enigmatic, Vesuvian.*
2. According to Bennett, what special problem do women poets face?
3. What does Bennett mean by saying that a female poet may remain a "stranger to herself"?
4. What does Bennett mean when she says the poem captures the female poet's "self-redefinition"?
5. Bennett mentions that Dickinson speaks "through the voice of a gun." She sees this as a metaphor for the "Vesuvian" nature of Dickinson's poetry. Explain what Bennett means by her interpretation of the metaphor.
6. Bennett gives a feminist reading of the poem. Can you interpret the poem in any other way--one that might include all readers, not just women poets?
7. What effect does Dickinson's unusual punctuation have on your experience of the poem?

Analyzing vs. Summarizing

Many students, not knowing what to say about a story, take the easy route and simply summarize the plot. Once you head down that road, you can write a page or two without saying anything important. Assume that your readers have already read the story; in that case, what good does it do to tell them what they already know?

What can you say about a story instead of simply summarizing its plot? Begin with *why* questions: *Why* do the characters act the way they do? *Why* does the author set the story in the place and time it occurs? *Why* do the events happen as they do? *Why* does the ending occur, given the situation and previous events in the plot? In addition, look for what is *not* said. We are often told to "read between the lines," that is, to draw conclusions based on what is said and done in a story. Authors rarely tell us in so many words the meaning or meanings of their works; literature requires us to respond with emotion and imagination so that we understand what is not said as well as what is. A simple example is that an author almost never *tells* us that a bad character is bad; instead, the character does and says things that we dislike and disapprove of. The author does not *tell* us to admire a certain character, but rather evokes our admiration by describing the courageous and generous things that character does.

Developing a Point by Using the Text

In order to avoid the trap of plot summarizing, organize your essay in some pattern other than a narrative. Illustration or enumeration is one practical way to organize such an essay. If you want to prove that a story is about selfishness, elaborate on three or four examples of selfish behavior and their consequences, using a different paragraph for each example. If you want to argue that a story warns us against not standing up for ourselves as individuals, identify three or four negative consequences of meek conformity.

When you write about a poem, go beyond what the poem *says*. If you do not feel qualified to write about poetry, you will be tempted to paraphrase the poem and stop there. But, as with stories, assume that your readers have read the poem and that you want to reveal something they do not already know. What can you say about a poem?

Begin by noticing details: Poetry is about details. First, notice the language: Is there anything unusual about the language of the poem? Is it conversational, formal, full of suggested and hidden meanings? Also notice images: Do the images of things follow a pattern—are they of animals, plants, weather, clothes, money, food? What about the tone of the poem? Is it humorous, solemn, sarcastic, matter-of-fact? Does the tone change?

Above all, poetry works through double meanings and figures of speech—or as poet Robert Frost said, saying something by saying something else. When you write about a poem, explore the possible meanings of symbols, metaphors, and words that have multiple meanings. Interpreting a poem well requires almost as much creativity as writing a poem.

WRITING EXERCISES: Basic, Intermediate, Challenge

Basic Exercise: Writing about Literature

Read the poem below and write brief answers to the questions that follow it.

The Road Not Taken

Two roads diverged in a yellow wood,
And sorry I could not travel both
And be one traveler, long I stood
And looked down one as far as I could
To where it bent in the undergrowth;
Then took the other, as just as fair,
And having perhaps the better claim,
Because it was grassy and wanted wear;
Though as for that the passing there
Had worn them really about the same,
And both that morning equally lay
In leaves no step had trodden black.
Oh, I kept the first for another day!
Yet knowing how way leads on to way,
I doubted if I should ever come back.
I shall be telling this with a sigh
Somewhere ages and ages hence:
Two roads diverged in a wood, and I—
I took the one less traveled by,
And that has made all the difference.

—Robert Frost, 1916.

1. Describe the situation faced by the speaker in the poem.
2. Describe precisely the speaker's response to the situation.
3. Describe the natural setting in the poem.

4. Explain the metaphorical meaning of the choice of roads.

5. Identify a line that contains more than one meaning.

6. Identify at least two emotions expressed in the poem.

7. Tell about a situation in your life where you had to choose between two "roads."

Intermediate Exercise: Writing about Literature

Read the following short story and write brief answers to the questions that follow it.

The Story of an Hour

KATE CHOPIN, 1894

Knowing that Mrs. Mallard was afflicted with a heart trouble, great care was taken to break to her as gently as possible the news of her husband's death.

It was her sister Josephine who told her, in broken sentences; veiled hints that revealed in half concealing. Her husband's friend Richards was there, too, near her. It was he who had been in the news-paper office when intelligence of the railroad disaster was received, with Brently Mallard's name leading the list of "killed." He had only taken the time to assure himself of its truth by a second telegram, and had hastened to forestall any less careful, less tender friend in bearing the sad message.

She did not hear the story as many women have heard the same, with a paralyzed inability to accept its significance. She wept at once, with sudden, wild abandonment, in her sister's arms. When the storm of grief had spent itself she went away to her room alone. She would have no one follow her.

There stood, facing the open window, a comfortable, roomy arm-chair. Into this she sank, pressed down by a physical exhaustion that haunted her body and seemed to reach into her soul.

She could see in the open square before her house the tops of trees that were all aquiver with the new spring life. The delicious breath of rain was in the air. In the street below a peddler was crying his wares. The notes of a distant song which some one was singing reached her faintly, and countless sparrows were twittering in the eaves.

There were patches of blue sky showing here and there through the clouds that had met and piled one above the other in the west facing her window.

She sat with her head thrown back upon the cushion of the chair quite motionless, except when a sob came up into her throat and shook her, as a child who has cried itself to sleep continues to sob in its dreams.

She was young, with a fair, calm face, whose lines bespoke repression and even a certain strength. But now there was a dull stare in her eyes, whose gaze was fixed away off yonder on one of those patches of blue sky. It was not a glance of reflection, but rather indicated a suspension of intelligent thought.

There was something coming to her and she was waiting for it, fearfully. What was it? She did not know; it was too subtle and elusive to name. But she felt it, creeping out of the sky, reaching toward her through the sounds, the scents, the color that filled the air.

Now her bosom rose and fell tumultuously. She was beginning to recognize this thing that was approaching to possess her, and she was striving to beat it back with her will—as powerless as her two white slender hands would have been. When she abandoned herself a little whispered word escaped her slightly parted lips. She said it over and over under her breath: "free, free, free!" The vacant stare and the look of terror that had followed it went from her eyes. They stayed keen and bright. Her pulses beat fast, and the coursing blood warmed and relaxed every inch of her body.

She did not stop to ask if it were or were not a monstrous joy that held her. A clear and exalted perception enabled her to dismiss the suggestion as trivial.

She knew that she would weep again when she saw the kind, tender hands folded in death; the face that had never looked save with love upon her, fixed and gray and dead. But she saw beyond that bitter moment a long procession of years to come that would belong to her absolutely. And she opened and spread her arms out to them in welcome.

There would be no one to live for her during those coming years; she would live for herself. There would be no powerful will bending hers in that blind persistence with which men and women believe they have a right to impose a private will upon a fellow creature. A kind intention or a cruel intention made the act seem no less a crime as she looked upon it in that brief moment of illumination.

And yet she had loved him—sometimes. Often she had not. What did it matter! What could love, the unsolved mystery, count for in the face of this possession of self-assertion which she suddenly recognized as the strongest impulse of her being!

"Free! Body and soul free!" she kept whispering.

Josephine was kneeling before the closed door with her lips to the keyhole, imploring for admission. "Louise, open the door! I beg; open the door—you will make yourself ill. What are you doing, Louise? For heaven's sake open the door."

"Go away. I am not making myself ill." No; she was drinking in a very elixir of life through that open window.

Her fancy was running riot along those days ahead of her. Spring days, and summer days, and all sorts of days that would be her own. She breathed a quick prayer that life might be long. It was only yesterday she had thought with a shudder that life might be long.

She arose at length and opened the door to her sister's importunities. There was a feverish triumph in her eyes, and she carried herself unwittingly like a goddess of Victory. She clasped her sister's waist, and together they descended the stairs. Richards stood waiting for them at the bottom.

Some one was opening the front door with a latchkey. It was Brently Mallard who entered, a little travel-stained, composedly carrying his grip-sack and umbrella. He had been far from the scene of the accident, and did not even know there had been one. He stood amazed at Josephine's piercing cry; at Richards' quick motion to screen him from the view of his wife.

But Richards was too late.

When the doctors came they said she had died of heart disease—of the joy that kills.

—Kate Chopin, "The Story of an Hour," *Kate Chopin: Complete Novels and Stories.* Library of America, 2002: 756–8.

1. What does this story reveal about Mrs. Mallard's marriage? Did she and her husband love each other?
2. How is Mrs. Mallard's reaction to the news of her husband's death different from that of other women? What causes her to change from grief to joy?
3. What kind of future does Mrs. Mallard begin to imagine for herself, and how does it differ from her past married life?
4. What kind of man is Brently Mallard? Describe his strengths and weaknesses.

5. What images of nature are present in the story, and what do they tell us about Mrs. Mallard's emotions?

6. How is Mrs. Mallard's heart trouble significant to the plot of this story? What is symbolic about it?

7. What is ironic about the last sentence in the story? What do the people present at the end—her sister, her husband, and Richards—not realize about the cause of her death?

Challenge Exercise: Writing about Literature

Choose a short story that you like and respond briefly to the following directives.

1. Describe the setting, explaining which details create a particular emotional effect.

2. Identify the main character and tell why this person comes across sympathetically or unsympathetically.

3. Identify the actions by the characters in the story that convey the meaning of the story.

4. State the main theme of the story.

5. Identify subordinate or conflicting themes.

6. Identify physical details, actions, or statements that foreshadow the outcome of the story.

7. Explain whether the author reveals his or her point of view in the story.

Essay Topics: Writing about Literature

1. Find two poems on the same theme (love, death, courage, etc.). Write a comparison essay examining the similarities and differences between them.

2. Find two short stories whose main characters face similar problems. Write a comparative essay exploring the similarities and differences in the way the two characters face their problems. Then explain how you have dealt with a similar problem.

3. Find two poems you like that were written by the same author. Research information about the author's life and try to determine which poem reflects more of the author's biography. Write an essay explaining your findings. Do not forget to cite your biographical source.

4. Find a story that you like. Look up information about the author's life and write an essay explaining what biographical facts are reflected in the story. Be sure to cite your source correctly.

5. Read a play, poem, or story and look up two critics' opinions of that work. Write an essay explaining which critic you agree with more. Be sure to cite your two sources correctly.

6. Read a well-known play and write a scene of your own showing what happens to the characters in their lives after the play ends. Try to remain true to the characters as they behave in the play itself.

7. Find a story or novel that has been made into a film. Write an essay explaining how the story changes in the film version. Find two reviews of the film and explain whether you agree with the reviewers' comments about the filmmaker's adaptation of the story. Be sure to cite the reviewers' articles correctly.

PEER REVIEW QUESTIONS: WRITING ABOUT LITERATURE

1. The overall purpose of your essay seems to be the following:

2. Your introduction is interesting. ☐ Yes ☐ No
   Your introduction identifies the work of literature by title and author and indicates what you are saying about it. ☐ Yes ☐ No
   The sentence that most nearly expresses your main point is the following:

3. You make use of details from the work to support your point without merely summarizing the plot. ☐ Yes ☐ No

4. You quote effectively from the work to support your points. ☐ Yes ☐ No

5. Your conclusion (is/is not) effective for the following reason:

6. What I like best about your essay is the following:

7. I recommend you make the following changes:

Proofreading Practice: Quoting Correctly from Literary Works

When you write about literature, check to make sure you have identified titles properly. Titles of short works such as stories and poems should be set in quotation marks: Kate Chopin's "The Story of an Hour" or Shelley's "Ode to the West Wind." Titles of long works such as novels or plays should be italicized: Tennessee Williams's *The Glass Menagerie* or Chinua Achebe's *Things Fall Apart*. Also check to make sure you have begun and ended your quotations correctly, remembering to put quotation marks before and after the phrase or sentence quoted and to introduce each quotation properly.

TEST YOURSELF: Quoting Correctly from Literary Works

Identify the three correct sentences below and correct the other four.

1. One novel that pits man against nature is Hemingway's "The Old Man and the Sea."
2. *The Black Cat* is my favorite story by Edgar Allan Poe.
3. Cervantes' *Don Quixote* is sometimes called the model for all later novels.
4. Richard Cory, at the end of Robinson's poem, "Went home and put a bullet through his head."
5. *The Stranger*, Camus' famous novel, begins today my mother died."
6. Langston Hughes's poem entitled "Harlem" begins with the question, "What happens to a dream deferred?"
7. Guy De Maupassant's story, "The Necklace," has an ironic ending.

Answers: 1. The Old Man and the Sea 2. "The Black Cat" 3. correct 4. correct 5. begins, "Today my 6. deferred?" 7. correct

---

PROOFREADING EXERCISES: Basic, Intermediate, Challenge

Basic Exercise: Quoting Correctly from Literary Works

Correct the error in each sentence. One sentence is correct.

1. Edgar Allan Poe's poem, The Raven, is eerie and haunting.
2. Poe continually repeats the phrase, Quoth the Raven, "Nevermore."

3. Poe also wrote many short stories, including The Pit and the Pendulum.
4. In his story called "The Tell-tale Heart," is about a man who commits a murder.
5. In "The Cask of Amontillado" is a story about a man who seeks revenge.
6. The main character in this story says "I must not only punish, but punish with impunity."
7. Poe often portrays emotional disturbance, for example, the "excessive nervous agitation" of the young man in "The Fall of the House of Usher."

Intermediate Exercise: Quoting Correctly from Literary Works

Read the following poem and find the seven errors in the passage that follows it.

We Real Cool
The Pool Players
Seven at the Golden Shovel
Gwendolyn Brooks, 1960

We real cool. We
Left school. We

Lurk late, We
Strike straight. We

Sing sin. We
Thin gin. We

Jazz June. We
Die soon.

In the poem "We Real Cool" by Gwendolyn Brooks is about a group of adolescents who like to hang out and play pool instead of going to school or working. The adolescent speaker in the poem brags, "We real cool. We/Left school. The poem is written in street language that expresses the lack of education and the hip attitudes of these young people, who "Lurk late" and "Strike straight." The tone of the poem is swaggering and strutting, "We real cool." These young people are proud of the way "they like to Jazz June." Although first published in 1960, the poem contains the kind of rhyme used by rap artists and slam poets later. The jazzy pause before the end of each line creates a syncopated rhythm, and most lines use alliteration, for instance, in phrases like "Sing sin" and Jazz June." The poem, in other words, expresses the creativity of these young people as well as their spirit of defiance, and both their boldness and their defeatism. After bragging about all their daring acts of rebellion; "Sing sin. We/Thin gin" they ruefully predict they will "Die soon."

Challenge Exercise:
Quoting Correctly from Literary Works

For practice in quoting from literature, complete the following exercises.

1. Write a sentence in which you quote a phrase of three or four words from a story, mentioning the author's name and fitting the quote smoothly into the wording of your sentence.
2. Write a sentence in which you quote a whole sentence from a story, mentioning the author's name, introducing the quotation properly, and beginning it with a capital letter.
3. Write a sentence in which you quote a phrase of two or three words from a poem, mentioning the poet's name and fitting the phrase smoothly into the wording of your sentence.
4. Write a sentence in which you quote two lines from a poem, introducing the quotation properly and indicating the line ending with a forward slash (called a virgule).
5. Write a sentence in which you include the name of an author and his or her poem or short story, mention the title, and make a statement about the work without quoting from it.
6. Write a sentence in which you include the name of an author and the title or his or her novel or play and make a statement about the work without quoting from it.
7. Write a sentence beginning with a quoted statement from a story or poem and concluding with your own words after the quotation.

Key Words from Chapter 16 for Review

fiction, genre, interpretation, literary criticism, primary and secondary sources

PUNCTUATION HANDBOOK

The Elements of Punctuation

The major elements of punctuation are commas, apostrophes, end punctuation (the marks at the end of sentences), semicolons, and colons.

Commas

Know the rules for commas and use them only as rules require. Putting in too many commas does more harm than leaving some out.

Use commas:

1. in dates and place names
2. to separate items in a series
3. to separate coordinate adjectives
4. after introductory phrases and clauses
5. before and after interrupters
6. before and after nonrestrictive relative clauses
7. before and after appositives
8. before short conjunctions in compound sentences
9. before and after persons spoken to
10. before and after contrasting parts
11. before and after direct quotations
12. in correspondence
13. to prevent confusion

1. Commas in Dates and Place Names

Put commas between the day of the week, the date, and the year, as well as after the year.

She was born on Tuesday, January 6, 1975, and grew up in California.

It is not necessary to put a comma between the month and year if no day is given.

An earthquake occurred off the coast of Japan in <u>March 2011</u>.

Separate a street address from the city and the city from the state or country, but do not put a comma before the ZIP code.

He worked at 199 Chambers <u>Street,</u> <u>New York,</u> New York 10007.

2. Commas to Separate Items in a Series

Place a comma after each element in a series except the last one; the comma before the conjunction (*and, or,* etc.) is optional, depending upon which style you are following.

They ate <u>sandwiches,</u> <u>potato salad,</u> and pie for lunch.

Or

They ate <u>sandwiches,</u> <u>potato salad</u> and pie for lunch.

(Keep in mind, however, that most academic style guides require a comma before the conjunction.)

A series can contain words or phrases.

Nouns:	*Books, records,* and *magazines* lay on the table.
Verbs:	We *ate, drank, sang,* and *danced* at the party.
Pronouns:	I think that *you, we,* and *they* all look alike.
Adjectives:	The letters were *terse, hard-hitting,* and *factual.*
Adverbs:	The Jets played *aggressively, efficiently,* and *shrewdly.*
Prepositions:	The detective looked *in, around, over,* and *under* the safe.
Phrases:	The company preferred sales managers who *were cordial with employees, knew the business,* and *demonstrated loyalty to the organization.*

3. Commas Separating Coordinate Adjectives

Several adjectives in a row modifying the same noun are called *coordinate adjectives.* They should be separated by commas if you could put *and* between the adjectives in place of the comma: *a large, comfortable* room (compare with a *large and comfortable* room). Do not put a comma between the last adjective and the noun.

an <u>intimidating, overpowering</u> defense
an <u>enchanting, imaginative, subtle</u> performance
a <u>squat, talkative</u> official
a <u>large, hairy, playful</u> sheepdog

In the last example, you could put *and* between the adjectives: a large *and* hairy *and* playful sheepdog. When you cannot put *and* between adjectives, do not use commas.

a <u>fine old</u> chair (not a fine *and* old chair)
a <u>navy blue beach</u> towel (not a navy *and* blue *and* beach towel)

4. Commas after Introductory Phrases and Clauses

Put commas after most introductory words, phrases, and clauses.

<u>Well,</u> you can never be sure.
<u>No,</u> that is not a good idea.
<u>Otherwise,</u> the plan will work.
<u>A few hours later,</u> she began to cry.
<u>When you have finished reading the article,</u> may I borrow the magazine?

When interjections (single words such as *well, yes, oh,* and *ah*) and interrupting words (such as *however, otherwise, meanwhile, first, nevertheless,* and *consequently*) begin a sentence, they should be followed by a comma. Interrupting phrases, also called *parenthetical phrases* (such as *of course, by the way, after all,* and *in a sense*) normally also take commas when they begin a sentence. Short descriptive phrases (such as *in a minute, after the game, next to the produce, along the railing,* and *during the performance*) are usually followed by commas, too. Sometimes, however, short descriptive phrases fit smoothly into a sentence and don't require the use of commas. Compare these two examples.

<u>After a 30-minute wait,</u> she saw the doctor.
<u>In the section behind third base</u> was a row reserved for celebrities.

In the first sentence, the introductory phrase has a pause after it and should be followed by a comma. In the second sentence, the introductory phrase is necessary to the statement and should not have a comma after it.

Dependent clauses (word groups containing subject-verb combinations) normally are followed by commas when they begin sentences.

> Although the pay was good, the job was unsatisfactory.
> When she thought about the past year, she felt pleased.
> Since you joined the faculty, the students have been ecstatic.
> Because the message was translated, we could understand it.

5. Commas before and after Interrupters

Sentence interrupters, or *parenthetical expressions* (think of *parentheses* before and after a phrase), are separated from the rest of the sentence by commas. When they appear in the middle of a sentence, put commas before and after them.

Here are some common interrupters.

however	of course	as a matter of fact
consequently	by the way	for example
nevertheless	in a sense	in fact
to be sure	in my opinion	in the first place

These interrupters are set off by pairs of commas, as shown here.

> She knew, by the way, that the computer did not work.
> The sound track, in my opinion, is exciting.
> The new model, however, will not be available until March.

Descriptive phrases containing past participles and present participles (*–ing* verb forms) after a noun often serve as interrupters as well.

> The captain, puzzled by the strange blips on the radar screen, cut the speed of the craft.
> An immigrant stonemason, hoping for steady work, appeared in the office.

Adjective phrases that come after nouns are also set off by pairs of commas.

> The instructions, dense and hard to read, gave them little aid.
> Two fathers, anxious about their sons' grades, called the principal.

6. Commas before and after Relative Clauses

Descriptive clauses beginning with *who, which,* or *that* are called *relative clauses.* Relative clauses beginning with *who* or *which* are sometimes set off by commas. The rules are:

Do not set off restrictive clauses with commas.
Do set off nonrestrictive clauses with commas.

What are restrictive clauses? Restrictive clauses contain information necessary to the meaning of the sentence (i.e., they "restrict" the meaning) and therefore should not be separated from the rest of the sentence by punctuation.

Example 1:

Students who receive A grades may skip the second course.

The clause *who receive A grades* should not be separated from the rest of the sentence by commas because without it the sentence "Students . . . may skip the second course" means something completely different.

Example 2:

The essay that won the prize was about illiteracy.

The clause *that won the prize* is restrictive; without it, the sentence does not specify which essay was about illiteracy.

Example 3:

The town in which the research took place was in California.

The clause *in which the research took place* is restrictive because the sentence has no specific meaning without it.

What are nonrestrictive clauses? Nonrestrictive clauses are relative clauses beginning with *who* or *which* (clauses beginning with *that* are always restrictive). Nonrestrictive clauses add extra details to the sentence but are not crucial to the meaning.

Example 1:

Electronic mail, which sends messages instantaneously, is beginning to replace "snail mail," which is what some people call the postal service.

The clause *which sends messages instantaneously* is nonrestrictive because it merely adds information and does not change the meaning of the sentence.

Example 2:

Philip Johnson, <u>who designed some of America's most interesting buildings,</u> failed the New York State licensing examination.

The clause *who designed some of America's most interesting buildings* is nonrestrictive because it adds information but is not necessary to identify the subject, Philip Johnson, whose name is already given.

7. Commas before and after Appositives

Appositives are phrases that come after nouns or pronouns and describe or identify them. They are usually set off by pairs of commas.

Arno, <u>the great cartoonist,</u> was voted America's best-dressed man in 1941.

Neil Armstrong, <u>the first man to step on the moon,</u> earned his pilot's license when he was 16.

Some very short appositives are not separated by commas.

The Emperor <u>Nero</u> was a psychopath.

My sister <u>Karen</u> will join us.

8. Commas before Short Conjunctions in Compound Sentences

Use a comma plus a short conjunction to link independent clauses in compound sentences. The short conjunctions are *and, but, or, for, nor,* and *so.* Remember to put commas *before* these conjunctions—not after them.

Independent Clause   Independent Clause

1. The location was desirable, <u>and</u> the price was reasonable.
2. Efforts were made by the police, <u>but</u> no suspects were found.
3. You may pay by check today, <u>or</u> you may have the store bill you later.
4. The first group stayed in the city, <u>for</u> they wanted to explore the museums.
5. The passengers were not injured, <u>nor</u> was the boat seriously damaged.
6. Sally had visited Puerto Rico before, <u>so</u> she knew where to eat in San Juan.

9. Commas before and after Persons Spoken to (Direct Address)

When you speak directly to a person, using his or her name in a sentence, separate the name from the rest of the sentence. Use commas in pairs unless the name comes at the beginning or end of the sentence.

I remember, Maria, how you looked in high school.
Maria, I remember how you looked in high school.
I remember how you looked in high school, Maria.

Many writers omit these commas and ignore the difference in meaning: *I remember Maria* is not the same as *I remember, Maria.*

10. Commas before and after Contrasting Parts

Use commas before and after contrasting phrases beginning with *not.*

The Red Sox, not the Yankees, won that series.
The weather was cooler, not warmer, than predicted.
The capital of Pennsylvania is Harrisburg, not Philadelphia.

11. Commas before and after Direct Quotations

Before quoting a whole statement, put a comma after the introductory word *said, stated, asked,* and so on.

He said, "This is the road to Seattle."
She asked, "Will this book explain how to sell real estate?"
The catalog stated, "This course includes intermediate algebra."

Put commas after quotations when the quotations come at the beginning of sentences. Commas belong inside quotation marks.

"After dinner, let's play Scrabble," Sue suggested.
"Don't leave any questions blank," the instructor said.

Short quoted phrases often fit smoothly into the sentence and should not be set off by commas.

Trevor called his brother a "universal genius."
Joanne was often called an " Anne Hathaway look-alike."
Shakespeare called music the "food of love."

12. Commas in Correspondence

In business letters and personal letters, the closing is always followed by a comma.

Business Letters	Personal Letters and Notes
Sincerely yours,	Yours truly,
Yours very truly,	Yours,
Yours truly,	As always,
Cordially yours,	Best wishes,
	Love,
	Yours,

In personal letters, put commas after the greeting.

Dear Janet,	Dear Mom,
Dear Tom,	Dear Grandpa,

13. Commas to Prevent Confusion

Occasionally, you may need a comma to separate words that might appear to belong together when the meaning requires that they be separated. Watch especially for prepositions (*in, around, over, through,* etc.) that appear to go with the words after them when they do not.

Inside, the room looked bright and airy. (*Inside the room* is not a phrase to be read together.)

Not long <u>after,</u> the candidates gave speeches. (*After the candidates gave speeches* is not meant to be a clause.)

All <u>around,</u> the landscape looked lush and mysterious. (*Around the landscape* should not be read as a phrase.)

Apostrophes

Apostrophes are used for two purposes.

1. In contractions, where letters have been left out
   do not = don't
   should not = shouldn't
2. In possessive forms
   's for singular possessives: Karen's dress
   s' for plural possessives: four students' grades

Exception: Plurals that do not take *s*, such as *men* or *children*, take *'s* in the possessive.

men's hats
children's games

Some common mistakes that people make when using apostrophes are:

Carelessly leaving apostrophes out of contractions: dont, instead of don't; shes, instead of she's; wouldnt, instead of wouldn't
Writing possessives without apostrophes: Karens dress, instead of Karen's dress; womens opinions, instead of women's opinions
Putting apostrophes in the wrong place: my mothers' attitudes, instead of my mother's attitudes; its' cold, instead of it's cold
Using apostrophes with personal pronouns: write hers, not her's; yours, not your's (impersonal pronouns do take apostrophes: everyone's opinions; somebody's car)

End Punctuation: Periods, Question Marks, and Exclamation Points

Use periods to end statements and indirect questions.

Statement: The store had a sale on January 2.
Indirect question: Sam asked whether the store was having a sale.

Use question marks after direct questions.

Is this book overdue?
When will you be back?
Why, if no one objects to the proposal, are we waiting until March to begin?

Do not forget to put the question mark at the end of long, complicated questions like the last one.

Use periods, not question marks, after requests.

Would you please send me an application form.
Would you please let me know if you are interested.

Use exclamation points after sentences that express excitement or strong feeling.

Get out of my sight!
Watch out for that elephant!
That was a fabulous performance!

Use exclamation points after single words or phrases that express astonishment or strong emotion.

Help!
Stop!
No more war!

Semicolons

Use a semicolon (;) to separate independent clauses in a compound sentence when there are no short connectives.

Children of illegal aliens often attend public schools; some states have asked the federal government to pay for the cost of their education.
Buying on credit has disadvantages; one may overestimate one's ability to pay.

Semicolons, not commas, should also be used to separate independent clauses when there is a long connective word (a conjunctive adverb) such as *however, therefore, meanwhile, nevertheless, consequently,* or *moreover* between the clauses. Use a comma after the connecting word.

Separate conference rooms are available for the two meetings; however, you may convene together afterward if you like.
We have already sent you a brochure; meanwhile, we are awaiting your request.

Use semicolons to separate independent clauses with the word *then* between them. *Then* is not a short connecting word like *and;* do not put a comma before it.

Not: We always swim at four o'clock, then we do aerobics.
But: We always swim at four o'clock; then we do aerobics.

Use semicolons to separate items in a series when the individual parts have commas within them.

She had lived in Dallas, Texas; San Mateo, California; and Stamford, Connecticut.
You will have to pass three examinations: a reading test, in multiple-choice format; a writing test, in the form of a one-hour essay; and a mathematics test, given on a computer.

Colons

The colon (:) is used to introduce something. Use colons after *as follows* or *the following* to introduce lists.

She called out the following names: Roberta, Carl, Tracy, Janice, and Lamont.

Open the bottle as follows: press down on the lid, align the arrows, and turn lid to the left.

Use colons when you introduce a list formally.

The ceremony will proceed in this order: first the procession into the auditorium, next the speeches, and fi nally the presentation of degrees.

A reader can enjoy the book except for a few shortcomings: its unrealistic plot, its difficult style, and its improbable ending.

Use colons to separate main clauses in compound sentences when the second clause explains the first.

Joan approached the interview with only one thought in mind: she intended to show them that she understood the job.

Don't use colons after informal introductory expressions (*like*, *such as*, *including*, or the abbreviation *e.g.*).

Not: We ordered five books, including: *Eat, Pray, Love.*

Better: We ordered five books, including *Eat, Pray, Love.*

Not: You need three liberal arts electives, such as: sociology, history, and literature.

Better: You need three liberal arts electives, such as sociology, history, and literature.

Not: You need to eat more nutritious food, e.g.: oat bran and citrus fruit.

Better: You need to eat more nutritious food, e.g., oat bran and citrus fruit.

credits